The Right to Resist

Also Available from Bloomsbury

The Ethics of Resistance: Tyranny of the Absolute, Drew M. Dalton
Hegel and Resistance: History, Politics and Dialectics,
ed. Bart Zantvoort and Rebecca Comay
*Resistance, Revolution and Fascism: Zapatismo and
Assemblage Politics*, Anthony Faramelli
The Primacy of Resistance: Power, Opposition and Becoming, Marco Checchi

The Right to Resist

Philosophies of Dissent

Edited by Thomas Byrne and
Mario Wenning

BLOOMSBURY ACADEMIC
LONDON • NEW YORK • OXFORD • NEW DELHI • SYDNEY

BLOOMSBURY ACADEMIC
Bloomsbury Publishing Plc
50 Bedford Square, London, WC1B 3DP, UK
1385 Broadway, New York, NY 10018, USA
29 Earlsfort Terrace, Dublin 2, Ireland

BLOOMSBURY, BLOOMSBURY ACADEMIC and the Diana logo are trademarks of Bloomsbury Publishing Plc

First published in Great Britain 2023
This paperback edition published 2024

Copyright © Thomas Byrne, Mario Wenning and Contributors, 2023

Thomas Byrne and Mario Wenning have asserted their right under the Copyright, Designs and Patents Act, 1988, to be identified as Editors of this work.

For legal purposes the Acknowledgements on p. vii constitute an extension of this copyright page.

Cover image: A mural by the artist Banksy covers a wall in the West Bank village of Beit Sahour, June 18, 2014. (© Ryan Rodrick Beiler / Alamy Stock Photo)

All rights reserved. No part of this publication may be reproduced or transmitted in any form or by any means, electronic or mechanical, including photocopying, recording, or any information storage or retrieval system, without prior permission in writing from the publishers.

Bloomsbury Publishing Plc does not have any control over, or responsibility for, any third-party websites referred to or in this book. All internet addresses given in this book were correct at the time of going to press. The author and publisher regret any inconvenience caused if addresses have changed or sites have ceased to exist, but can accept no responsibility for any such changes.

A catalogue record for this book is available from the British Library.

A catalog record for this book is available from the Library of Congress.

ISBN: HB: 978-1-3502-6526-4
PB: 978-1-3502-6530-1
ePDF: 978-1-3502-6527-1
eBook: 978-1-3502-6528-8

Series design by Charlotte Daniels

Typeset by RefineCatch Limited, Bungay, Suffolk

To find out more about our authors and books, visit www.bloomsbury.com and sign up for our newsletters.

Contents

Acknowledgments — vii

Introduction *Thomas Byrne and Mario Wenning* — 1

Part 1 Justifications for Resistance

1. Kantian Conditions for the Possibility of Justified Resistance to Authority *Stephen R. Palmquist* — 15
2. Justifying Resistance *Christian Schmidt* — 31
3. Beyond Morality: On the Relation of Indifference and Resistance *Philip Hogh* — 53

Part 2 Resistance, Revolution and Social Change

4. On the Temporal Structure of Resistant Practices: A Hermeneutical Proposal *Stefan Deines* — 73
5. Resistance and Social Transformation in Walter Benjamin's "On the Critique of Violence" *Alexei Procyshyn* — 93
6. Passive Resistance: A Daoist Approach *Mario Wenning* — 113
7. Resistance through Transformation: Spiritual Practices as a Pedagogy of Unlearning and Becoming *Jinting Wu* — 131

Part 3 Resistance in the Media, the Arts and Religion

8. Network Resistance in China *Shih-Diing Liu and Lin Song* — 157
9. "Probability and Reality Do Not Always Coincide": Uncanny Modernity in Kleist's *Michael Kohlhaas* *Louis Lo* — 173
10. Resistance in the Mysticism of Kabir and Jaspers *Amita Valmiki* — 191

11 On Dissent Against Public Health Interventions:
    A Phenomenological Perspective During the COVID-19 Pandemic
    Tarun Kattumana and Thomas Byrne   207

Notes on Contributors   235
Index   239

Acknowledgments

The editors would like to express their gratitude to the editorial team at Bloomsbury, and especially to Lucy Russell and Liza Thompson, for their support and patience throughout the publication process. We would also like to thank Lisa Carden for her copy-editing work. The book has profited from the constructive comments of two anonymous reviewers. Xianzhe Hui and Mark Kourie have provided invaluable assistance during different stages of preparing the manuscript for publication. The book has also benefited from financial support from the University of Macau.

Chapter 6 contains modified extracts from the article "Manifest Reason: Walter Benjamin on Violence and Collective Agency" by Alexei Procyshyn, published in *Constellations* (2014). These are included here with the kind permission of John Wiley and Sons.

Chapter 11 was supported by the following bodies: Centre for Access to Medicines, KU Leuven; The Transvaxx Project; and the Talent Program, University of Macau. The authors thank Kenneth Knies, Deva Waal, Hanika Froneman, Catherine Koekoek, Robert Alvarez, and Adele Guyton for their helpful comments on previous drafts of this work.

Introduction

Thomas Byrne and Mario Wenning

"Resistance" has become a form of shorthand for all kinds of practices of contestation and revolt that challenge existing forms of power. Whether this umbrella concept has sufficient analytic focus to identify and differentiate the increasingly complex nature of protest movements at a global level is, however, up for debate. First, the concept of resistance can be too broad to exclusively identify progressive transformative practices that change social orders in a generally positive direction. Thus, the concept is being claimed by individuals and movements as diverse as the Black Lives Matter Movement in the US, the global environmental movement, the Occupy Movement, different forms of feminism, and initiatives against pandemic-prevention measures, to name just a few. Moreover, the concept does not distinguish between forms of protest that are based on democratic principles and raise legitimate demands for social change and those that are nondemocratic, lack legitimacy, or do not contribute to emancipatory projects. It groups a variety of diverse political tactics and ideological perspectives into one catch-all concept.

In addition to being too broad, the concept of resistance is also too narrow. Forms of everyday resistance go unnoticed when there is an exclusive focus on publicly visible acts of contestation. However, those everyday forms of civic resistance that may happen behind closed doors or in remote regions are essential parts of a comprehensive conception of dissent and cannot be relegated to the realm of the private and marginal. Neither are practices such as meditations for peace commonly considered as constituting acts of resistance.

Part of the conceptual difficulty stems from the fact that the term "resistance" has become fashionable in a culture that cherishes nonconformism and dissent as an expression of one's individual authenticity or one's group identity. As Hegel was already aware, to be modern essentially includes not only experiences of negativity, but the capacity to say "no." As a consequence of the modern ethos to resist, it has become difficult—if not impossible—to claim or reconcile with social and political reality without thereby appearing to be a defender of the status quo, a "yes man" or "yes woman" who suffers from naiveté or conformism. Paradoxically, in an age where resistance has become both the norm and thereby also increasingly meaningless, it needs to take on—or at least *pretend* to take on—the impossible role of a veto player in a political game that does not permit veto players. Resistance is thus condemned to be a tragic and yet potentially valuable and necessary pursuit.[1]

It is the fate of contemporary practices of resistance that, once identified as such, they are subjected to cooptation for neoliberal, commercial, or ulterior goals. Moreover, the focus on resistance often fails to capture the creativity of the insurgent practices it aims to circumscribe. The prefix "re-" in "resistance" emphasizes its reactive nature. Resistance is identified as a reaction that challenges prevailing forms of power, rather than as being a form of activity that is connected to creative dynamics. The need to move beyond the traditional paradigms of resistance has thus been obvious for some time. This volume seeks to revisit the question of what constitutes resistance as an emancipatory practice and thereby to concretize what it means to resist well.

Due to the ambiguous and reactive nature of resistance, we consider it necessary to return to the question of why, and in what form, resistance can be considered a fundamental human right with which subjects constitute themselves as members of a political community. It is common to think of people engaged in resistance following the models presented by emblematic heroic figures of resistance such as Antigone in her defiance against Creon and Socrates in the defence of philosophy against Athenian politics. The thinkers paving the way for the codification of a right to resist draw on an older tradition of civil and religious resistance that has been articulated since the Roman theory of a social contract that included resistance to violations of what has been explicitly or implicitly agreed to by the members of a political community. The concept was further developed in terms of a distinctive right to resist (*ius resistendi*) against abuses of power in the late medieval natural right tradition, culminating in the discussion of civil resistance as an essential form of political agency. To counteract the abuses of power and to advance the common good, the Jesuit Francisco Suarez insisted on a right to defy and, if necessary, overthrow, illegitimate forms of authority. The theories of tyrannicide proposed by the Monarchomachs in France during the sixteenth and seventeenth centuries were a further step toward countering the imposition of absolutist rule and the persecution of religious minorities. Finally, the French Revolution contributed to a universalization of the right to resistance and its transformation into a duty. Thus, while the 1789 version of the *Declaration of the Rights of Man and Citizens* recognized a right of resistance of "Man" to oppression, the 1793 version proclaimed that insurrection is not only "the most sacred of rights," but that it belongs to all human beings as "the most indispensable of duties."[2] The Western discourse of resistance has been further developed by Locke, Mill, Marx, Benjamin, and Martin Luther King, Jr., among others, while authors such as Heidegger and Foucault have attempted to seek unexplored potentials for resistance in what they perceived as an increasingly irresistible, powerful, and self-destructive modernity. In addition to this philosophical focus on resistance, the right to assembly and petition peacefully has entered constitutional documents as a codified right. What this resistance discourse shares in common is that it has conceived of resistance largely as a defensive strategy against tyrants and other forms of social and political injustice.

One attempt to bypass the defensive conception of resistance that has often been diagnosed as a shared feature of protest movements has been the emphasis on constituent power. Rather than unquestionably adopting the reactive dimension of resistance, the constituent power paradigm emphasizes bottom-up and creative rather than top-down forms of predictable contestation. It focuses on processes of democratic self-activation. Specifically, dynamic forms of resistance from below display previously unexplored features of social and political agency. They are enacted by the oppressed and structurally disadvantaged, including minorities, women, refugees excluded from citizenship, and precarious members of a community. Practices of contestation take place at a national, international, and ultimately at a global level where human beings arrive with distinctive horizons of memory entangled with complex histories of often invisible oppression, as well as potentials for emancipation that are being identified, created, and transformed by diverse cultural influences.

The advantage of this conceptual move towards constituent power is to become aware of pre- or extra-institutional modes of creatively occupying and reclaiming political spaces, which goes beyond the mere capacity for expressing a "no-stance," which has dominated resistance strategies that are primarily or even exclusively defined in terms of their reaction against the perceived targets of protest. Yet, even though the turn to resistance as a feature of constituent people-centric power that emphasizes creative agency from below as well as from the margins has emphasized the need for a transnational protest culture, its theoretical vocabulary is frequently burdened by conceptual predecisions. In particular, the "official" vocabulary of resistance movements and acknowledged practices of dissent is limited by the cultural preoccupations of the Global North that has emerged with the articulation of resistance in the liberal as well as in the Marxist and Neo-Marxist traditions. The blind spot of these approaches is that they have been insufficiently attentive to phenomena of resistance that reflect non-Western theoretical paradigms, especially those forms of resistance that have emerged in the East as well as in the global South. Moreover, these traditional paradigms of conceptualizing resistance may not be adequate to capture the transformation of defiant practices in light of new media such as the internet and the seemingly enduring success of authoritarian forms of governance drawing on new forms of technologies and AI for the purpose of expanding technological surveillance and political control.

Given the above considerations, this volume departs from the methodological assumption that it is necessary to, first, remain aware of the need to critically address the challenge of the umbrella concept of resistance to be neither too broad nor too narrow. Second, it aims to focus on the often implicit biases of theories of resistance to predominantly draw on established Western conceptions of what constitutes modern political resistance and, third, it seeks to identify forms and practices of largely invisible and under-theorized forms of resistance.

The contributions in this volume set out to present a complex constellation of paradigms of resistance that aims to break new ground by rethinking what it means to resist. They take into account dimensions of resistance that have not been adequately noticed such as spiritual and network resistance. Moreover, they broaden the conceptual scope of theories of resistance by including non-Western, and specifically Asian, models of dissent. Asian traditions of conceptualizing and practicing resistance have emphasized passivity over activity, as well as the importance of mind–body cultivation and spiritual awareness. Rather than focusing exclusively on questions of legitimacy, power, and redistribution, the goal is to focus on the transformatory potential of these practices that are not commonly associated with resistance. At the risk of generalization, one can say that the Asian constellation of resistance practices has undermined the duality of the distinction between individual and group as well as the distinction between internal and external reality, often by way of linking resistance to sophisticated practices of meditation and cultivation, activities that are not normally linked to political contestation. Rather than idealizing these "exotic" conceptions and spaces of resistance due to their difference to the classical Western tradition of heroic resistance against political power and injustice, we believe that they present timely contributions to the need to establish a dialogue between Western and Eastern resistance discourses and contribute to the cosmopolitan attempt to broaden the theoretical concern for resistance by focusing on global cultures of contestation.[3] We see this methodological shift not as an alternative to a focus on traditional conceptions of dissent, e.g. in the liberal and Marxist traditions, but as complementary.

Let us conclude by briefly summarizing the contributions included in this volume. The first section, "Justifications for Resistance," contains three chapters. The first of these, written by Stephen Palmquist, is titled, "Kantian Conditions for the Possibility of Justified Resistance to Authority." In this text, Palmquist explores and problematizes Kant's theory of justifiable resistance to authority. To begin, he notes that there is a fundamental distinction in Kant's theory between the role of authority and resistance in public and private contexts. According to Palmquist's Kant, when one enters into a private contract, they are forbidden from resisting authority. In contrast, in contexts involving the public use of reason, resistance is sometimes required. Palmquist points out two problems that arise with this theory of resistance. The first difficulty concerns a contradiction that can be found in Kant's philosophical writings. Palmquist points out that in *Metaphysics of Morals*, Kant—in contrast to his previous claims—argues that a citizen *never* has the right to resist the edicts of the government. After detailing this contradiction, Palmquist addresses the second problem, which concerns Kant's personal activities. Despite the fact that Kant extolled the American and the French revolutions, when his philosophical treatise on religion were taken by the government to conflict with the laws of the King, Kant did not seek to resist, but rather simply gave up his right to free expression. Palmquist concludes his piece by arguing that we may be able to avoid these contradictions and discrepancies, which Kant could not. We can do so by recognizing and working towards the ideal, that universities and their professors promote a robust public conflict between philosophers, on the one hand, and those who would seeks to capitalize or monetize the private use of reason, on the other hand.

In Chapter 2, "Justifying Resistance," Christian Schmidt examines the historical evolution of the concept of resistance in the Republican Tradition. He begins his analysis by discussing how modern thinkers, such as Hobbes and Spinoza, interpreted practices of resistance as signs of a malfunctioning social order. Schmidt shows how these thinkers, in being unwilling to concede a "right to resist," laid the foundation for modern forms of civil disobedience. The result of this trajectory can be found in the writings of Hegel, who developed a justification of resistance by portraying the state as an entity of the bourgeois. Yet, Schmidt argues that Hegel's conception of resistance cannot suffice. For the Republican Tradition, resistance cannot be justified without proposing institutions beyond resistance. Conceptions of historical openness and the institutions beyond resistance were only developed by thinkers such as Benjamin, Heidegger, and

Foucault. These authors proposed these new institutions by situating their philosophies outside of the Republican tradition. Schmidt's sets for himself the task of reconceiving of post-republican institutions. As he shows, such institutions would allow for resistance against their fundamental principles, while still working for the demands of the public.

Phillip Hogh concludes the section with "Beyond Morality. On the Relation Between Indifference and Resistance." Hogh explores different aspects of the relationship between Kant's "fully moralized" society and everyday acts of resistance in our current world. His account is grounded in the insight that any act of resistance has the goal of dismantling that which is the reason for that act in the first place—for some examples, a continuing cruel event, an obtaining unjust institution, or the cruel rule of a dictator. The one who resists, seeks to make all resistance unnecessary, by eradicating the event, institution, or rule. Yet, resistance could attain such success—where all resistance would be unnecessary—only when a fully moral society is realized. Here, morality would *be* reality. In this society, the categorical imperative and the moral law would be instantiated in the activities of each individual. Hogh investigates the implications of a "fully moral" society in three stages. To do so, he draws on the insights of Wilde, Adorno, and Amery. First, Hogh explores the possibilities and impossibilities of such a society by drawing extensively from Kant's philosophy. Second, he shows that there are concrete limitations that concern the realization of a fully moral society. Finally, Hogh advances the original argument that a fully moral society would in fact not be perfectly moral at all, but rather, counterintuitively, it would be amoral, because it would have entirely detached itself from questions of morality and immorality. That is to say that Hogh concludes his essay by defending the observation, that a completely moral society would be amoral.

The second section of the volume, "Resistance, Revolution, and Social Change," comprises four chapters. Stefan Deines begins this section with "On the Temporal Structure of Resistant Practices: A Hermeneutical Proposal." In this chapter, Deines advances a radically new way to conceive of acts of resistance. To begin, he explores two contemporary approaches to resistance, which have normally been taken as contradictory. On the one hand, there is the approach proposed by Butler, Rorty, and Arendt, according to which resistance is a clear break from existing conditions of society and politics. On the other hand, Gadamer and Walzer emphasize that resistance is still primarily a continuation of tradition. Deines outlines that there are shortcomings with both accounts. The former seemingly cannot explain how resistance is a form of practice, while the latter cannot show why resistance is important for social progress. In this text, Deines does not counter these objections, but rather proposes a new middle ground, which draws from both accounts. Deines' novel theory is grounded in his unique methodology. Specifically, he focuses his study on the temporality of the acts of resistance. He understands (and grasps the problems of) the two standard theories of resistance by interpreting them as representing two paradigmatic ways of exploring the temporality of resistant practices. On that basis, he proposes his own theory, which can recognize how resistance acts are both preserving *and* altering. He shows how this new philosophy provides a framework for understanding actions and practices of resistance, along with tradition and discourse.

Next, the reader will find Alexei Procyshyn's chapter, "Resistance and Social Transformation in Walter Benjamin's 'On the Critique of Violence.'" In his text, Procyshyn presents an original interpretation of Benjamin's work. In contrast to both Derrida's and Agamben's reading, Procyshyn reveals that Benjamin's text was written as a critique of and alternative to Weber's account of politics. Weber, Benjamin asserts, concluded that political and practical action is always mediated by structures and institutions. As Prochyshyn shows, this leads Weber to conclude that all political acts of resistance are, in part, self-defeating. In contrast, Prochyshyn's Benjamin puts forward an analysis that denies that political actions must be mediated by such institutions or structures. This observation allows for Benjamin to uncover an intersubjective political agent, which was definitively hidden for Weber's mediatory account. By reading *On the Critique of Violence* in this way, Proscyshyn accomplishes two goals. First, he sees that Benjamin thinks of violence in a new way. While violence can aid in attaining certain socio-historical goals, he notes that it has other purposes as well. Second, Proscyshyn discloses that Benjamin focuses on collective action over individual resistance activities. By making these two points, the author can show that Benjamin's work presents a non-mystical form of resistance and engagement with society.

In the chapter "Passive Resistance: A Daoist Approach," Mario Wenning turns to the classical Chinese tradition of philosophical Daoism to rethink the nature of passive resistance. While passive resistance is often associated with civil disobedience—as in the case of Gandhi's anti-colonial struggle and King's civil rights movement—the chapter reconstructs the importance of Daoist motifs for a new conception of transcultural resistance. By turning to the resistance against National Socialism by the resistance fighters of the White Rose movement and the Marxist poet Bertolt Brecht, the chapter distinguishes between heroic and nonheroic forms of resistance to then discuss the potentials of resistance-in-place in today's economy of ambition. The Daoist concept of "wuwei" presents a heuristic tool that helps to identify and interpret otherwise marginalized forms of subversive practice that embrace silent, passive, and rogue forms of dissent over direct modes of political contestation.

The second section concludes with Jinting Wu's chapter, "Resistance through Transformation: Spiritual Practices as a Pedagogy of Unlearning and Becoming." Wu approaches the question of resistance from a different perspective than the other chapters in this volume. She does not investigate what are normally considered acts of resistance, such as civil disobedience or subversion targeted at institutions, but rather rethinks the concept of resistance by exploring how spiritual practices can be forms of transformation from within. Wu studies how spiritual practices, such as meditation, can be the location of a different kind of resistance—a resistance that can radically re-map subjectivity. Her analysis can be broken into two parts. First, she discusses the ways spiritual practices can be acts of resistance. She shows that these forms of resistance are characterized by a suspension of the self-world duality. These practices root out deep-seated behavioral and cognitive biases by expanding the potentiality of one's consciousness. Spiritual practices allow for us to unmake subjectivity and reconceive of its possibilities. Second, Wu applies her insights practically to show how spiritual practices can serve as a site of pedagogical resistance and transformation in educational settings. She reveals that these practices can provide valuable alternatives to solving structural material problems for pupils. In this context, Wu argues that it is only when we reach a collective consciousness that true, lasting wellbeing can be cultivated for students.

The final section of the volume, "Resistance in the Media, the Arts, and Public Health," begins with Liu Shih-Diing and Lin Song's chapter, "Network Resistance in China," which draws on several case studies to reveal novel ways of understanding resistance in the digital age. Specifically, they investigate Internet-based communication in China, studying how Chinese citizens have resisted and reacted online when confronted with the government response to issues such as COVID-19, the #MeToo movement, and recent land seizures, amongst others. Their analyses demonstrate that Internet-based communication opens up new spaces for resistance. Moreover, the resultant social energy found in these digital venues can help create a new kind of political subjectivity. Shih-Diing and Song show that communication networks such as the Internet and mobile devices allow for the possibility of subverting existing power regimes in new and potent ways. At the same time, Shih-Diing and Song temper their conclusions, by rejecting the idea that the internet user can—via their specific forms of resistance—become "post-national subjects." They argue that in the constitution of public discourse, the state still remains an important subject-producing apparatus. In the end, the chapter makes a case for internet resistance as the expression of people's sovereignty under neoliberal depoliticization, while still cautioning against its possible problems in a context of rising populist nationalism.

In the following chapter, "'Probability and Reality Do Not Always Coincide': Uncanny Modernity in Kleist's *Michael Kohlhaas*," Louis Lo draws out the philosophical implications of Kohlhaas's— the main and eponymous character of the novella—paradoxical acts of resistance. Lo seeks to clarify Kohlhaas' radical activities, which appear simultaneously to resist *and* conform to the laws of the state. Lo situates his analysis of this paradox within a discussion of two notions of modernity. He juxtaposes "calculating modernity" or modernity proper, which highlights reason, freedom, and technology, to "uncanny modernity" or antimodernity, which emphasizes the primitive and excessive. According to Lo, the former inspires revengeful thinking, while the latter suppresses resistance and revenge. Lo argues that we can understand von Kleist's descriptions of the actions of Kohlhaas, by recognizing that these two notions of modernity are not fully opposed to each other, but rather blend together in the novel. Lo's von Kleist synthesizes these two concepts of modernity and in doing so, problematizes the concepts of revenge and resistance. Lo argues that we can understand this synthesis and its resultant difficulties by turning to the works of Deleuze and Guattari on the one hand, and Nietzsche, on the other hand. During his investigation of these authors' works, Lo utilizes Nietzsche's insights to disclose that the main emotion of this act of revenge is *ressentiment* or rancor. With these ideas in mind, Lo goes on to ask if it is possible for revenge to be impersonal, in the sense that the hero does not take full control of his revenge? His work asks if there is revenge that is not developed from *ressentiment* and can be taken irrespective of the avenger's motivation.

Next, the reader will find Amita Valmiki's work, "Resistance in the Mysticism of Kabir and Jaspers," wherein she explores what we can learn from the mystics and saints, who revolutionize the space for religious freedom, by resisting traditional religious paradigms. Valmiki examines the insights of two thinkers, before synthesizing their philosophies. The chapter first concentrates on the writings of Kabir Das, who was a weaver mystic from North India. Valmiki shows that Kabir's resistance to social orthodoxy went against the six systems of Indian philosophy. Kabir denied both the common rituals of the faith and the compartmentalizing of religious identity into Hindu and Muslim. Second, she investigates the works of the German philosopher Karl Jaspers. Under the influence of North German Protestantism, Kant, and Kierkegaard, Jaspers argued—contra religious authorities—that there is not a single true faith. Moreover, he emphasized that the subject possesses spontaneously decisive freedom and can attain authentic inner life by exercising that freedom. Despite the temporal and geographical distance between them, Valmiki argues for her original claim, that these two thinkers share more than has yet been acknowledged. On the one hand, she demonstrates that Kabir and Jaspers both resisted the doctrinal approach to religion. They concluded that Eastern and Western traditions offer relative truth. On the other hand, both addressed the "existential problems" of the people who seek to resist intellectualism in spirituality. Finally, Valmiki highlights that the notion of resistance in the social field articulated by Kabir and Jaspers is critical for communal harmony in these troubled times.

The final chapter of the volume, "On Dissent Against Lock-Downs: Phenomenology and Public Health during the COVID-19 Pandemic," is written by Tarun Kattumana and Thomas Byrne. The text examines the conditions that set the stage for resistance against government lockdowns, which were mandated in 2020 and 2021 (and which may return). The text can be broken down into two parts. First, the chapter uncovers the historical and societal conditions, which led to the crisis of trust in public health recommendations and the resulting protests against lock downs, by exploring the insights of Edmund Husserl. This analysis of the historical and societal development of the sciences is necessary because the international protests against lockdowns did not occur in a vacuum, but are rather the result of a long historical process. By analyzing Husserl's theory of the history of the sciences, along with some resonances from feminist, social epistemological, and critical treatments of science, the authors present novel insights concern about the relationship between the world of science and the everyday experience of the subject, as they are currently conceived. Second, Byrne and Kattumana extend these insights to reveal why there has arisen a distrust of science generally and public health recommendations more specifically. The authors uncover why individuals might find valuable and necessary public health recommendations to be alienating. They then conclude by directly applying their observations to shed new light on concrete cases of protests against lockdowns in different countries around the world.

Notes

1 See Armin Nassehi, *Das große Nein: Eigendynamik und Tragik des gesellschaftlichen Protests* (Hamburg: Kursbuch, 2020).
2 Cited in James D. Ingram, "Radical Cosmopolitanism and the Tradition of Insurgent Universality," in *Routledge International Handbook of Cosmopolitan Studies*, ed. Gerard Delanty (Abingdon: Routledge, 2018), 21–9, citation on p. 24.

3 For such an attempt, see Esther Peeren, Robin Celikates, Jeroen De Kloet, and Thomas Poell (eds), *Global Cultures of Contestation: Mobility, Sustainability, Aesthetics and Connectivity* (Cham: Palgrave, 2018); Tamara Caraus and Elena Paris (eds), *Migration, Protest Movements and the Politics of Resistance: A Radical Political Philosophy of Cosmopolitanism* (Abingdon: Routledge, 2018); Tamara Caraus and Camil Parvu (eds), Cosmopolitanism and Global Protests: Special Issue of *Globalizations Journal* vol. 14, no. 5 (2017).

Bibliography

Caraus, Tamara and Elena Paris (eds). *Migration, Protest Movements and the Politics of Resistance: A Radical Political Philosophy of Cosmopolitanism.* Abingdon: Routledge, 2018.
Caraus, Tamara and Camil Parvu (eds). Cosmopolitanism and Global Protests: Special Issue of *Globalizations Journal* vol. 14, no. 5 (2017).
Ingram, James D. "Radical Cosmopolitanism and the Tradition of Insurgent Universality," in *Routledge International Handbook of Cosmopolitan Studies*, ed. Gerard Delanty. Abingdon: Routledge, 2018, 21–9
Nassehi, Armin. *Das große Nein: Eigendynamik und Tragik des gesellschaftlichen Protests.* Hamburg: Kursbuch, 2020.
Peeren, Esther, Robin Celikates, Jeroen De Kloet, and Thomas Poell (eds). *Global Cultures of Contestation: Mobility, Sustainability, Aesthetics and Connectivity.* Cham: Palgrave, 2018.

Part One

Justifications for Resistance

1

Kantian Conditions for the Possibility of Justified Resistance to Authority

Stephen R. Palmquist

Immanuel Kant's theory of justifiable resistance to authority is complex and, at times, appears to conflict with his own practice, if not with itself. He distinguishes between the role of authority in "public" and "private" contexts. In *private*—e.g., when a person is under contract to do a specific job or accepts a social contract with one's government—resistance is forbidden; external behavior must be governed by *policy* or *law*. In contexts involving the *public* use of reason, on the other hand—e.g., when a person is faced with a moral decision or is engaged in a philosophical dispute—the freedom of conscience sometimes *requires* resistance, especially in cases where other persons inappropriately attempt to usurp authority over matters that are rightfully up to the individual to decide. In texts such as *Perpetual Peace*, Kant looks forward to a political situation wherein no political resistance (e.g., in the form of *war*) would be necessary. Yet in *Metaphysics of Morals*, he argues that a citizen never has the right to revolt against one's government, suggesting we must cooperate even with war. On a personal level, Kant favored both the American and the French revolutions; yet when the censor accused his writings on religion of conflicting with the king's edict, Kant did not resist the (arguably unjust) authority; instead, he waived his (apparently public) right to free philosophical expression. I shall argue that a key to resolving these tensions lies in the principle that *universities* must promote a healthy, "public" *conflict* between philosophers and the guardians of all "private" employments of reason. The only ground for disallowing private resistance, therefore, is the underlying presence of genuine *philosophical* resistance.

1. The Problem of Conflicting Values in Authority-based Contexts

Kant's theory of justifiable resistance to authority has several facets, some of which appear at times to conflict with his own practice, if not also with the theory itself. In texts such as "The Doctrine of Right" (Part I of *The Metaphysics of Morals*), he argues that citizens never have the right to revolt against their government, suggesting we must cooperate even with situations involving politically motivated abuse, such as war.[1] Similarly, individuals in various types of contractual relationship, such as that between an employer and an employee, are duty-bound to cooperate with whatever policies or laws those in authority over them may impose.[2] In other texts, such as *Perpetual Peace*, where Kant envisions a future world situation that will leave no room for political resistance of state against state (i.e., no room for *war*), he argues that this ultimate goal of human history can be reached only if states first agree to form themselves into a Federation of States. He envisions a world situation whereby this over-arching governing body would serve as a *higher* authority whose international laws each state would be obligated to obey, just as individuals within any given state must obey that state's internal laws.[3]

By means of theories such as these, Kant weaves into the very fabric of his vision of a civil society a seemingly absolute requirement of *obedience* to whatever person or body may hold a position of authority over us. Many commentators have pointed out that this highly *conservative* message to individuals seems incongruent with the fact that Kant is widely regarded as one of the founding fathers of political *liberalism*. The main thrust of Kant's political theory seems clearly designed to enshrine *freedom* and individual *liberty* as necessary requirements of an enlightened political community, so why does he repeatedly emphasize obedience to authority?

Turning our attention to Kant's personal views, we find a similar tension. Kant openly praised both the American and the French revolutions.[4] Yet in 1794, when his own writings on religion were deemed to be inconsistent with the king's edict imposing religious censorship, Kant failed to resist the censor's authority, even though the ruling was arguably unjust; instead, he *gave up* his presumed right to free public philosophical expression, promising never to write or speak on religion again during the king's reign.[5] Kant has often been accused of lacking courage by responding to the censorship issue by simply caving in to such unjust pressure. It is worth noting here at the outset, however, that his personal response in this case is actually *consistent* with his official theory, that we are to obey those in authority over us, even when we feel as if we are being abused. The tension remains, however, between his seemingly wimpish response to being censored and his seemingly wholehearted endorsement of revolutions around the world. In relation to both his private views and his official theories on the issue of resisting authority, commentators have therefore tended to be perplexed when attempting to explain how the sage of Königsberg could have held such divergent positions.

In what follows, I shall argue that we can resolve these tensions by coming to a proper understanding of three important perspectival distinctions. (A perspectival distinction is a description of two or more opposing ways of viewing one and the same subject matter, such that *true statements* can be made from each opposing viewpoint, even though the statements seem mutually contradictory if considered in the abstract.[6]) The first key distinction is between the "private" and "public" spheres of rational discourse. As we shall see, Kant's call to absolute obedience relates only to actions that occur in the *private* sphere; the proper attitude adopted by those engaging in the sphere of *public* discourse is rational conflict. The second distinction is between the higher and lower faculties of the *university*: philosophy, the so-called lower faculty, governs discourse in the public sphere, while all official pronouncements made by members of the three higher faculties (namely, theology, medicine, and law) must follow government restrictions, which are ultimately established by members of the three principal private professions (namely, priests, doctors, and lawyers), in order to protect the welfare of the ordinary citizens who solicit their assistance. And the third is between assessing one's own moral obligations to those in authority and appreciating reason's influence on the historical development of the human race. I shall argue that for Kant the role of universities in general, and of the lower faculty (i.e., of philosophers) in particular, is crucial to a proper understanding of both his official theory (that disobedience to authority in the private sphere is never justified) and his personal expressions of support for various actual revolutionary movements (on the grounds that they are an inevitable expression of *public reason* at certain crucial turning-points in human history).

2. Two Perspectival Distinctions: Private vs. Public Spheres and Higher vs. Lower Faculties

In several publications dealing with political issues—most notably, his short essay entitled "An Answer to the Question: What is Enlightenment?"—Kant crucially distinguishes between the way authority functions in the "public" (*öffentlich*) and "private" (*privat*) contexts. His distinction tends to be somewhat confusing because in certain respects he uses these terms in a way that is opposite to the way we typically use their contemporary English equivalents. For Kant, we are acting in the *private* sphere in any situation where we are under contract to do a specific job or have entered (at least implicitly) into a social contract with whatever political authority governs the place where we live. As I mentioned at the outset, Kant famously and controversially argues that resistance is *forbidden* in such contexts; external behavior *must* be governed by *law* (in the case of citizens living in a civilized state) or *policy* (in the case of freely chosen employer–employee relations), inasmuch as these are private agreements that can always be terminated by the subordinate individual, if the requirements imposed by the authority become too harsh to bear. Among the few absolute requirements that Kant's theory of statecraft requires of all just governments is that *slavery* is forbidden and that citizens must always be free to emigrate.[7] The reason Kant is so insistent on these points—whereas he is not so insistent that, for example, a democratic system is necessarily better for the people than a monarchical system—is that individuals *must* be free to terminate their relationship with the country of their citizenship, just as employees must be free to quit their jobs, if their situation is to avoid being a form of enslavement.

We are acting in the *public* sphere, by contrast, whenever we are faced with a moral decision or are engaged in an open, philosophical discussion of issues relevant to ourselves or to all citizens of our state. In these contexts, Kant claims, the freedom of conscience sometimes *requires* resistance, especially in cases where other persons attempt to usurp authority over matters that are rightfully moral and are therefore up to the individual to decide. Despite the common caricature of Kant as an extreme individualist, his moral philosophy is actually community-oriented to a large extent, depending as it does on the principle of *universal* values; this is why he regards a situation that poses a *moral* challenge as a matter of "public" concern, even though in a sense moral decisions relate to each individual's "inner" rationality and are in that sense personal matters. Ideally, we work out the details of our moral obligations through free and open dialogue with others who are part of our social network of relationships. Kant is well known for regarding certain types of lying as one of the primary examples of an immoral act.[8] So it should come as no surprise when he argues that our ethical (public) obligation takes precedence over our political (private) obligation in the case of lying: presumably even if one's employer or government were to *order* a lie, we would be justified to resist.[9]

This first perspectival distinction suggests two basic conditions for the possibility of justified resistance to authority, although Kant himself does not spell them out very explicitly. First, if one's government or one's employer does *not* permit its citizens or employees to terminate their contracts, then this would seem to be a sufficiently irrational situation to justify a person in resisting the authority's policies or laws. Citizenship, like employment, is a *private choice*, and on this assumption alone does it make sense to demand that those who accept the terms of the contract must obey the policies imposed on them by the recognized authorities. Second, a government (and, arguably, an employer) that leaves no room for philosophical debate also provides the citizen (or employee) with a justified rationale for resistance—though in this case it seems likely that Kant would say the only wise form of resistance would be to terminate the contract (i.e., to emigrate or to quit one's job). After all, a government or an employer who refuses to engage in philosophical debate is unlikely to respond to any *other* form of resistance with anything but harsh and heavy-handed punishment.

Kant discusses the second perspectival distinction in several publications, culminating in his late work, *The Conflict of the Faculties* ([1798] 1996). In this book, Kant comments on the significance of the fourfold division in the structure of the Prussian universities of his day. The three "higher" faculties (theology, law, and medicine) were charged with the task of educating professionals who would have a direct influence on the welfare of the general public. Priests and their churches are to care for the spiritual welfare of the citizens in any state; lawyers and law enforcement agencies are to care for the welfare of people's property; and doctors and other health care professionals are to care for people's physical welfare. In each case, these professionals are under contract, ultimately with the government, to follow pre-established guidelines to ensure that they treat the people properly. As such, governments (and so also, specific employers) have not only the *right* but also the *obligation* to set up standards and to require (e.g., through government legislation) that the members of each profession obey these standards. As Kant points out in *What Is Enlightenment?* ([1784] 1996), there would be a subtle irony in a situation where these professionals were *never* under *any* circumstances allowed to question the status quo. The irony is that ordinary citizens look to such professionals to *establish* the guidelines for good practice, but if they are duty-bound to *obey* those very guidelines, then how will the guidelines ever improve as knowledge develops?

Kant's key to resolving this problem, how the higher faculties can both obey the rules as they now stand and yet also question them in an effort to promote constructive change, lies in the role of the *lower* faculty, the faculty of philosophy. The task of philosophers in the university is not merely to debate amongst themselves, but also to promote a healthy "conflict" with members of the *higher* faculties. Philosophers' debates with theologians, lawyers, and doctors constitute a *public* employment of reason, even though the matters they are debating relate to the *private* sphere that, as such, commands absolute obedience. In other words, Kant's ultimate rationale for never allowing private individuals to resist the status quo is his assumption that an undercurrent of genuine *philosophical* resistance is present in the public sphere. As Kant again puts it in *What Is Enlightenment?* (a relatively short work that was written largely as a tribute to the enlightened policies of King Friedrich Wilhelm I):

> But I hear from all sides the cry: *Do not argue!* The officer says: Do not argue but drill! The tax official: Do not argue but pay! The clergyman: Do not argue but believe! (Only one ruler in the world says: *Argue* as much as you will and about whatever you will, *but obey!*)[10]

When the private use of reason is at issue, arguing with the rules is simply inappropriate: the duty of the good citizen or employee is to obey the rules. But such a stance is tolerable only in a context where the authorities do not regard *public argument* as threatening to their authority. Kant's position, in other words, is that society in general ought to imitate the healthy conflict that should be exemplified by the university structure, wherein students can at one and the same time be trained (from within their own faculties) to be responsible, law-abiding members of professions such as lawyers, doctors, and priests, and yet they can also learn (when undertaking concurrent philosophical studies) systematically to question the very policies and procedures they have been trained to trust. A political system that can ensure peace and stability, and thereby minimize the risk of being toppled by revolutionary forces from within, must seek to imitate this balance between public freedom of expression and private compliance with the law.

The key distinction provided by *What Is Enlightenment?* is between the use of *coercion*, which is based on the state (*civil* coercion being possible only in virtue of the state's existence), and the use of *persuasion*, which is a distinctively *human* power and therefore can be done only by those who have preserved their own humanity. A state cannot *allow* individuals to use violent resistance, because to do so would be to contradict its own sovereignty. A revolution that succeeds is in this sense taking a step backwards, reverting from the civil state to the state of nature. Resistance at this level is therefore justifiable, on Kantian grounds, only if its purpose is not to overthrow the state but rather to *communicate* with it, with the state's ultimate *improvement* as the goal.

Several commentators have argued that, provided one's resistance to authority takes the form not of active subversion, but of what we would nowadays call *civil disobedience* (at least in the passive form of refusing to obey), then it serves as an essentially *communicative act* and as such is justified and not subject to the charge of being subversive of authority. One who disobeys in a *civil* manner (i.e., non-violently) is not attempting to cheat the system or set oneself up as an authority that is somehow *above* the law (this being the core of Kant's objection to individuals deciding unilaterally to break the law), but is attempting to communicate a message to those who make the policy, that the purposes of justice are not being served as adequately as they could be, so that certain aspects of the existing policy or existing law need to be reformulated. Understood in this way, civil disobedience, especially when performed by groups rather than by individuals, can be regarded as a *public* rather than a *private* act; as such, it does not necessarily contravene Kant's principle that in the private sphere one must always obey.

3. The Third Perspectival Distinction: Individual Morality vs. the Role of Reason in History

The foregoing two perspectival distinctions, between the private and public spheres of rational discourse and between the higher and lower university faculties, enable us to grasp the conditions that qualify Kant's (otherwise seemingly absolute) insistence on obedience to authority. It turns out that Kant is not rejecting any and all forms of disobedience; instead, his point is that, viewed from the political perspective alone, it would be self-contradictory to formulate a law or policy giving citizens or employees the *right* (within the private sphere) to disobey. Rights, and the laws or policies on which they are based, function as tools of coercion. If I disobey a traffic law, for example, the existence of the law gives a policeman and the courts the *right* to employ coercive force against me. A right to *disobey* would empower an individual to apply a similar degree of coercive force against a policeman or a judge. Kant rejects *this* justification for resisting authority because it would undermine the entire basis for civil society.[11]

Rather than appealing to coercive force (a tool of the *private* sphere), justified resistance must transcend private political agreements by appealing to *public reason*. In other words, any acceptable form of civil disobedience must be an essentially communicative act, whose main purpose is not to *force* the authorities to change but to make the general public more aware of one's reasons; if civil disobedience is effective and if one's government is good, then such acts will eventually lead to some change of policy that addresses the underlying concerns.[12] The goal of all such public communication, according to Kant, is to learn to "think in the position of everyone else";[13] when a person is not in a position to form an actual group that is powerful enough to influence the sovereign, this mindset can still be used as the key to determining when an individual person is justified in resisting authority. The problem here is that the general public, even (or perhaps, especially) in a democracy, is often influenced by *non*-moral incentives *not* to think from the unprejudiced position of the common good; people all too often have in mind only the rewards they stand to gain by supporting a particular faction, and in this way the unforced force of public reason tends to be ignored.

This deeper understanding of Kant's position only highlights the strangeness of the fact that Kant himself openly declared his support for actual revolutions of his day, such as those in the United States and France. In order to understand how this could be more than just blatantly inconsistent—or even worse, an indication that some of his theories themselves were disingenuous—we must call attention to a third perspectival distinction, between an individual's moral self-understanding and the historical evolution of the human race.

In those passages where Kant admits that an individual might in some situations have a right to resist authority, he bases his proviso on what he calls an "internal juridical duty," stemming from the "right of humanity in our own person";[14] this is closely related to what Kant calls "duties to oneself." Kant holds that these *take precedence over* our external duty to obey the sovereign power of the land.[15] This is because to disobey our duties to ourselves causes us to turn ourselves into a mere thing, and we lose all dignity, essentially sacrificing the humanity in ourselves. Kant states at one point that we must avoid any situation that involves "debasing humanity in one's person (*homo noumenon*), to which the human being (*homo phenomenon*) was nevertheless entrusted for preservation."[16] Kant's point is that *human beings* should view their *political rights* as an opportunity to preserve *humanity* and its *moral duties*. Morality is what is being preserved here, not the state. As Kant writes near the end of *Metaphysics of Morals*: "Be no man's lackey.—Do not let others tread with impunity on your rights."[17] Thus, he earlier makes an explicit allowance for at least a passive form of what we today call civil disobedience: "Obey the government (in everything which does not conflict with inner morality that has authority over you)."[18] In an article discussing these issues, Sven Arntzen interprets these passages to mean that "the exercise of political authority must, for its own preservation, observe the limits expressed by the principle of humanity.…. Political authority requires for its own preservation that the subject resist under the relevant circumstances."[19] But this interpretation misunderstands the referent of Kant's distinction between the noumenal (moral) and phenomenal (political) perspectives on this issue. Civil disobedience is justified only if its purpose is to preserve the (moral) *goodness* of the political authority, not to preserve the existence of a political system *per se*. From *that* perspective, as we have seen, resistance will always be inherently self-contradictory. In other words, Kant's point when insisting on obedience is that the *political* perspective on its own gives us no justification for resistance to its authority.

A proper understanding of Kant's meaning is crucial, because the phenomenal side of this third perspectival distinction, which will enable us to understand the self-consistency of his views on justified resistance, is that what is true for the individual's moral obligations in the present situation is not necessarily the same as what is true for the overall evolution of the human race. According to Kant, reason itself develops, and we may therefore look forward to human history eventually reaching an inevitable goal, as described most fully in *Perpetual Peace*. The rational (though perhaps unreachable) goal of the human race is to build a society where people are good enough so that fewer and fewer (and ideally, *no*) external laws will be needed in order to coerce us to be good. The categorical imperative stipulates that being good means cooperating with other rational beings (including animals and even nature, insofar as these can be conceived at least indirectly as in some sense rational agents). Laws are needed only insofar as people are *not* cooperative. So, not cooperating with a so-called "bad law," or even with a "bad regime," displays a disposition that will ironically cause the political situation to become worse—i.e., to be supplemented with more and more fine-tuned laws that will restrict the people's freedom (by forcing them to cooperate) still further.

The only exception is the type of situation where one is so overwhelmed by the *moral evil* one is being ordered to perform that those in power will clearly recognize your act of passively refusing to obey as posing a challenge to the status quo. In the cases of both the American and French revolutions, the motivation was not merely a lack of justice for an individual or for a small interest group, but outrageous moral acts that raised the level of concern from one of ordinary treason to one of promoting humanity's historically-significant moral evolution. As noted above, Kant accepts the distinction introduced by Hobbes and others, between the "state of nature" (where brute force and the will of the most powerful determine what is right) and the "civil state" (where people enter into a contractual agreement with governing authorities). The reason he officially rejects the legitimacy of revolution is that a revolution inevitably requires, at least temporarily, the destruction of a civil state and a return to the state of nature. By contrast, gradual reform from within is always preferable. Revolution can be justified, it seems, only if all other avenues of change have been attempted without success, and if the public use of reason by the people confirms that the status quo has become too immoral to tolerate.

We are now in a position to suggest two reasons that Kant could have given to clarify why he approved of the American and French revolutions, as cases of justified resistance to the government authority. First, he was not a citizen of those countries, so he was also not subject to their social contract. In this very practical sense, he would not have found himself duty-bound to obey or affirm the principles of their regimes. In other words, unlike citizens of the British colonies that became the United States or of pre-revolutionary France, Kant the citizen of Prussia was in a position that enabled him to observe events in these other countries in a more objective matter. While he would have been obligated to obey the authorities in those countries, had he been a citizen there, his distance enabled him to assess the events from the perspective of their historical implications. Therefore, even though individuals involved in these events acted immorally when viewed from a purely political perspective, the basic moral values they enshrined can be appreciated as empirical evidence confirming Kant's belief in the inevitable progress of human history toward more rational (i.e., moral) social structures.

A second rationale that Kant might have cited is that the British and French regimes were *not* allowing their people to terminate their collective contract with their government. If he perceived the British and French governments as putting their subjects into a situation that virtually amounts to collective slavery, then Kant's admiration for the ideals of these revolutions is not as inconsistent as it initially seems. His statements regarding the illegitimacy of revolt all refer to the *internal consistency* of the law or constitution: the sovereign cannot build into the law of the land a *right* to overthrow the government, for this would undermine the force of the law itself and create a paradoxical situation whereby the sovereign is not sovereign. This, Kant thinks, would be a recipe for disaster. It makes no sense for a government to have a law, or for a company to have a policy, that amounts to saying "if you disagree with the rules, you do not need to follow them." Instead, Kant's position is that enlightened governments will encourage their citizens to *debate* the rules as much as they wish in public settings, provided they privately obey the rules until such a time as the rules may change as a result of such public debate. This is not inconsistent with the view that in some—hopefully rare—cases, the only recourse an enlightened public has is to revolt. There is no necessary inconsistency in rejecting revolution in general as a legitimate political strategy, because it lacks civility and requires a return to the brutality of the state of nature, thus involving its perpetrators in morally questionable actions, but at the same time admitting that from the perspective of the long term historical development of humanity, revolt may be the only way forward when a highly oppressive regime refuses to heed public reason.

4. Conclusion: Summary of the Kantian Conditions for Justified Resistance to Authority

Having defended the consistency of Kant's position on the necessity of obedience to proper authorities with his admiration for successful democratic revolutions, I shall now conclude by summarizing the basic Kantian conditions for the possibility of justified resistance to authority. First and foremost, we have seen that resistance is itself a fundamental condition for the possibility of an enlightened government. In much the same way that resistance functions in the physical world as a constructive expression of the balance between the opposing forces of attraction and repulsion,[20] every political authority *needs* resistance in some form. In a healthy, enlightened society (or a company or any other structured social organization), resistance occurs through the agency of rational public debate, for which philosophers ought to be the exemplars. This is why properly functioning philosophy departments in properly functioning universities are crucial to Kant's vision of the enlightened state. In the context of such enlightened societies, citizens are *always* obligated to obey the law, even if they disagree with it—the sole exception being those rare cases when obeying a law would require a person to act immorally. No citizen in such a society would ever be justified in staging a revolution, because it will always be more productive, from the standpoint of human history, to change the system from within. The highest degree of legitimate resistance in such contexts would be a passive form of civil disobedience, which must always remain peaceful in order to be called "civil" but which may well include deliberately disobeying the morally offensive laws.

In a society that does *not* enjoy the freedom of expression that makes all of this possible, resistance of other types may be needed. In oppressive, totalitarian contexts, for example, it is far more likely that a person might be required to do something he or she regards as immoral. Kant's position is that subjects in such a society should still obey the law even when they disagree with it (just as Kant himself assented to the king's censor when he was accused of having expressed views on religion that were deemed subversive of the government's edict requiring public figures to teach only approved religious doctrines). This is because obedience is good, and making moral goodness real in human society is the rational goal of human history. But in extreme circumstances, when even civil disobedience (i.e., passive non-compliance) on the part of large portions of the population fails to persuade the sovereign authority to change its ways, the ultimate expression of resistance, revolution, may be the only option that will honor our human duty to preserve the humanity that ought to be reflected in every political system. In cases where the sovereign wrongly attempts to squash all resistance, revolution is justified by the broadest demands of human evolution, because ultimately no political system can thrive without resistance.[21]

Notes

1 Kant [1797] 1996: 6.320–3. Even if the constitution of one's political state is clearly defective, "it is still absolutely unpermitted and punishable to resist it" (6.372). For enlightenment comes not through revolution but gradual reform (Kant [1784] 1996: 8.36; Kant [1797] 1996: 6.355). See also Kant [1798] 2006, where Kant associates revolution with "barbarism" (7.326). Interestingly, he elsewhere admits that "violent revolution" may be the only way a republican constitution can arise out of a democracy (Kant [1795] 1996: 8.353; cf. 8.372). References to Kant's writings cite the volume and page numbers of the standard Berlin Academy edition, which are provided in the margins of the English translations.
2 For "it is an external duty to keep a promise made in a contract" (Kant [1797] 1996: 6.220), even if the other party has no power of coercion to force me to comply (6.219). Kant thus devotes a whole section of the Doctrine of Right to "Contract Right" (6.271–6). As applied to states: even though a revolution may in a sense be justified "by a bad constitution" (Kant [1795] 1996: 8.372-3), "during the revolution anyone who took part in it by violence or intrigue would be subject with right to the punishment of rebels." Kant [1797] 1996: 6.353.
3 In the "Second Definitive Article for Perpetual Peace," Kant calls this body a "league of nations" ([1795] 1996: 8.353–7). He makes similar suggestions in a number of places: e.g., [1797] 1996: 6.349; [1784] 2007: 8.28; and [1793] 1996: 8.311.
4 See Kuehn 2001: 4, 155, 340–3, 375–8, 400, 405.
5 For Kant's own account of this event, see Kant [1798] 1996: 7.5–10.

6 For a thoroughgoing examination of this principle and its relation to Kant's philosophical system, see Palmquist 1993: 27–65 (Chapter II).
7 Kant distinguishes carefully between *slavery*, which is forbidden, and the practice of employing domestic *servants*, which is allowed ([1797] 1996: 6.282–4). This distinction is not surprising, given that Kant himself employed a domestic servant for most of his adult life. The only exception to the rule forbidding slave-type situations is that the state can treat certain kinds of criminals as if they were slaves (6.333). On the right of emigration, see 6.338.
8 The duty never to make a "lying promise," as Kant puts it, is the standard example he uses to illustrate one of the four basic types of duty (namely, perfect duties to others) in both *Groundwork* ([1785] 1996: 4.402–3, 419) and the second *Critique* ([1788] 1998: 5.21, 61).
9 This, I take it, is one of the key points made in Kant's infamous essay, *On a Supposed Right to Lie from Philanthropy* ([1797] 1996: 8.425–30), though his choice of examples makes Kant easy prey for those who think he is justifying a cold disregard for the welfare of others. Kant makes the duty to disobey explicit in *Religion* ([1793/1794] 2016: 6.100n), where he argues that "when human beings command something that is in itself evil (immediately opposed to the moral law), one need not, and ought not to, obey them." See also 6.154n.
10 See Kant [1784] 1996: 8.36–7.
11 As Sven Arntzen points out (1996: 410), commentators agree that Kant's main point is to argue that "there can be no *positive* law according to which a subject has a right of resistance."
12 For an excellent account of how Kant's position leads to just such a view of civil disobedience, see the concluding chapter of Maliks (2008). See also Kant [1793] 1996: 8.304.
13 Kant [1790] 2000: 5.294. This is the second of three "maxims of the common human understanding" that Kant lists in his *Critique of the Power of Judgment*. It is closely related to the first of the three characteristics of "the freedom to think" that Kant defends in his essay *What Does it Mean to Orient Oneself in Thinking?* ([1786] 1996: 8.144): "how much and how correctly would we *think* if we did not think as it were in community with others to whom we *communicate* our thoughts, and who communicate theirs with us!"
14 See Kant [1797] 1996: 6.236.
15 In *Lectures on Ethics* (Collins), Kant says: "the duties that stem from right and benevolence are not so binding as those towards myself" ([1784–5] 1997: 27.433).
16 Kant [1797] 1996: 6.423. Arntzen (1996: 414–19) rightly emphasizes the importance of this passage but misunderstands the preservation as being about the juridical state, not the *moral* state.
17 Kant [1797] 1996: 6.436.

18 Kant [1797] 1996: 6.371.
19 Sven Arntzen, "Kant on Duty to Oneself and Resistance to Political Authority," 424.
20 Kant [1786] 2002: 4.527, 552–3.
21 I received valuable feedback on earlier versions of this chapter, when it was presented in various forms and under a variety of different titles, on the following occasions: the international conference on Rethinking Resistance, organized by the Philosophy and Religious Studies Program at the University of Macau (December 2011); a monthly meeting of the Fringe Branch of the Hong Kong Philosophy Café (December 2011); a public lecture organized by the Hong Kong Association for European Studies and the Government and International Studies Department at Hong Kong Baptist University (October 2012); a session of the American Philosophical Association's Pacific Division Meeting, held in San Francisco, California (March 2013); a seminar in the Chair of Judeo-Christian Studies series, sponsored by the Department of Judeo-Christian Studies at Tulane University in New Orleans, Louisiana (November 2014); the "Kantian Peace" Section of the General Conference of the European Consortium for Political Research, held at Charles University in Prague, Czech Republic (Sept. 2016); the International Workshop on Punishment and J. S. Mill, focusing on themes from C. L. Ten, sponsored by the Centre for Bioethics at the Chinese University of Hong Kong (October 2018); and a seminar sponsored by the Philosophy Department at Keio University, Tokyo, Japan (May 2019). My thanks to the many participants at these various events who offered valuable suggestions and feedback, to Hong Kong Baptist University for providing funding for me to travel to some of the events, and to Hong Kong's University Grants Committee for providing grants from the General Research Fund that supported many of the chapter's evolving iterations.

Bibliography

Arntzen, Sven. "Kant on Duty to Oneself and Resistance to Political Authority." *Journal of the History of Philosophy* vol. 34, no. 3 (1996): 409–24.

Kant, Immanuel. *Metaphysical Foundations of Natural Science*, trans. G. Hatfield & M. Friedman, in *Theoretical Philosophy after 1781*, edited by H. Allison and P. Heath, 171–270. Cambridge: Cambridge University Press, 2002.

Kant, Immanuel. *Critique of Practical Reason*, trans. M. Gregor, in *Practical Philosophy*, edited by M. Gregor, 137–271. Cambridge: Cambridge University Press, 1998.

Kant, Immanuel. *Critique of the Power of Judgment*, trans. P. Guyer and E. Matthews, in *Critique of the Power of Judgment*, edited by P. Guyer. Cambridge: Cambridge University Press, 2000.

Kant, Immanuel. *The Metaphysics of Morals*, trans. M. Gregor, in *Practical Philosophy*, edited by M. Gregor, 363–603. (Cambridge: Cambridge University Press, 1996.

Kant, Immanuel. *Anthropology from a Pragmatic Point of View*, trans. R. B. Louden. Cambridge: Cambridge University Press, 2006.

Kant, Immanuel. "Moral Philosophy," trans. P. Heath, *Lectures on Ethics*, edited by M. Gregor, 37–222. Cambridge: Cambridge University Press, 1997.

Kant, Immanuel. *Religion within the Bounds of Bare Reason*, trans. S. R. Palmquist (revising W. Pluhar), in *Comprehensive Commentary on Kant's Religion within the Bounds of Bare Reason*. Chichester: John Wiley & Sons, 2016.

Kant, Immanuel. *Groundwork of the Metaphysics of Morals*, trans. M. Gregor, in *Practical Philosophy*, edited by M. Gregor, 41–108. Cambridge: Cambridge University Press, 1996.

Kant, Immanuel. *An Answer to the Question: What is Enlightenment?*, trans. M. Gregor, in *Practical Philosophy*, edited by M. Gregor and A. Wood, 15–22. Cambridge: Cambridge University Press, 1996.

Kant, Immanuel. *Idea for a Universal History with a Cosmopolitan Aim*, trans. A. W. Wood, in *Anthropology, History, and Education*, edited by R. Louden and G. Zöller, 108–20. Cambridge: Cambridge University Press, 2007.

Kant, Immanuel. *What Does it Mean to Orient Oneself in Thinking?*, trans. A. W. Wood, in *Religion and Rational Theology*, edited by A.W. Wood & G. Di Giovanni, 7–18. Cambridge: Cambridge University Press, 1996.

Kant, Immanuel. *On the Common Saying: That May Be Correct in Theory, but it Is of No Use in Practice*, trans. A. W. Wood, in *Practical Philosophy*, edited by M. Gregor, 277–309. Cambridge: Cambridge University Press, 1996.

Kant, Immanuel. *Toward Perpetual Peace*, trans. A. W. Wood, in *Practical Philosophy*, edited by M. Gregor, 315–51. Cambridge: Cambridge University Press, 1996.

Kant, Immanuel. *On a Supposed Right to Lie from Philanthropy*, trans. A. W. Wood, in *Practical Philosophy*, edited by M. Gregor, 609–15. Cambridge: Cambridge University Press, 1996.

Kant, Immanuel. *The Conflict of the Faculties*, trans. M. Gregor, in *Religion and Rational Theology*, edited by A. Wood and G. Di Giovanni, 237–327. Cambridge: Cambridge University Press, 1996.

Kuehn, Manfred. *Kant: A Biography*. Cambridge: Cambridge University Press, 2001.

Maliks, Redar K. *Making the Center Hold: Kant on Sovereignty and Resistance*. New York: Columbia University PhD dissertation, 2008.

Palmquist, Stephen R. *Kant's System of Perspectives: An Architectonic Interpretation of the Critical Philosophy*. Lanham, MD: University Press of America, 1993.

Palmquist, Stephen R. "'The Kingdom of God is at Hand!' (Did *Kant* really say *that*?)." *History of Philosophy Quarterly* vol. 11, no. 4 (1994): 421–37.

2

Justifying Resistance

Christian Schmidt

1. The Impossibility of Legitimate Resistance

In his book *The Ruin of Kasch*, Roberto Calasso quotes the formula: "The secret nature of the principles of legitimacy is the power to exorcise fear."[1] Originally referring to the fear of those who govern, the formula prompts me to express a deeper truth about modern forms of sociality. In modernity we know a deeply troubling disquiet akin to Hobbes' reflections on the English revolution, namely that upheavals and rebellions may subvert any possibility of a decent human life.

> In such condition, there is no place for industry; because the fruit thereof is uncertain; and consequently no culture of the earth; no navigation, nor use of the commodities that may be imported by sea; no commodious building; no instruments of moving, and removing such things as require much force; no knowledge of the face of the earth; no account of time; no arts; no letters; no society; and which is worst of all, continual fear, and danger of violent death; and the life of man, solitary, poor, nasty, brutish, and short.[2]

This specific fear exceeds by far the concern of any ruling class to lose influence and privileges. It has become a common anxiety, which was fueled by the French Revolution and has been part of popular culture ever since. We find it, for instance, in Charles Dickens' *A Tale of Two Cities*, where the revolutionary jurisdiction in France is described in a way

> that the usual order of things was reversed, and that the felons were trying the honest men. The lowest, cruelest, and worst populace of a city, never without its quantity of low, cruel, and bad, were the directing spirits of the scene: noisily commenting, applauding, disapproving, anticipating, and precipitating the result, without a check.[3]

More recently these images of revolutionary events were revived by Christopher Nolan's movie *The Dark Knight*. According to these dystopian fantasies, all social coordination comes to a halt when resistance to one or more fundamental principles of a current society succeeds. And fundamental is every principle

> by which subjects are bound to uphold whatsoever power is given to the sovereign, whether a monarch, or a sovereign assembly, without which the commonwealth cannot stand; such as is the power of war and peace, of judicature, of election of officers, and of doing whatsoever he shall think necessary for the public good.[4]

Theoreticians and historians of revolutions rarely challenge the appropriateness of the Hobbesian fear of the revolutionary dissolution of the commonwealth by hinting at widespread incidents of spontaneous organisation throughout all revolutionary episodes. Hannah Arendt is one of the few counterexamples. She argued against a misconception of revolutionary events common to both the left and the right that "a revolution did not end with the abolition of the state and government but, on the contrary, aimed at the foundation of a new state and the establishment of a new form of government."[5]

Yet, even in circumstances which could account for such a view, public opinion today is likely to see dangers to the common good in acts of resistance. The rebel movements of the Arab Spring—and in Libya and Syria especially—are cases in point that even uprisings against dictatorship and violently undemocratic government invite the question of whether the outcome of the rebellion will lead to any improvements at all. Rather, one expects chaos and civil war, or the seizing of power by a hitherto suppressed organization, instead of supposing that the resistant subjects will found a new form of society. Only a mixture of emphatically peaceful protests and a pre-existing model of democracy, as in the Eastern European former socialist states or—more recently, although with lesser success—in Myanmar and Belarus, is able to temper such fears.

Hobbes' inability to justify any kind of fundamental opposition to the current state of affairs, let alone active resistance, seems to be excessive at the first sight. Considering the actual hostility against revolutionary changes in current societies, Hobbes' reluctance has proven overly influential. Even Hannah Arendt dismissed Jefferson's idea that every generation should have its revolutionary moment in order to actively affirm the constitutional rules under which it lives.[6]

In order to understand the Hobbesian fear, which underlies structurally conservative worries even today, it is important to notice its foundation in real experience. During the seventeenth century, the inter-confessional wars devastated

Europe. In the especially hard-hit countryside of Brandenburg, local traditions were completely erased. There were simply not enough people left to pass on customs, folk tales, or songs to the next generation.[7] The gruesome details of murders, robberies, and violations that caused this eradication circulated—in an often exaggerated manner—via pamphlets, newspapers, and broadsheets across Europe. It would therefore be misleading to assume that some of Hobbes' biographical peculiarities gave rise to the theoretical dominance of fear in his political thinking. Even Spinoza, who questioned and opposed practically all the intuitions that ground Hobbesian social theory, agrees on the importance of eliminating the specific kind of Hobbesian fear from the social field. To reduce this fear, one has to increase the power bestowed on the commonwealth; and instituting a political order is—in the eyes of those thinkers—the best way to do it.

From the immense stock of collective human potential concomitant with social coordination, Spinoza concludes that while people may quarrel over the given civic order, they are not actually able to completely abandon it.

> Accordingly, from the quarrels and seditions which are often stirred up in a commonwealth, it never results that the citizens dissolve it, as often happens in the case of other associations; but only that they change its form into some other.[8]

At first sight, Spinoza's position seems to be a perfect starting point to justify resistance. Giving a hardly qualified assent to an external sovereign power is no longer necessary without the Hobbesian fear of losing the social bond completely. Instead, citizens might call for the present social order to be justified according to their own standards. But Spinoza is quite clear on the point that no state whatsoever could grant its citizens the right to oppose its juridical form, or even its actual rulings.

> Moreover, we cannot even conceive, that every citizen should be allowed to interpret the commonwealth's decrees or laws. For were every citizen allowed this, he would thereby be his own judge, because each would easily be able to give a colour of right to his own deeds.[9]

Even though the political order might be corrupt enough to necessitate its abolition, Spinoza denies the *right* to resistance in such cases. None other than the person who holds government office—"*qui imperium tenet*"[10]—may effectively judge the status of a given political order. Otherwise the storming of the United States Capitol by Trump supporters in January 2021 would not only be justified (as it certainly was in the minds of the rioters) but would represent the paradigm for politics—leading almost inevitably to civil war. To avoid this path, the decline of a corrupt order is not a matter of justified resistance, but of that order's dissolution due to the civic public's increasing fear and indignation.

Spinoza's position on this issue might be hard to grasp, since he even provides examples of social orders that are undoubtedly in a state of dissolution. These are communities who fail to uphold the reasons for the indispensable fear and reverence which goad their citizens to conform to its regulations. Equally doomed are states where the government loses its ruling dignity due to its officials behaving in ways which are contrary to the strong moral sentiments of the public (for example, if one or several government officials publically appear drunken, naked, in the company of whores, or making fools of themselves—examples which might have lost some of their persuasiveness after the successful electoral campaign of Donald Trump bragging about his abusive behavior towards women). And finally no order can survive if the deprivation of goods or the rape of young girls and women establishes a fear that contradicts the original sense of communal order.[11]

But no matter how unbearable the social conditions might be, resistance is not, for Spinoza, a legitimate reaction to the corruption of the state. When resistance occurs, it is a symptom of the malfunctioning of social institutions. As such, it might even have a liberating effect. When Minneapolis' Third Precinct police building burned to the ground during the protests following the murder of George Floyd in May 2020, the liberating effect became palpable even in the photographs of the tense but at the same time jubilant crowd.

However, it is important to mark the difference. Spinoza regards acts of resistance and rebellion as consequences, at times even inevitable ones, of an inappropriate political order. Still, there cannot be a *right* to resist or contest for logical reasons. Such a right would subvert the very possibility of forming a community at all. It would realize, as Spinoza argues, what no human can consistently try to achieve: the abolition of not just a concrete but of *every* social order.

Why is it logically impossible that a right to resistance exists? Spinoza seems to imply that such a right would necessarily undermine what constitutes the communal state, which is that the whole multitude acts as lead by one mind—"*una veluti mente ducitur.*" The right to judge the common rules effectively for oneself dissolves the unity which brings about the power of a polity. It would introduce divides in the political body of the multitude by virtue of diverging interpretations of each rule. Therefore it would disable the multitude's capability to act as one. Spinoza goes so far as to claim that every contestation of the public order is not only illegitimate, but also unreasonable. The coordination and cooperation in a political body increases the personal power of every individual—his or her capabilities to transform and control external objects—to such a degree that damage to these capabilities resulting from unreasonable norms and orders seems to be insignificant. "For it is reason's own law, to choose the less of two evils; and accordingly we may conclude, that no one is acting against the dictate of his own reason, so far as he does what by the law of the commonwealth is to be done."[12]

What generates this view for the republican tradition as a whole, as recognized by Philip Pettit, is an understanding of law and rules not as restraints of personal freedom, but as its prerequisites.[13] Thus each and every individual is bound by the laws of its commonwealth without any qualification. However, there are qualifications on the political order in Spinoza's thinking which stem from exactly the same source. The common rules and laws are the condition of an effective political unity. But resistance will emerge regardless of its illegitimate character if law and rules fail to produce social concord. Therefore, the political order in itself is subject to dynamic forces which will undermine its stability if they are not controlled by a well-designed structure. Hence, to propagate a new kind of constitutional order is not a matter of legitimate resistance, but of scientific inquiry and insight.

It is obvious from this reconstruction how the foundation of political theory in the republican tradition excludes not only the possibility of a right to resist, but at the same time introduces a scientific discourse of its own right which positions itself by its unqualified respect of the law and of the actual rules outside of their scope. It might suffice here to recall Kant's approval of the formula "Argue as much as you will and about what you will; only obey!"[14] in order to demonstrate the tremendous influence exerted by this new way of conceiving the relation of political theory and political order. Assuredly there are also important differences in the political theories of Kant and Spinoza, since the latter wants to establish more direct ways of political influence by all members of the community than the former. Yet, the status of their reasoning itself is astonishingly similar.

2. The Progression Toward the End of Resistance

As we know today, scientific discourse never was (and never became) a separate space for reasoning. Instead from the outset it developed its own dynamics of interference with actual politics. There is and always has been an "aspiration to power that is inherent in the claim to being a science."[15] Hence the scientific production of knowledge claims was, and still is, a powerful means of either stabilizing or destabilizing any kind of state authority. The scientific assertion that it is rather the fact of the matter, which undercuts the authority, makes the point even worse. Reclaiming for itself the perspective of objective truth, political science pretends to stand outside of the political field when it contributes substantially and effectively to it. Unsurprisingly, this rhetorical instrument was soon adopted by all political players; and it is commonplace today whenever factual expertise is presented to support a political decision. Thereby the interrelations of political convictions and knowledge claims become quite volatile, for they follow the ever changing necessities of daily political decision making. In philosophy of the early modern period, however, the questions around constitutional orders or the fundamental social structure prevailed, thus framing the relation of knowledge claims and political reasoning in a much more stable way.

Equipped with the less volatile truth of its scientific reasoning, the republican tradition begins to develop a different attitude towards the question of resistance. But a major shift in this matter did not take place until a new understanding of history had evolved. In the pre-modern model of history, as we can find it in Machiavelli and Spinoza, history served only as a repository for human experience. Social constellations were made comprehensible by a discussion of historical instances of the very same constellation. Spinoza explicitly declares:

> I am fully persuaded that experience has revealed all conceivable sorts of commonwealth, which are consistent with men's living in unity, and likewise the means by which the multitude may be guided or kept within fixed bounds. So that I do not believe that we can by meditation discover in this matter anything not yet tried and ascertained, which shall be consistent with experience or practice. [...] And so it is hardly credible, that we should be able to conceive of anything serviceable to a general society, that occasion or chance has not offered, or that men, intent upon their common affairs, and seeking their own safety, have not seen for themselves.[16]

From this perspective, developments can lead only to another already known political order. Stability, on the other hand, is a political value since it helps to avoid the severe personal and social dangers of any transitory process[17] (while the transition in itself does not entail any gain). A transition just replaces one accommodation of communal life's fundamental necessities with another one. This is demonstrated by the fact which is astonishing at least for today's readers that a multitude can establish a republican order under the political forms of a monarchy, an aristocracy, or a democracy alike.

As we know, Spinoza did have a theoretical preference for democracy because he thought that the republican elements therein might receive the greatest support from the process of political decision-making.[18] Yet, he put great effort into making proposals for a republican monarchy and a republican aristocracy; and, unlike his democratic model, he succeeded in doing so. His time's common conception of history led him to the conviction that any kind of government has to grant its subjects ways to make themselves heard, both in contemplating questions about the future or by making complaints. While Spinoza does not consider their voices to be ultimately decisive, he nevertheless maintains that they should certainly have a significant effect on the ultimate decision of the ruling authority.

This kind of integrating participation of the citizens in the legislative and decision-making process is the early republican answer to the threat of resistance. It is impossible to justify resistance on this view, but any kind of government has to take into account the reasons that produce resistance. Since these reasons are actual powers—powers that constitute the governed community—there is no choice to ignore or to oppress them if the stability of the political order is to remain secure.

Obviously, this concept of public participation has not lost its significance since the early republican theories first articulated it. Today it still captures the way the procedures of constitutional democracies produce legitimacy. Accordingly, Jürgen Habermas describes "the political public sphere as a sounding board for problems that must be processed by the political system because they cannot be solved elsewhere":

> To this extent, the public sphere is a warning system with sensors that, though unspecialized, are sensitive throughout society. From the perspective of democratic theory, the public sphere must, in addition, amplify the pressure of problems, that is, not only detect and identify problems but also convincingly and *influentially* thematize them, furnish them with possible solutions, and dramatize them in such a way that they are taken up and dealt with by parliamentary complexes.[19]

Another feature of our time with roots in Spinoza's republicanism is how different models of constitutional democracies vary in the degrees and modes of public influence they permit. However, all of these models claim to realize the self-ruling and self-government of the citizens unified in their specific constitutional democracy—in short: to realize their autonomy.

Surely resistance still occurs in such societies. And some thinkers, such as Robin Celikates, even grant it a necessary status, since "structural deficits are unlikely to be addressed from within existing institutions."[20] Nevertheless, such acts of illegal but legitimate resistance are restricted in their means as well as in their ends. As acts of civil disobedience they become essentially another mode of participation. In exceptional ways they demonstrate discontent and give voice to positions which cannot make themselves heard in institutionalized procedures, or that do not gain what their proponents consider to be adequate influence. This includes that they function to correct active institutions without challenging the existence of those very institutions. Regularly, they appeal to the authorities or demand a restitution of correct institutional procedures. In an exemplarily republican fashion their exceptionality is legitimized by their function to stabilize the political community at large:

> In the context of existing political systems, political processes of deliberation and decision making are distorted by almost unavoidable structural democratic deficits—for instance in the dimensions of representation, participation, and deliberation, but also due to the influence of asymmetrical power differences in the public debate, hegemonic discourses, and ideological self-conceptions. This fact constitutes the starting point of the radical democratic concept of civil disobedience.[21]

As already mentioned, restricting or replacing resistance with models of political participation was originally tied closely to a pre-modern conception of history. When history becomes the narration of progressive development, the role of political science changes dramatically. We can trace this transition in one of Hegel's early works: his drafts on a constitution for Germany. The introduction of the second draft starts with the declaration: "Germany is no longer a state."[22] Hegel has to argue against the appearance of the factual existence of state institutions in order to justify his strong claim. In a manner reminiscent of Spinoza, he contrasts the given institutions of his time with the concept of a state. The war against the French Republic demonstrated quite clearly to Hegel that in Germany the unifying bond necessary to constitute a state was lost. There existed traditional institutions which once established such a bond. However, they fell prey to particular interests in Hegel's time, and thus became an obstacle to the effective unity of a multitude who acts as if lead by one mind.

This diagnosis presents Germany as an institutional order which on the one hand works perfectly well in its juridical procedures, yet on the other hand cannot create an effective political unity from these juridical actions (despite the absence of actual resistance). At first sight, this description of an institutional order, which does not cease to exist despite its dysfunction, might appear only as a shift of emphasis in comparison to Spinoza. We would then read Spinoza as someone who describes such an order only as constantly threatened by instability, and not necessarily as unable to exist for a certain historical period of contingent duration.

Nonetheless, it is also possible to interpret the shift from Spinoza to Hegel in a stronger fashion than a simple shift of perspective. We would then read Hegel as someone who sees a partial, but never perfect, realisation of the concept of the state in every actual state. According to this new perspective, history is no longer confined to the transition from one pre-established form of government to another. This transition is rather one that progresses towards the fulfilment of a rational idea of the state. Hegel re-interprets different forms of government as ways to realize the ideal of the state under different concepts (e.g. monarchy, aristocracy, democracy, and their respective variations) which all belong to one and the same idea.

> In considering the Idea of the state, we must not have any particular states or particular institutions in mind; instead, we should consider the Idea [...] in its own right [*für sich*]. Any state, even if we pronounce it bad in the light of our own principles, and even if we discover this or that defect in it, invariably has the essential moments of its existence [*Existenz*] within itself (especially if it is one of the advanced states of our time). But since it is easier to discover deficiencies than to comprehend the affirmative, one may easily fall into the mistake of overlooking the inner organism of the state in favour of individual [*einzelne*] aspects.[23]

This new perspective on the relation of existing political orders and the scientifically established idea of what it is to be a political order not only adds another option to the varieties of institutional change in history, but also sets up an entirely new paradigm of what happens in the history of politics. Institutional change is the gradual realization of an idea in an ongoing progress (although this process may be subject to interruption or reversal).

Obviously, scientific knowledge remains of extraordinary importance under this new historical paradigm. Now the determination of political concepts even has the power to transcend all previous political experiences. Therefore the question of the scientific method becomes pressing, since that method provides us relevant conceptual knowledge. Hegel's method of gaining scientific knowledge starts with the analysis of institutions that occurred throughout history. By way of abstraction, he determines their essence, i.e. what makes them count as the institutions they are. This abstract concept or idea of an institution is the yardstick to assess the quality of an actual institution, i.e. the degree to which the actual institution realizes its conceptual essence. His claim is that the essence of an institution is also the driver for institutional and conceptual developments resulting in a concept that is perfectly congruent with reality.

> It has already been shown and will again emerge in the course of this enquiry that the history of the world is a rational process [...] This, as I have said, must be the result of our study of history. But we must be sure to take history as it is; in other words, we must proceed historically and empirically.[24]

Hegel takes actual institutions as factual evidence for what he extracts as their essential determination. Different historical periods—by virtue of their contrast—may help during the construction of complex political concepts such as "state" or "liberty"[25] in order to clarify specific aspects of these concepts.

Because scientific concepts are related closely to certain historically existing institutions, it is immediately clear why science is a field that witnesses both arguments and the contestation of knowledge claims. The difficult framework of scientific knowledge remained widely unacknowledged throughout the nineteenth century. Instead, science acquired the reputation of providing unquestionable and objective reasons for choices in all fields of human activity. This furnished revolutionary movements with a new self-confidence. Many of them felt backed up by scientific insights, justifying themselves as necessary developments in the course of history.[26] Revolutions were no longer figured as the destruction of the social order, but rather as a (perhaps final) step along the progress of history.

It was one of the most powerful justifications for acts of rebellion and resistance that they were integral parts of change on the world stage, and in turn were justified as a scientifically approved necessity. Political science no longer provided mere impartial commentary on the field of politics, but rather offered an alternative set of rules and laws aimed at replacing actual state institutions. Whereas hitherto these state rules and laws framed the autonomy of its citizens, now the laws of history assumed this role. The laws of history were not seen as oppressing autonomy and replacing autonomy with historical determination. They were thought of as enabling real autonomy by establishing its institutional pre-conditions.

The scientific back-up of resistance was such an extraordinarily strong means of justification throughout the twentieth century that its political opponents attacked it regularly by questioning the scientific character of its theoretical background. The allegation of ideology stressed the political essence of such theories and rejected at the same time their legitimate participation in the realm of scientific discourse. In the end, the whole Hegelian scheme of politics as a science was either rejected as a proto-totalitarian conception[27] or re-interpreted in a Kantian manner.

The Kantian option, which refers us back to Jürgen Habermas' already quoted political theory, determines the concept of a state by equating it with constitutional democracy. It thereby implies that the historical development of social institutions are geared toward this end. The need for institutional adjustment and rearrangement is always possible; or the final institutional form might not have yet been fully realized despite our acquaintance with what it should be in principle. Still, the rule of law, or the communicative procedures of decision-making, have already presented themselves to us as the logical end of history's progress. Consequently, resistance in a strong sense, i.e. resistance as the destruction of old constitutions and the institution of new ones, is an activity of the past. In Western democracies at least, the institutional progression is said to be so advanced that other forms of social development have taken over.

In Hegel's works there is some evidence that he too saw himself at the threshold of a new epoch, one in which social progression was no longer brought about by brute and often blind force, but by the analysis of and debate on the idea behind the political institutions. One can conclude this from examining his lectures on the philosophy of world history from 1830–1, which we know only from student's notes.

In his lectures, Hegel argued that a new "intellectual principle" had been at work since the Reformation and the French Revolution "to serve as a basis for the state": "the principle of Certainty, which is identity with my self-consciousness, stopping short however of that of Truth."[28] Hegel recognized the new foundation of the state as "the will of its individual members," which does not have to conform to the state as "an independently substantial Unity, and the truth and essence of Right in and for itself."[29] Yet, in order to coordinate diverging views and interests, the free will of individuals had to conform to the project of developing common freedom. Rational and peaceful institutional improvement is possible, for Hegel, only if citizens and government exhibit a certain disposition [*Gesinnung*]:

> an *ex animo* acquiescence in the laws; not the mere customary observance of them, but the cordial recognition of laws and the Constitution as in principle stable [*überhaupt das Feste*], and of the supreme obligation of individuals to subject their particular wills to them. There may be various opinions and views respecting laws, constitution and government, but there must be a disposition on

the part of the citizens to regard all this opinions as subordinate to the substantial interest of the State.[30]

It is important not to construe the priority of individual free will as contradictory to one's obligation to subject one's will to law and the constitution. The subordination of the will refers to the substantial interest of the state. And this substantial core of the concept of the state is the realization of the freedom of its citizens.

The simultaneous realization of these two categories, certainty and disposition, would allow a political discourse on institutional change to proceed on that basis that existing institutions aim consciously at the realization of freedom. Therefore, whoever proposes an institutional improvement would have to demonstrate the common advantage of her suggestions. On the other side, everyone who argues for a specific institutional change could be sure that the whole society is unanimous with regard to the realization of freedom as the objective of institutional transformations. This would also ensure that suggestions that invoke the realization of freedom have a good chance to be heard and taken seriously. Institutional changes would no longer require the exercise of force because of consent to the essence of the state and its institutions is already in place. So, at least in my reading, Hegel does not have to be so sure of the ultimate structure of the social in order to establish the realization of certainty and disposition as the ultimate goal of historical progress.

But whatever the exact relation of Hegel's own thinking and the interpretation of his political philosophy might be, his bourgeois utopia remains extremely influential today. It resonates especially in current Kantian interpretations of his theory. Regardless of its appropriateness to the modern reality of institutional changes, identifying constitutional democracy with Hegel's utopia and the end of history delegitimizes all forms of resistance which aim at transcending the status quo and its concomitant interpretation of autonomy as best articulated through the rule of law and democratic policy-making.

We are now in a situation that seems to offer even fewer options than the original republican model of history. Whereas in Spinoza and Machiavelli forms of government might change on the basis of a permanent republican demand for participation, the constitutional democracy appears to be the only option left for the moment. There is no other republic than the political state we are in. Accordingly, the nineteenth- and twentieth-century science of a political history amounted to a mere temporal interruption in the continuous rejection of resistance by the republican tradition.

3. Refraining from the Illusion of Stability

If we define resistance in its strongest sense to imply destroying social interrelations and instituting new ones, and we define its justification as the presentation of resistance as a legitimate activity, then we must conclude that there can be no real justification for resistance. While there are conceptions of history that accord resistance a role in actual development of social institutions, these developments are always directed to a situation in the future where resistance is replaced by processes of social change based on consent.

Yet apart from republican ideas, we know of philosophical approaches that are less concerned with the rule of law and the aforementioned Hobbesian fear. In the early twentieth century, thinkers like Martin Heidegger and Walter Benjamin tried to restore a consciousness of historical openness. Both had realized that republican institutions establish a reproductive complex which gives the theory of the end of history a practical dimension. Benjamin even called it the "experience of our generation: that capitalism will not die a natural death."[31] This small, seemingly insignificant note provides the key to understanding essential aspects of Benjamin's thinking and of his more widely recognized formulations, such as:

> That things go "on like this" is the catastrophe. It is not an ever-present possibility but what in each case is given.[32]

> Humanity figures there as damned. Everything new it could hope for turns out to be a reality that has always been present; and this newness will be as little capable of furnishing it with a liberating solution as a new fashion is capable of rejuvenating society.[33]

Benjamin felt that in his time, the whole idea of progress was completely absorbed in capitalist society, where it had developed a phantasmagorical form. Progress had become reduced to solely the ongoing renewal of commodities and of their phantasmagorical incorporation of human wishes. Therefore, he could not subscribe to faith in progress.

He observed that this ever accelerating renewal "shattered the wish symbols [...], even before the monuments representing them had collapsed."[34] Benjamin thought that this process might even initiate a jolt out of the historical continuum by shocking the integrity of the phantasmagorical structure multiple times. Nevertheless, he maintained that such a leap could not be the fulfilment of an ongoing progress according to an eternal law of history. Rather it had to bring all such processes to a halt in order to open up the closure of the future and to allow a new time to start.

Yet Benjamin did not identify capitalism and its culture of commodities as the only fields of mythical thinking and historical closure in his time. He also considered the rule of law and the parliamentary form of lawmaking as manifestations of a mythical violence. Benjamin recognized violence as the decisive driving force behind the nonviolent facades of juridical procedures and the parliamentary production of consent by compromise. With resolute determination, he wrote in his "Critique of Violence":

> We are above all obligated to note that a totally nonviolent resolution of conflicts can never lead to a legal contract. For the latter, however peacefully it may have been entered into by the parties, leads finally to possible violence. It confers to both parties the right to take recourse to violence in some form against the other, should he break the agreement.[35]

And:

> Nevertheless, however desirable and gratifying a flourishing parliament might be by comparison, a discussion of means of political agreement that are in principle nonviolent cannot be concerned with parliamentarism.[36]

The latter becomes clear if we understand that Benjamin detected the camouflage of inherent violence especially in the work of parliaments, which—due to their own way of handling political affairs—"lack the sense that a lawmaking violence is represented by themselves."[37] This violent aspect of lawmaking is rather obvious, if one sees that the compromise produced by a parliament is only the reflection of—at least impending—violent clashes within a society. The compromise does not abolish this threat of violence, but rather transforms one kind of violence into another. Open violence and conflict change to lawful relations of oppression and inequality. This new kind of violence is more opaque; and it endures. On these grounds, Benjamin called it "mythical." It not only establishes a social order, but also remains silently present in already instituted social relations.

The function of violence in lawmaking is twofold. Lawmaking pursues as its end, with violence as the means, *what* is to be established as law. But at the moment of instatement, lawmaking does not dismiss violence. Rather, at this very moment of lawmaking, it specifically establishes as law not an end unalloyed by violence, but one necessarily and intimately bound to it under the title of power. Lawmaking is powermaking and, to that extent, an immediate manifestation of violence.[38]

As a result, the institution of law and of a lawmaking authority actually is not the eminent reduction or even the exorcism of fear that the republican tradition believed it to be. It is, according to Benjamin's analysis, the *perpetuation* of fear. It is the expression of the failure to solve social conflicts in a nonviolent manner, or at least in a way that violence is pacified by the process.

Consequentially, the rule of law and the laws of history are equally modes of social determination and domination. Autonomy, on the other hand, has become a notion so closely tied to the legal context that its meaning of self-determination gets lost under the influence of Kantian concepts.

In this institutional, practical, and theoretical situation, the idea of an open undetermined future was intentionally a-theoretical. A science of history was rejected, as was any universal argument for any institution. Benjamin's aim was the critical subversion of the capitalist subsumption of all aspects of modern life in order to revive the felt need for change and thereby produce a readiness for action.

Heidegger—opting for the adversarial political camp but being close to Benjamin with regard to the philosophy of history—searched for ways to re-institute social life without relying on a theoretical foundation. He explicitly wanted to acknowledge the absence of any ultimate foundation in the sphere of basic social choices.

> In the usual horizon of "logic" and of the predominant thinking, the projection of the grounding of truth remains pure arbitrariness [...] Here truth is taken as an object of calculation and computation, and ultimate intelligibility by an everyday machinational understanding is claimed as the measure. [...] *But the essential projection of the "there" is the unprotected carrying out of the thrownness that first emerges in the throwing.*[39]

Here, "the essential projection of the 'there'" refers to a different founding of our daily orientations which in their combination constitute the world (our world) and designate our respective places in this world (the "there" of our being). This different founding (Heidegger wrote of the "other beginning" of human history) shall not take refuge in a justification such as mythical extrapolations of the present scientific worldview, religious dogma or metaphysical revelations. On the contrary, the real truth is that metaphysics, religion, and the sciences, are results of our foundational choices and not—not even *post hoc*—justifications for our basic orientations. These orientations are not (and cannot be) safeguarded by such insights. Their results and limitations have to show themselves in the process of carrying out a form of life based on these orientations.

Yet our orientations are so intervened with justificatory practices that we do not recognize free choices as the fundament of the way how we lead our collectively determined life. In order to realize this fundamental truth, the "task is not to 'explain' the projection but to transfigure it in its ground and abyss [...] and thus to show human being the other beginning of its history."[40]

But how is the recognition of free practical choices as the post-foundational foundation of social life to be realized? In both Heidegger's and Benjamin's case, the aim was neither a change for the final good nor change for its own sake, but an altered attitude toward the collective forms of life.

This attitude could of course not remain an individual issue. The demand for self-reflection had—or to be more precise, still has—to find an institutional expression. At least in my reading, Benjamin and Heidegger in all their differences strive for institutions that bear the possibility of their fundamental transformation and even their abolition in themselves. Such institutions would not have the republican function to channel and overcome resistance. They would rather demonstrate the recognition that no constitution of a collective action evolves without friction.

Thus, the demand for such institutions is a radicalization of Spinoza's realism. Spinoza rejected the construction of political bodies as long as their theorizers did not take into account the disturbing of human emotions and interests. However, he approved of considerations which tried to confront or regulate such obstacles to a peaceful, stable, and rational order.[41] The radicalization of this realism in political theory lies in the belief that every organization of human collaboration is seriously threatened by the frictions it brings about. The production of resistance is inevitable. And no authority can govern this unavoidable resistance eternally.

The wish to eliminate or control resistance is the deeper reason why modern forms of governing and policing the multitude arose. The rule of law, and the democratic procedures of participation, did not banish the danger of destructive resistance. New ideas of controlling crowds through influencing individual behavior in almost all aspects of social life were efforts to regain the control which the republican theories had promised as a result of their constitutional innovations. Yet within the anti-republican camp, we find substantial doubt that such a situation is, in principle, reachable.

The diagnosis is that a persistent resistance never ceases to provoke new and ever more excessive ways of social regulation. Thus, acts of resistance are beyond the focus of such philosophical approaches. The more urgent philosophical task is to renew our understanding of institutions.

There is no doubt that people need institutions. However, their dominating character might be the result of a misunderstanding of the conditions under which they exist. The idea of stability, the exorcism of fear—comprehensible as it is—has proven to be misleading (at least to some thinkers). Therefore, the alternative option to republicanism is worth reconsidering.

If nothing else, here we can find efforts to think of institutions differently. The holy grail would be institutions that have enough binding power to enable collaborative action but do not become quasi-natural forces beyond human control.

One final word of qualification is required concerning the disapproval of institutional stability. Today there is a philosophical discourse that Oliver Marchart called Left-Heideggerianism[42] and which rejects institutional continuity in favor of radical change. Under the label of Left-Heideggerianism, Marchart subsumes mainly French philosophers such as Alain Badiou, Jacques Rancière, and Claude Lefort, but he also includes Ernesto Laclau, Chantal Mouffe, and Giorgio Agamben, who adds Benjaminian motifs to this discursive field. Given this revival of ideas brought forward in the first half of the twentieth century, one is inclined to forget that the respective horrors of German National Socialism, the Soviet Union, and Maoist China each provided different but compelling reasons to abandon the unreserved celebration of fundamental historical rupture and readopt the idea of stability. All of them consciously tried to reinstitute a form of social life that would result in the kinds of repression that perverted any idea of liberation with which they were once associated. The idea to limit social change regained plausibility in this context.

Given the historical developments of the twentieth century, it is impossible to take up the political ideas of Benjamin and Heidegger without serious consideration of the aforementioned political orders and the devastation which accompanied them. Such considerations entail at least the inclusion of self-reflection on the effects of power generated by an altered way of institutionalizing human collaboration. Michel Foucault describes this self-reflection as the search for a means to reduce and control the excrescences of power, "to establish a limit to this too much of power, to this overproduction of power, every time and by all means if it is at risk to become a menace."[43]

But does this not mean that one is obliged to reduce and control exactly the effect that Spinoza identifies as the ultimate goal of communality: the increase of power? A closer look reveals that power is capability in Spinoza, and Foucault is far from demanding a reduction or even just a stagnation of our capabilities. Foucault would rather have us control and reduce those power relations that tie the gain of capabilities to an increased heteronomy in our relations to others. "What is at stake, then, is this: How can the growth of capabilities be disconnected from the intensification of power relations?"[44]

Therefore, a post-republican institution would have to do more than merely incorporate the possibility of its change and even its abolition. To qualify as post-republican in the sense that I would like to suggest, it would also require more than allowing contestation and resistance against its fundamental principles. Over and above all this, it would be necessary to create an institutional structure that strengthens and encourages autonomy, together with the individual disposition thereby induced. And as much as that is required, we would also want such an institution to increase the capabilities of the multitude by which it is constituted through the collaboration it facilitates. In other words: The stakes are quite high for post-republicanism.

Notes

1. Roberto Calasso, *The Ruin of Kasch*, trans. William Weaver and Stephen Sartarelli (Manchester: Carcanet Press Ltd., 1994), 54. For the original context, see Guglielmo Ferrero, *The Principles of Power: The Grat Political Crisis of History*, trans. Theodore R. Jaeckel (New York: G. P. Putnam's Sons, 1942), 39.
2. Thomas Hobbes, *Leviathan* (Oxford: Oxford University Press, 1996), 84.
3. Charles Dickens, *A Tale of Two Cities* (London: Penguin, 2003), 292.
4. Hobbes, *Leviathan*, 191.
5. Hannah Arendt, *On Revolution* (London: Penguin, 1990), 261.
6. Hannah Arendt, *On Revolution*, 234.
7. See Christopher Clark, *Iron Kingdom: The Rise and Downfall of Prussia: 1600–1947* (London: Allen Lane, 2006), 36.
8. Benedict de Spinoza, *Political Treatise*, ed. R. H. M. Elwes, trans. A. H. Gosset (London: G. Bell & Son, 1883), VI, 2.
9. Benedict de Spinoza, *Political Treatise*, III, 4.
10. Benedict de Spinoza, *Political Treatise*, IV, 6.
11. For all examples, see Benedict de Spinoza, *Political Treatise*, IV, 4.
12. Benedict de Spinoza, *Political Treatise*, III, 6.
13. See Philip Pettit, *Republicanism: A Theory of Freedom and Government* (Oxford: Oxford University Press, 1997), 40: "The general opinion was that without law there was no liberty—no liberty in the proper, civil sense."
14. Immanuel Kant, "Answer to the question: What is Enlightenment? (1784)," in *Practical Philosophy*, ed. and trans. Mary J. Gregor (Cambridge: Cambridge University Press, 1996), , 11–22, here: 22.
15. Michel Foucault, *Society Must Be Defended: Lectures at the College de France, 1975–1976*, trans. David Macey (New York: Picador, 2003), 10.

16 Spinoza, *Political Treatise*, I, 3.
17 See Spinoza, *Political Treatise*, VII, 26; VIII, 9; X, 1.
18 See Spinoza, *Political Treatise*, VII, 5: "It is certain, that everyone would rather rule than be ruled. [...] And, therefore, it is clear, that a whole multitude will never transfer its right to a few or to one, if it can come to an agreement with itself, without proceeding from the controversies, which generally arise in large councils, to seditions. [...] However, [...] a king [...] cannot by himself [...] know what will be to the interest of the dominion: but for this purpose [...] will need many citizens for his counsellors."
19 Jürgen Habermas, *Between Facts and Norms. Contributions to a Discourse Theory of Law and Democracy*, trans. William Rehg (Cambridge, MA: MIT Press, 1998), 359.
20 Robin Celikates, "Civil Disobedience: Between Symbolic Politics and Real Confrontation," in *Demonstrations: Making Normative Orders*, ed. Frankfurter Kunstverein and Exzellenzcluster, "Die Herausbildung normative Ordnungen" an der Goethe-Universität Frankfurt am Main (Nuremberg: Verlag für moderne Kunst, 2012), 358–62, here: 362.
21 Robin Celikates, *Demonstrations: Making Normative Orders*, 361 .
22 Georg Wilhelm Friedrich Hegel, "The German Constitution (1798–1802)," in *The Political Writings*, ed. Laurence Dickey and Hugh Barr Nisbet, trans. Hugh Barr Nisbet (Cambridge: Cambridge University Press, 1999), 6–101, here: 6.
23 Georg Wilhelm Friedrich Hegel, *Elements of the Philosophy of Right*, ed. Allen W. Wood, trans. Hugh Barr Nisbet (Cambridge: Cambridge University Press, 1991), § 258 Add., 279 (translation slightly altered).
24 Georg Wilhelm Friedrich Hegel, *Lectures on the Philosophy of World History: Introduction*, trans. Hugh Barr Nisbet (Cambridge: Cambridge University Press, 1980), 29.
25 In addition, we might recognize that Marx—not only in this respect a faithful adherent to the Hegelian concept of science—reinforced the bond of factual evidence and scientific concepts in "The German Ideology" without losing sight of the insight that factual evidence alone, i.e. without a structuring principle, can never represent a scientific fact.
26 Lenin's notorious formula: "The Marxist doctrine is omnipotent because it is true." See Vladimir Ilyich Lenin, "The Three Sources and Three Component Parts of Marxism," in *Collected Works*, vol. 19 (Moscow: Progress Publishers, 1977), 21–8, here: 21.
27 See for an overview M. W. Jackson, "Hegel. The Real and the Rational," in *The Hegel Myths and Legends*, ed. Jon Stewart (Evanston: Northwestern University Press, 1996), 19–25.
28 Georg Wilhelm Friedrich Hegel, *Lectures on the philosophy of history*, trans. J. Sibree (London: Henry G. Bohn, 1861), 465.

29 Georg Wilhelm Friedrich Hegel, *Lectures on the Philosophy of History*, 465.
30 Georg Wilhelm Friedrich Hegel, *Lectures on the Philosophy of History*, 468 (translation slightly altered).
31 Walter Benjamin, *Über den Begriff der Geschichte*, Werke und Nachlaß: Kritische Gesamtausgabe 19, ed. Gérard Raulet (Berlin: Suhrkamp, 2010), 132: "Die Erfahrung unserer Generation: daß der Kapitalismus keines natürlichen Todes sterben wird." The remark is marked and crossed out; however, the significance of both indications remains obscure since Benjamin also crossed out passages which he later reused in other contexts.
32 Walter Benjamin, *The Arcades Project*, ed. Rolf Tiedemann, trans. Howard Eiland and Cavin McLaughlin (Harvard, MA: Harvard University Press, 1999), [N9a,1], 473 (translation altered).
33 Walter Benjamin, *The Arcades Project*, 15.
34 Walter Benjamin, *The Arcades Project*, 13.
35 Walter Benjamin, "Critique of Violence," in *Reflections: Essays, Aphorisms, Autobiographical Writings*, ed. Peter Demetz (New York: Schocken, 1986), 277–301, here: 287 f.
36 Walter Benjamin, *Reflections: Essays, Aphorisms, Autobiographical Writings*, 288.
37 Walter Benjamin, *Reflections: Essays, Aphorisms, Autobiographical Writings*, 288.
38 Walter Benjamin, *Reflections: Essays, Aphorisms, Autobiographical Writings*, 295.
39 Martin Heidegger, *Contributions to Philosophy (Of the Event)*, trans. Richard Rojcewicz and Daniela Vallega-Neu (Bloomington and Indianapolis: Indiana University Press, 2012), § 204, 260.
40 Martin Heidegger, *Contributions to Philosophy (Of the Event)*, § 203, 258.
41 Spinoza, Political Treatise, I, 1 and 6.
42 Oliver Marchart, *Post-Foundational Political Thought: Political Difference in Nancy, Lefort, Badiou and Laclau* (Edinburgh: Edinburgh University Press, 2007), ch. 1.
43 Michel Foucault, "La philosophie analytique de la politique (#232)," in *Dits et écrits: 1954–1988*, ed. Denis Defert and François Ewald (Paris: Gallimard, 1994), 3 (1976–9): 534–51, here: 537: "poser une limite à ce trop de pouvoir, à cette surproduction du pouvoir chaque fois et dans tous les cas où elle risquait de devenir menaçante."
44 Michel Foucault, "What is Enlightenment?," in *The Foucault Reader*, ed. Paul Rabinow (New York: Pantheon Books, 1984), 32–50, here: 48.

Bibliography

Arendt, Hannah. *On Revolution*. London: Penguin, 1990.
Benjamin, Walter. "Critique of Violence," in *Reflections: Essays, Aphorisms, Autobiographical Writings*, edited by Peter Demetz. New York: Schocken, 1986.

Benjamin, Walter. *The Arcades Project*, ed. Rolf Tiedemann, trans. Howard Eiland and Cavin McLaughlin. Cambridge, MA: Harvard University Press, 1999.

Benjamin, Walter. *Über den Begriff der Geschichte*, Werke und Nachlaß: Kritische Gesamtausgabe 19, ed. Gérard Raulet. Berlin: Suhrkamp, 2010.

Calasso, Roberto. *The Ruin of Kasch*, trans. William Weaver and Stephen Sartarelli. Manchester: Carcanet Press Ltd., 1994.

Celikates, Robin. "Civil Disobedience: Between Symbolic Politics and Real Confrontation," in *Demonstrations: Making Normative Orders*, edited by Frankfurter Kunstverein and Exzellenzcluster, "Die Herausbildung normative Ordnungen," Goethe university Frankfurt. Nuremberg: Verlag für moderne Kunst, 2012.

Clark, Christopher. *Iron Kingdom: The Rise and Downfall of Prussia: 1600–1947*. London: Allen Lane, 2006.

Dickens, Charles. *A Tale of Two Cities*. London: Penguin, 2003.

Ferrero, Guglielmo. *The Principles of Power: The Great Political Crisis of History*, trans. Theodore R. Jaeckel. New York: G. P. Putnam's Sons, 1942.

Foucault, Michel. "La philosophie analytique de la politique (#232)," in *Dits et écrits: 1954–1988*, edited by Denis Defert and François Ewald. Paris: Gallimard, 1994.

Foucault, Michel. "What is Enlightenment?," in *The Foucault Reader*, edited by Paul Rabinow (New York: Pantheon Books, 1984).

Foucault, Michel. *Society Must Be Defended: Lectures at the College de France, 1975–1976*, trans. David Macey. New York: Picador, 2003.

Habermas, Jürgen. *Between Facts and Norms. Contributions to a Discourse Theory of Law and Democracy*, trans. William Rehg. Cambridge, MA: MIT Press, 1998.

Hegel, Georg Wilhelm Friedrich. "The German Constitution (1798–1802)," in *The Political Writings*, edited by Laurence Dickey and Hugh Barr Nisbet, translated by Hugh Barr Nisbet. Cambridge: Cambridge University Press, 1999.

Hegel, Georg Wilhelm Friedrich. *Elements of the Philosophy of Right*, edited by Allen W. Wood, translated by Hugh Barr Nisbet. Cambridge: Cambridge University Press, 1991.

Hegel, Georg Wilhelm Friedrich. *Lectures on the Philosophy of World History: Introduction*, trans. Hugh Barr Nisbet. Cambridge: Cambridge University Press, 1980.

Hegel, Georg Wilhelm Friedrich. *Lectures on the Philosophy of History*, trans. J. Sibree. London: Henry G. Bohn, 1861.

Heidegger, Martin. *Contributions to Philosophy (Of the Event)*, trans. Richard Rojcewicz and Daniela Vallega-Neu. Bloomington and Indianapolis: Indiana University Press, 2012.

Hobbes, Thomas. *Leviathan*. Oxford: Oxford University Press, 1996.

Jackson, Michael W. "Hegel. The Real and the Rational," in *The Hegel Myths and Legends*, edited by Jon Stewart. Evanston: Northwestern University Press, 1996.

Kant, Immanuel. "Answer to the question: What is Enlightenment? (1784)," in *Practical Philosophy*, edited and translated by Mary J. Gregor. Cambridge: Cambridge University Press, 1996.

Lenin, Vladimir Ilyich. "The Three Sources and Three Component Parts of Marxism," in *Collected Works*, vol. 19. Moscow: Progress Publishers, 1977.

Marchart, Oliver. *Post-Foundational Political Thought: Political Difference in Nancy, Lefort, Badiou and Laclau*. Edinburgh: Edinburgh University Press, 2007.

Pettit, Philip. *Republicanism: A Theory of Freedom and Government* (Oxford: Oxford University Press, 1997).

Spinoza, Benedict de. *Political Treatise*, ed. R. H. M. Elwes, trans. A. H. Gosset. London: G. Bell & Son, 1883, VI, 2.

3

Beyond Morality: On the Relation of Indifference and Resistance

Philip Hogh

Most of us have probably encountered the situation when someone begs for money on the street. Although the variety of possible reactions to this is fairly broad, there are two reactions that I would call typical. The first type of reaction is: I ignore the question and walk away. The second type is: I give some of the change I have to the person who is asking. If we are to judge these types of reactions, we could say that the first type is determined by indifference towards the suffering of a human being and his request for help, whereas we would have to classify the second type as an act of charity and helpfulness. And if we want to make our judgments even clearer in a moral sense, then Kant's "End-in-itself"-formulation of the categorical imperative may be useful: "So act that you use humanity, whether in your own person or in the person of any other, always at the same time as an end, never merely as a means."[1] If I am called on to use humanity toward any person not merely as a means but also at the same time as an end in itself, my indifference towards the suffering of a human being must doubtlessly be classified as a violation of the moral law. On the other hand, helping the someone in financial distress by giving him or her money could be judged as an action according to the moral law: I do what that person asks because moral law demands treating him or her as an end not merely as a means. If someone's humanity is endangered because of their suffering, I must act and help.

It may not be problematic to accept the aforementioned moral judgment of the first reaction, but the question is whether the second reaction is lawful in the sense of the moral law, since it is plain to see that the financial gift, this act of charity, will only help the other person in the very short term, moment, perhaps enabling them to buy something they need. However, it will not be sufficient to end their dependency on outside help. In *The Soul of Man under Socialism*, Oscar Wilde relentlessly pinpointed this problem. Against the backdrop of Kant's idea of morality, Wilde's line of reasoning may seem astonishing as it is neither egoism nor indifference that is criticized here, but altruism:

> They [the people, P.H.] find themselves surrounded by hideous poverty, by hideous ugliness, by hideous starvation. It is inevitable that they should be strongly moved by all this. The emotions of man are stirred more quickly than man's intelligence; and [...] it is much more easy to have sympathy with the suffering than it is to have sympathy with thought. Accordingly, with admirable though misdirected intentions, they very seriously and very sentimentally set themselves to the task of remedying the evils that they see. But their remedies do not cure the disease: they merely prolong it. Indeed, their remedies are part of the disease.[2]

By helping the poor by giving money to them, I achieve the opposite of what I intended, because I leave the social conditions of poverty untouched and unchanged. According to Wilde, poverty is not a natural state but caused by the capitalist institution of private property, which is why he argues that "it is immoral to use private property in order to alleviate the horrible evils that result from the institution of private property."[3] A social order that necessarily produces poverty because of its formation, its inner structure, does not deserve to be prolonged. But acts of charity, in the sense of using private property to alleviate its horrible results, have exactly this effect. Through acts of charity, the poor are kept alive while at the same time the social order that is responsible for the emergence of poverty is also maintained.

Considering Wilde's perspective, our hitherto clear moral judgments of the two typical reactions to begging are thrown into turmoil. Now it seems that in the initial situation, both indifference *and* charitable acts are immoral because they leave the social roots of poverty, and thus immorality, intact. According to Wilde, the solution to this problem is theoretically clear: "The proper aim is to try and reconstruct society on such a basis that poverty will be impossible."[4] However, this is a difficult task: the first practical step would have to be the reduction of suffering respectively poverty and, as we have seen, this would at the same time be a contribution to the stabilization of the existing social order. So there seems to be no way out of the immoral whole, because even actions carried out with the intention to be in accordance with the moral law ultimately defy it. How, then, is resistance possible?

The aim of any kind of resistance lies in the abolishment of its own causes, a status quo in which resistance would no longer be necessary. Referring to Kant, one could call this state a "fully moralized"[5] society. Here, resistance would no longer be necessary as all human subjects would live according to the moral obligations imposed on them by the categorical imperative. Moral law would no longer stand in contrast to an immoral society. Morality and reality would be unified, so resistance would not be necessary as there would be no unjustified and unreasonable restrictions of one's free will. Instead of being imposed on the human subjects, moral law would be realized in actions whose actors would have made that law their reason to act. There would be no longer any need to confront the human subjects with the moral ought, as they would find it realized—and realize it themselves—in everything they do.

With this in mind, in this chapter I will discuss the thesis that it is a constitutive function of morality to guide actions so that the necessity for an imposition of the moral law disappears. As long as this is not realized, the "fully moralized" society can only be a counter-image of the present state of things. As this insight does not solve the concrete practical problems an immoral and unjust society reveals, it is necessary to understand how acts of resistance are possible in such a society and how they can be morally judged.

In the first part of this chapter, I will try to shortly outline the possibilities and impossibilities of a "fully moralized" social order based on Kant's philosophy of history and his political writings. The second part will then confront the idea of a "fully moralized" society, with the limits its practical implementation would have to face in present societies that are marked by what I will call the subjective and objective aspects of social indifference, and further discuss the question of how much space of action for resistance remains. I will then come back to Wilde's critique of acts of charity before concluding with the argument that a "fully moralized" society would not only have freed itself from immorality, but also from the necessary existence of the moral law, which is to say that a free society would be amoral.

1. (Im)Possibilities of a "Fully Moralized" Society

Even though the question whether or not a "fully moralized" society is possible is a practical-political one that cannot be answered without referring to the institutions a society has given itself, Kant focuses at first on the anthropological issue of how far the moralization of human nature can go.

"[A]s the only rational creature on earth,"[6] human beings are not determined by the physical processes that define their bodies. Instead, as bearers of reason, humans are able to give and take reasons for their actions. These actions are consequently understood as "appearances of the free will"[7] and the latter has to be assumed as existing if human actions are to be understood as not merely natural processes.[8] Kant then assumes that there are two kinds of "natural predispositions" in human beings: those that can be shaped by reason through "experimentation, practice and instruction," and those that are governed by instinct and cannot be controlled by reason.[9] As Kant additionally assumes that all "natural predispositions are destined eventually to develop fully and in accordance with their purpose,"[10] this must be valid for the reasonably shapeable predispositions too. Now, how do we have to understand the full development of these predispositions?

As "reason knows no limits in the scope of its projects," the full development of all "natural predispositions' that are "aimed at the use of [...] reason"[11] cannot be easily anticipated. What rational creatures do with their reasonable predispositions is left up to them, to their free will, which is the cause for their actions (but of course the freedom of their will must not be understood as indeterminacy or randomness). Although it cannot be determined by empirical factors, the will is free only through its determination by the moral law which governs every human subject or rational creature. Thus, Kant calls the consciousness of the determination of free will through moral law a "fact of reason."[12] That said, this determinacy does not force every rational creature to act upon the moral law practically, but it is the only thing that makes reasonable actions possible at all.

Before I can answer the question of what would be the full development of the reasonable predispositions of human nature, it is important to look at Kant's further assumptions on human nature. Although the free will is determined by reason human nature is not *a priori* reasonable. On the contrary, human beings can act out of inclinations, and often do so. As a constitutive part of human nature, these inclinations have an antagonistic character:

> Here I take antagonism to mean the unsociable sociability of human beings, that is, their tendency to enter into society, a tendency connected, however, with a constant resistance that continually threatens to break up this society. This unsociable sociability is obviously part of human nature. Human beings have an inclination to associate with one another because in such a condition they feel themselves to be more human, that is to say, more in a position to develop their natural predispositions. But they also have a strong tendency to isolate themselves, because they encounter in themselves the unsociable trait that predisposes them to want to direct everything only to their own ends and hence to expect to encounter resistance everywhere, just as they know that they themselves tend to resist others.[13]

It is important to stress that both association with others and isolation *from* others are inclinations. Kant does not want to argue that associating with others is reasonable but isolation from others is not. As inclinations, they both have to be understood as parts of the "lower faculty of desires"[14] and as such they can never function as a "determining ground"[15] for moral actions. Instead the "unsociable sociability," the antagonism between the two mentioned inclinations, is a trait of human nature and thus cannot be abolished. As empirical beings, human subjects will always have inclinations and this is why the moralization of society cannot be guaranteed. It will not be established automatically but rather result from a confrontational historical process.

> Here the first true steps are taken from brutishness to culture, which consists, actually, in the social worth of human beings. And here all of the talents are gradually developed, taste is formed, and, even, through continual enlightenment, the beginning of a foundation is laid for a manner of thinking which is able, over time, to transform the primitive natural predisposition for moral discernment into definite practical principles and, in this way, to ultimately transform an agreement to society that initially had been pathologically coerced into a moral whole.[16]

For Kant, the antagonistic nature of human beings is not a disadvantage. It is not an obstacle for the development of a moral whole but its condition of possibility. Without conflict and competition, human beings would never have a reason to advance their abilities.

> Humans wish to live leisurely and enjoy themselves, but nature wills that human beings abandon their sloth and passive contentment and thrust themselves into work and hardship, only to find means, in turn, to cleverly escape the latter. The natural motivating forces for this, the sources of unsociability and continual resistance from which so many ills arise, but which also drive one to the renewed exertion of one's energies, and hence to the further development of the natural predispositions, thus reveal the plan of a wise creator, and not, as it may seem, the work of a malicious spirit that has tampered with the creator's marvelous work or ruined it out of envy.[17]

As the "natural motivating forces" [*Triebfedern*] leading human beings "to direct everything only to their own ends"[18] cannot be abolished, they become means in the ongoing antagonistic struggle of individual interests, in the practical expression of individual inclinations. Hence the competition between these interests then results in the continuous development of those natural predispositions which are shapeable by reason, ultimately in the historical progress of humanity.

So a total moralization of human nature is impossible as the antagonism of inclinations will never disappear. "[N]othing entirely straight can be fashioned from the crooked wood of which humankind is made. Nature has charged us only with approximating this idea."[19] As there will always be an irreducible part of human nature which defies full moralization, the approximation of this idea Kant proposes has to be carried out as juridification of human relations. The form of freedom which can hereby be achieved is called external or juridical freedom: "[I]t is the authority to obey no external laws than those to which I have been able to give consent:."[20] As long as the actor obeys these laws, it does not matter whether he or she does it out of inclination or out of moral insight and conviction. The ideal result of the juridification would be "a civil society which administers right universally."[21] Here all human relations would be governed by the mutual recognition of all subjects as bearer of rights. If this aim is achieved, then the treatment of others as ends in themselves would be practically and socially realized even if the subjects involved would only reluctantly obey the external laws.

Kant's moral law then works both as a counter-image of an immoral society and as practical guideline towards which the juridification of an immoral society has to be oriented. Although a fully moralized society is a utopian idea which may never be realized, we are forced to deal with it pragmatically and determine our external relations as juridical.

2. On the Social Limits of Moralization and the Space for Resistance

For Kant, human nature—as we have seen—prevents the full moralization of society. Juridification, as the pragmatic consequence drawn from the "natural" limits of moralization, does not have to take human nature into account as it is only concerned with the subjects' external relations. The obstacles juridification has to deal with are not natural but social. Why is that? The currently existing forms of right seem to be a juridical implementation of the moral law only if the mutual mediation of right and social domination is ignored. Kant's idea of juridification and right was that every human subject should have equal rights anywhere and anytime. It is an idea of a reconciled totality which unifies all individual human beings as humanity: "[O]riginally no one has more of a right to be at a given place on earth than anyone else."[22]

However, it is the law-governed society of the present that produces poverty, homelessness, starvation, war, and suffering. Juridical solutions have produced what it originally was meant to overcome. At this point, it becomes necessary to leave Kant's abstract moral and juridical considerations respectively to confront these considerations with the social reality of the present. The aspect of contemporary capitalism I will concentrate on is best understood as the replaceability of every human subject, an aspect which becomes even more obvious in times of crisis.

There is nothing natural about being a subject; it is a social acquirement but one that is so fundamental that no subject can get rid of it simply by deciding to do so. While it is not natural, it is but nature-like, or a second nature. Although it cannot be lost like money, keys, or smartphones, the opportunities to realize one's subjectivity can be restricted socially, meaning that although every subject will always have the potential to be the author of their actions, acting itself can be made impossible by social, political, and economic, sanctions. A subject that can no longer act, that cannot realize its freedom, would be a subject only in a formal sense; it would not experience itself as a vital member of society and would cease being a subject in a material sense. This means that the subject's formal freedom that is at the center of Kant's moral philosophy does not prevent it from being replaceable. Only the concrete formation a society gives itself can prevent that. This imminent replaceability marks the objective indifference of every human subject in contemporary capitalism.[23]

If the subject's material freedom is not guaranteed because of its objective indifference, then this has consequences for the subject's relations to other subjects and to itself. To prevent the loss of subjectivity in a material sense, the subject has to ignore its own and others' suffering, caused by the efforts everybody necessarily has to put in if they do not want to be replaced by anybody else. Considering the objective indifference of every human being in capitalism and the danger of being replaced at any moment, subjective indifference towards others and oneself is what follows. Then objective indifference marks the (ir)relevance of every individual subject for society as a whole, and subjective indifference marks the way the subject deals with it. Ironically, subjective indifference as an attitude becomes necessary for the subject to prevent the loss of its material freedom. This means that by trying to prevent its own replacement, the subject contributes to a social process which necessarily and imminently threatens everybody with exactly this replacement. To remain a subject in a material sense, the subject has to cause harm to itself and simultaneously has to ignore the suffering resulting from this. With reference to Kant's moral law, the subject has to ignore itself as an end-in-itself and instead regard itself as a means. This ignorance towards itself is equiprimordially given with the subject's ignorance towards other subjects. "Being hard, the vaunted quality education should inculcate, means absolute indifference toward pain as such. In this the distinction between one's own pain and that of another is not so stringently maintained. Whoever is hard with himself earns the right to be hard with others as well and avenges himself for the pain whose manifestations he was not allowed to show and had to repress."[24] In its exaggerating tone, Adorno's consideration makes one thing clear: This deformation, which Adorno calls "bourgeois coldness,"[25] is not a damage that is inflicted on a complete and healthy human being by social powers but is the normal way of the constitution of subjectivity in late capitalism. From Adorno's purely negative perspective, one could say that subjective indifference is not an immoral exception, but a necessary condition of the current realization of freedom.

Sophie Loidolt proposes a differentiation between active indifference as a subjective attitude towards others, the world, and oneself, and passive indifference as something which is happening between and in human beings, and which cannot be reduced to an effect of subjective actions.[26] Although I agree with this differentiation, I think that both aspects are mediated in what I called subjective and objective indifference, because although subjective indifference becomes visible as an effect of subjective attitudes it is nevertheless the result of a social formation of subjectivity which is why objective indifference must be understood as its presupposition. On the other hand, objective indifference would not exist if it were not reproduced by subjective actions in which indifference is consciously or unconsciously effective. Therefore, the passivity which could be ascribed to objective indifference is in itself a result of subjective actions.

So, it is clear to see that we would be misled if we understood subjective indifference as an attitude of a socially isolated subject. Instead, at this time of numerous wars and environmental catastrophes, we witness a great willingness to help and to give in the wealthier regions of this earth. For every catastrophe, there is a charity event and an organization trying to raise as much money as possible to help the victims. But again, we have to ask if these global acts of charity make subjective and objective indifference disappear, or—to ask in a more or perhaps even less modest way—are these acts of charity to be seen as expressions of the recognition of moral law, and furthermore as expressions of its social realization? As we have seen, Wilde argues that such acts of charity are to be seen as use of "private property in order to alleviate the horrible evils that result from the institution of private property"[27] as these "remedies do not cure the disease" of poverty. Instead, "they merely prolong it."[28] Acts of charity can only be used to alleviate the outcomes; they ignore the cause.

So, on the one hand, acts of charity are the reactions of indifferent subjects to horrible effects of indifference which even indifferent subjects cannot bear, which is why they could be called indifferent resistance against indifference. On the other hand, they leave the source of indifference intact. So, they can be understood as indifferent actions obscuring their indifference. "All interest is nothing more than exercised routine: the sympathy for victims of a catastrophe mediated by television, the progress in one's career, the latest technical device with fantastic functions, the incessant amusement, which has more of a superficial pose than of real feeling. It is actually indifference which is behind this seeming interest and egoism."[29] From this point of view, acts of charity are a form of affirmation misunderstanding itself as resistance. This has consequences for the way in which these acts can be judged morally.

Wilde's judgment is that acts of charity are immoral. This is much stronger than the idea that they are contradictory or inconsistent because they unknowingly reproduce what they want to abolish. To understand the immorality Wilde has in mind, it is necessary to find a formulation of moral law that actually takes the present social conditions of the (im)possibilities of moral actions into account. Marx's reformulation of Kant's categorical imperative points in this direction: "The criticism of religion ends with the teaching that *man is the highest being for man*, hence with the *categorical imperative to overthrow all relations* in which man is a debased, enslaved forsaken, despicable being."[30]

If both Kant's and Marx's version of the categorical imperative must be understood as the only true moral reason a subject can have for its actions, then acts of charity are clearly immoral. Although the giving subject's intention may be different, the subject that receives money or other things as an act of charity does not have the status of a subject. It lives in dependency from the good will of the wealthy and can keep itself alive only through them. Instead of treating subjects as autonomous beings, the social organization of acts of charity keeps the receiving subjects in their heteronomous status. A subject that cannot realize its freedom socially becomes a mere object of administration, and the treatment of a subject as an object through acts of charity can, according to Wilde, never lead to the realization of freedom. As the subjects are regarded as mere recipients of acts of charity they are not treated as ends but as things. This is why acts of charity are violations of the moral law both in its Kantian and in its Marxian version.

But where does this lead us now? One could argue: "If acts of charity are immoral, then stop them. Stop giving money to the poor, because they will never become autonomous beings through this. Instead, they will maybe start to rest on the money they get an thereby increase public spending." This is exactly the argument that is used to argue for cutting social welfare. Of course, this does not offer a solution because this argument would overlook the fact that charity's immorality does not lie in charity itself, but rather in the social order that has produced poverty. If every subject has to use other subjects primarily as a means of ensuring its survival, and has to ignore their and its own suffering, then life in capitalism is immoral. And it is this fundamental kind of immorality that affects even on those actions aimed at helping the needy.

So, from this point of view, the categorical imperative demands too much. The social order of present societies forces its members to treat themselves and each other as objects which can be useful or useless means to achieve subjective ends. If this is the initial situation for every social action a subject wants to carry out, this means that subjectivity does not exist yet as the realized potential to make the categorical imperative the reason for one's actions. Of course, it is possible to treat other human beings not only as means but as ends, so that it is possible to act according to the categorical imperative in some cases. But the Kantian version of the moral law does not just say that we should treat some subjects not only as means but as ends, it says that we should treat any subject like that, and this is what is made impossible by the present social order.

Here Adorno's concept of "bourgeois coldness" comes into play again:

> If coldness were not a fundamental trait of anthropology, that is, the constitution of people as they in fact exist in our society, if people were not profoundly indifferent toward whatever happens to everyone else except for a few to whom they are closely bound and, if possible, by tangible interests, then Auschwitz would not have been possible, people would not have accepted it.[31]

Today, after Auschwitz, we are involved in the suffering of human beings thousands of miles away from us, and the moral obligation the categorical imperative imposes on us would be to stop not only the suffering of our loved ones but of every human being living in this world.

But what are we supposed to do with this insight? Shall we refrain from the moral demand because under the current circumstances no subject can make it its reason to act? Shall we identify it as illusionary because the subjects are not what they are supposed to be and instead be satisfied with the freedom and wealth we have achieved? The term this position could be identified with is "resignation". Here, the insight that every subject is responsible and to be blamed for the suffering of other subjects it cannot abolish leads to an acceptance of the current state of things.

In present capitalism the categorical imperative is an imposition or impertinence because although no existing subject can actually make it its reason to act, it is still demanded from every human subject just because it is a subject.

As a "fact of reason"[32] the existence of the moral law cannot be denied, not even in times which do not provide the social conditions of the possibility of moral action. So, we do not only have to bear the suffering of others but also the guilt of being responsible for that suffering in a mediated way as well as being unable to abolish it. The problem resulting from this is that we cannot refrain from this moral demand if we do not want to lose the possibilities for critique. But on the other hand, it is currently beyond the subjects' power to make the categorical imperative their reason to act, because the social conditions do not provide the possibilities for this. This means that the present is marked by an antinomy between the unconditional demand of the categorical imperative and the nonexistence of social conditions which would make it possible to act upon it.

This antinomy cannot be escaped. But what does this mean for us as acting subjects? At first this antinomy makes it impossible for us to know in advance what is the right thing to do, because that would mean drawing a plan which would guarantee the carrying out of moral actions. This would imply that the right thing to do is prescribed even before the situation appears that would force us to act. It is exactly this point where the technicalization of human action, where indifference becomes visible: when the suffering of a particular human being just becomes an example for a universal rule telling us how to act. In this case human impulses disappear; the subject makes itself hard against its own impulses and against the suffering of the other, and instead only tries to apply a universal rule.

If we look at the example I chose at the beginning of my paper, it becomes difficult to distinguish the two types of actions as indifferent and moral, because neither in the first nor in the second case the needy person is treated as a particular human being. Instead, two different types of rules are applied. If one would really want to help the needy person and not just escape from a somehow uncomfortable situation, one would have to talk to that person for longer than 30 seconds and try to find possibilities to change this person's life. But hardly anybody ever does that. Most of the time we try to find ways how to avoid getting affected by situations like this, in short, we become indifferent.

If one takes this into account and thinks of one of Adorno's most quoted sentences: "Wrong life cannot be lived rightly"[33], then one could argue that considering this total negativity it does not make a difference what anyone does. When life is wrong or immoral—in the sense that I described above—then it does not matter whether you help a needy person or not. Everything is just a particular appearance of the same bad universal. And if one cannot change this universal why bother at all what is right or wrong?

In his reflections on torture Jean Améry says: "The boundaries of my body are also the boundaries of my self. My skin surface shields me against the external world. If I am to have trust I must feel on it only what I want to feel".[34] The speculative power of the self, meaning: of the mind, is bound to an unscathed body. If the body is tormented, the mind cannot escape to objects external to sensual experience. The body becomes the only thing that matters; it is all that is left. What becomes obvious in the case of torture, that mental and cognitive capacities have their limits where the body is tormented or suffering, gives us a crucial insight into the functionality of moral actions. Morally I might never be on safe grounds, but what I can have is a sense for what is unbearable for me as a living human being, a sense for situations in which I can no longer just stand there and watch and endure seeing other human beings punished, tortured and killed.

Kant's categorical imperative does not need a justification because as the "fact of reason"[35] it is in itself the unconditional. But as this unconditional is nothing but pure reason the question arises how pure reason can act, and the answer is: it cannot. For Adorno action needs an addendum, a material impulse as a reaction to a situation that is determined as a moral situation because the integrity of a human being is at stake. This impulse is nothing external to reason; instead the moral judgment—"What's happening here is unbearable—is an expression of that impulse. Adorno's reformulation of the categorical imperative—'to arrange [...] thoughts and actions so that Auschwitz will not repeat itself, so that nothing similar will happen"[36]—is not a fact of reason but an expression of historical experience: "Dealing discursively with it would be an outrage, for the new imperative gives us a bodily sensation of the moral addendum—bodily, because it is now the practical abhorrence of the unbearable physical agony to which individuals are exposed even with individuality about to vanish as a form of mental reflection".[37]

Indifference begins where this bodily sensation is either not felt anymore or where it does not lead to an impulse to action. This means that resistance against indifference starts as attention to situations in which the subject tries making the unbearable bearable and represses the bodily impulses which could make a difference. In opposition to Kant moral actions have to be thought of as a reconciliation of reason and inclination, not as a reasonable suppression of inclinations.

From Wilde's perspective, Adorno's reference to the bodily impulse—in Kant's words, to inclinations—as a *conditio sine qua non* of moral actions, could be called emotionally consequent but not intelligent, because (according to Wilde) it is the altruistic impulse expressing itself in acts of charity which prolongs the suffering of those who shall be helped. On the one hand, though, this would be a misunderstanding of Adorno's thought as the impulse he thought of is nothing immediate; no pure nature, no mere reflex, but rather the point where reasonable insight finds its end and expression in an action which at the same time results from the impulse that this particular situation is unbearable.

Wilde's radical critique of acts of charity, on the other hand, has its reason in his deep conviction that a different, better society was sure to come. From his point of view in 1891, establishing a just society that would no longer need acts of charity was the rational consequence of the wealth and freedom capitalism had already created, which is why to Wilde it was not intelligent to keep alive a social order when that social order had already produced the means for its own reasonable abolition. Carrying out acts of charity was a waste of time, so money and creativity would be put to better purpose in making those acts unnecessary, which Wilde thought was about to happen.

Seventy-five years later, Adorno could not be as optimistic as Wilde, because the turn to barbarism in Europe he had witnessed had destroyed all social revolutionary confidence. Given that barbarism was always possible, one could not have trust in the objective tendency of history to end up in a communist paradise. For Adorno, the question to be asked was: What do we have to do if on the one hand practical change or changing practice is "indefinitely delayed,"[38] and on the other hand humanity's ongoing suffering cannot be accepted either? In such a situation the starting point for resistance is nothing but the individual reflection on one's own involvement in its reproduction and on the damage one inflicts on oneself.

3. Conclusion

It is difficult to say what follows from this kind of resistance. It is easier to say what *should* follow: social practices that remove subjective and objective indifference. Between my sketch of how resistance in the aforementioned sense has to be understood and this resistance's aim, there is a gap. This gap could be closed by drawing up a plan for how to achieve this aim, but then resistance would become technical, a method independent from its actual fulfilment. But perhaps it may be illuminating to think about a situation where indifference has disappeared.

A social order without indifference would at first be an order without the fear of being replaced by somebody else; today, this means it is necessary to compete with others to ensure one's well-being. Human beings could be subjects and treat each other as subjects, not as more or less useful or useless things. So, on the one hand human beings would be able to act on the categorical imperative because the social conditions of the possibility to make it one's reason to act would exist. On the other hand, if these conditions are fulfilled, the moral obligation forcing the subjects to act on it would dissolve. As every subject could be sure that no other subject would be the victim of social irrationality—poverty, violence etc.— the moral necessity to permanently care for everybody else would disappear, too, as would the bad conscience which troubles so many people today and which leads to acts of charity. This means that the only truly moral deed nowadays would be to abolish the immoral present state of things, resulting in a society which would have freed itself not only from its diseases but from the impertinence of the moral law, too. This society would then be amoral but not immoral.

About the character of this new social order, which he called socialism, Oscar Wilde said: "The chief advantage that would result from the establishment of Socialism is, undoubtedly, the fact that Socialism would relieve us from that sordid necessity of living for others which, in the present condition of things, presses so hardly upon almost everybody."[39] Instead of being morally forced to look after other people, caring for each other would become an expression of freedom rather than duty or guilt. Here, the end goal of social relationships is making each other happy; not as an altruistic duty to cover "society's visible sores,"[40] but as a way to become happy oneself; as a way for individual freedom to become reality, not just the silencing of a troubled conscience. Instead, the other person's happiness would become one's own happiness and this would perhaps not be the worst understanding of the realization of Kant's utopian moral idea.

Notes

1 Immanuel Kant, "Groundwork of the Metaphysics of Morals," in Immanuel Kant, *Practical Philosophy*, ed. Mary J. Gregor (Cambridge: Cambridge University Press, 2006), 80.
2 Oscar Wilde, "The Soul of Man under Socialism (1891)," in Oscar Wilde, *The Soul of Man under Socialism and Selected Critical Prose*, ed. (with an introduction and explanatory notes) Linda Dowling (London: Penguin Books, 2001), 127.
3 Wilde, "The Soul of Man under Socialism," 128.
4 Wilde, "The Soul of Man under Socialism," 127/28.

5 Immanuel Kant, "Idea for a Universal History from a Cosmopolitan Perspective," in Immanuel Kant, *Toward Perpetual Peace and Other Writings on Politics, Peace and History*, ed. Pauline Kleingeld (New Haven and London: Yale University Press, 2006), 12.
6 Kant, *Idea for a Universal History*, 5.
7 Kant, *Idea for a Universal History*, 3.
8 See Kant, *Groundwork of the Metaphysics of Morals*, 49.
9 See Kant, *Idea for a Universal History*, 5.
10 Kant, *Idea for a Universal History*, 4.
11 Kant, *Idea for a Universal History*, 5.
12 Immanuel Kant, "Critique of Practical Reason," in Immanuel Kant, *Practical Philosophy*, ed. Mary J. Gregor (Cambridge: Cambridge University Press, 2006), 164. For an excellent examination of Kant's "fact of reason," see Michael Wolff, "Warum das Faktum der Vernunft ein Faktum ist. Auflösung einiger Verständnisschwierigkeiten in Kants Grundlegung der Moral," in *Deutsche Zeitschrift für Philosophie* vol. 57, no. 4 (2009): 511–49.
13 Kant, *Idea for a Universal History*, 6/7.
14 Kant, *Critique of Practical Reason*, 156.
15 Kant, *Critique of Practical Reason*, 157.
16 Kant, *Idea for a Universal History*, 7.
17 Kant, *Idea for a Universal History*, 7/8.
18 Kant, *Idea for a Universal History*, 7.
19 Kant, *Idea for a Universal History*, 9.
20 Immanuel Kant, "Toward Perpetual Peace. A Philosophical Sketch," in Immanuel Kant, *Toward Perpetual Peace and Other Writings on Politics, Peace and History*, ed. Pauline Kleingeld (New Haven and London: Yale University Press, 2006), 74.
21 Kant, *Idea for a Universal History*, 8.
22 Kant, *Toward Perpetual Peace*, 82.
23 For a substantial analysis of indifference in capitalism, see Georg Lohmann, *Indifferenz und Gesellschaft. Eine kritische Auseinandersetzung mit Marx* (Frankfurt am Main: Suhrkamp Press, 1991).
24 Theodor W. Adorno, "Education After Auschwitz," in Theodor W. Adorno, *Critical Models. Interventions and Catchwords*, trans. Henry W. Pickford (New York: Columbia University Press, 2005), 198.
25 Theodor W. Adorno, *Negative Dialectics*, trans. E. B. Ashton (New York: Continuum Press, 1973), 363.
26 See Sophie Loidolt, "Indifferenz. Räume des entmachteten Erscheinens," in *Profile negativistischer Sozialphilosophie. Ein Kompendium*, ed. Burkhard Liebsch, Andreas Hetzel, and Hans Rainer Sepp (Berlin: Akademie Press, 2011), 128–32.
27 Wilde, "The Soul of Man under Socialism,", 128.

28 Wilde, "The Soul of Man under Socialism," 127.
29 Loidolt, "Indifferenz," trans. lated by me, P.H.,136 .
30 Karl Marx, *Critique of Hegel's "Philosophy of Right,"* ed. J. O'Malley (Cambridge: Cambridge University Press, 1970), 137.
31 Adorno, "Education After Auschwitz," 201.
32 Kant, *Critique of Practical Reason*, 164.
33 Adorno, *Minima Moralia*, 39.
34 Jean Améry, *At the Mind's Limits: Contemplations by a Survivor on Auschwitz and Its Realities,* trans. Sidney Rosenfeld and Stella P. Rosenfeld (Bloomington: Indiana University Press, 1980), 28. For a contemporary and subtle philosophical interpretation of Améry's text, see Jay M. Bernstein, "Améry's Body: 'My Calamity ... My Physical and Metaphysical Dignity,'" in *On Jean Améry. Philosophy of Catastrophe,* ed. Magdalena Zolkos (Plymouth: Lexington Books, 2011), 39–60.
35 Kant, "Critique of Practical Reason," 164.
36 Adorno, *Negative Dialectics*, 365.
37 Adorno, *Negative Dialectics*, 365.
38 Adorno, *Negative Dialectics*, 3.
39 Wilde, "The Soul of Man under Socialism," 127.
40 Adorno, *Minima Moralia*, 42.

Bibliography

Adorno, Theodor. "Education After Auschwitz." in Theodor W. Adorno, *Critical Models. Interventions and Catchwords*, translated by Henry W. Pickford, 191–204. New York: Columbia University Press, 2005.

Adorno, Theodor. *Minima Moralia. Reflections from Damaged Life*, translated from the German by E. F. N. Jephcott. London and New York: Verso, 2005.

Adorno, Theodor. *Negative Dialectics*, trans. E. B. Ashton. New York: Continuum Press, 1973.

Améry, Jean. *At the Mind's Limits: Contemplations by a Survivor on Auschwitz and Its Realities*, trans. Sidney Rosenfeld and Stella P. Rosenfeld. Bloomington: Indiana University Press, 1980.

Bernstein, Jay M. "Améry's Body: 'My Calamity ... My Physical and Metaphysical Dignity,'" in *On Jean Améry. Philosophy of Catastrophe*, edited by Magdalena Zolkos, 39–60. Plymouth: Lexington Books, 2011.

Kant, Immanuel. "Critique of Practical Reason," in Immanuel Kant. *Practical Philosophy*, edited by Mary J. Gregor, 133–276. Cambridge: Cambridge University Press, 2006.

Kant, Immanuel. "Groundwork of the Metaphysics of Morals," in Immanuel Kant, *Practical Philosophy*, edited by Mary J. Gregor, 37–108. Cambridge: Cambridge University Press, 2006.

Kant, Immanuel. "Idea for a Universal History from a Cosmopolitan Perspective," in Immanuel Kant, *Toward Perpetual Peace and Other Writings on Politics, Peace and History*, edited by Pauline Kleingeld, 3–16. New Haven and London: Yale University Press, 2006..

Kant, Immanuel. "Toward Perpetual Peace. A Philosophical Sketch," in Immanuel Kant, *Toward Perpetual Peace and Other Writings on Politics, Peace and History*, edited by Pauline Kleingeld, 67–109. New Haven and London: Yale University Press, 2006.

Lohmann, Georg. *Indifferenz und Gesellschaft. Eine kritische Auseinandersetzung mit Marx*. Frankfurt am Main: Suhrkamp Press, 1991.

Loidolt, Sophie. "Indifferenz. Räume des entmachteten Erscheinens," in *Profile negativistischer Sozialphilosophie. Ein Kompendium,* edited by Burkhard Liebsch, Andreas Hetzel, and Hans Rainer Sepp, 125–44. Berlin: Akademie Press, 2011.

Marx, Karl. *Critique of Hegel's "Philosophy of Right,"* ed. J. O'Malley. Cambridge: Cambridge University Press, 1970.

Wilde, Oscar. "The Soul of Man under Socialism (1891)," in Oscar Wilde. *The Soul of Man under Socialism and Selected Critical Prose*, edited with an introduction and explanatory notes by Linda Dowling, 125–60. London: Penguin Books, 2001.

Wolff, Michael. "Warum das Faktum der Vernunft ein Faktum ist. Auflösung einiger Verständnisschwierigkeiten in Kants Grundlegung der Moral," in *Deutsche Zeitschrift für Philosophie* vol. 57, no. 4 (2009): 511–49.

Part Two

Resistance, Revolution, and Social Change

4

On the Temporal Structure of Resistant Practices: A Hermeneutical Proposal

Stefan Deines

1. Introduction

> When we think of the world's future, we always mean the destination it will reach if it keeps going in the direction we can see it going in now; it does not occur to us that its path is not a straight line but a curve, constantly changing direction.
>
> Ludwig Wittgenstein

What is resistance? One might think that there is little disagreement or conflict about how to answer this question. How to characterize resistant practices might also seem obvious. A resistant practice or a resistant stance is directed against specific social and political conditions or forces. This is done in the name of other social and political conditions or forces that are threatened, or made impossible, by these conditions. Resistance, then, is a normatively motivated counter-power directed against threatening forces. But even if one agrees with this minimalist definition, there are still serious differences in the fields of critical theory and social philosophy regarding how an elaborate conception of resistant practices might look.

These differences, I shall argue, stem from different conceptualizations of the temporal structure of the practices in question. Different theoretical accounts of resistant practices model the relation between past, present, and future in different ways.[1] Differences concerning the temporal structure of resistance can already be demonstrated with respect to the concept of resistance itself, which comprises the aspect of continuance as well as alteration.[2] Resistance can refer to the potential of an object or a person to remain as it is (to stand one's ground or to prevail against exterior and changing forces). But resistance is also associated with change, with the potential to alter or overcome prevailing conditions and structures, making room for something new.

In this chapter, I take a close look at two paradigmatic ways to conceive of the temporality of resistant practices in contemporary strands of critical theory and social philosophy. Both ways are mainly concerned with the question of how it is possible to resist existing societal and cultural conditions and how change comes about. The first offers a theoretical account that highlights the importance of the relation between resistant practices and their concomitant existing conditions. I call this the "structural-conservative model of resistant practice." The second offers a strand of theory that points out the aspect of overcoming existent conditions and stresses the importance of innovation and revolutionary transformation. I call this the "event-like (*ereignishaft*) revolutionary model of resistant practice." These two accounts differ radically according to their respective descriptions of resistant practices and the actions of resistant subjects. These differences are so extensive that the two theories even seem to accuse each other of not presenting an acceptable account of resistant practice at all. The first account is accused of failing to explain why the practice in question is resistant or critical at all, and the second of failing to explain why the resistant process can be understood as a practice in the first place. In light of these reciprocal objections, the demands placed on a plausible theory of resistant practices are much more easily explicated. First, the theory should be able to incorporate aspects of resistance and critique with aspects of practice and action. Second, it should be able to explain different forms of resistant practices, ranging from those practices that are conservative and preserving, to practices that are innovative and altering. In the final part of this paper, I outline in broad strokes how one of the existing accounts of resistant practice can be explicated and supplemented in such a way that it can live up to these two demands.

2. Resistance and Structural Conservatism

Resistance is certainly not a key term of Gadamer's hermeneutic philosophy, but a look at his theory can nevertheless help us to understand the relationship between practices of preservation and practices of transformation.[3] In *Truth and Method*, Gadamer criticizes a common prejudice which evaluates tradition on the one hand, and social change on the other, as different with regard to activity, liberality, and rationality. According to this prejudice, change is considered to be the result of an active engagement based on reasons and pursuits of positive goals. Thus, change is associated with emancipation and progress. In contrast, tradition is conceptualized as something that continues passively and without any specific reason. Tradition only persists, so to speak, because it escapes the activity and rationality of those agents which bring about change.

Gadamer wants to correct this view by pointing out that preservation, and not only transformation, should be conceived of as a practice that people engage in actively, freely, and with good reason. Gadamer's theory is thus equally applicable to the description of the practices of preserving resistance and of the practices of transformative resistance—there is no structural difference between them with respect to the aspects of activity, rationality, and freedom.[4] One consequence of the systematic valorisation of tradition is that Gadamer has often been unfairly portrayed as a conservative, reactionary thinker who advocates preservation and criticizes innovation.[5] But Gadamer does not favor—and nor does he recommend—tradition over change. He merely analyzes the conditions and possibilities of human practice.

Of course, it is not wrong to point out this specifically conservative trait in hermeneutic philosophy. But it is, nevertheless, important to keep in mind that the conservatism one finds here is neither a political conservatism nor a conservative attitude, but it is rather a *structural* conservatism. Structural conservatism means that all our practices are based on (and would be impossible without) a fore-structure consisting of beliefs, norms, values, and conventions, which have been handed down through history. Even the practices of change and transformation necessarily draw on traditional elements and features of society, since, without the application of existing norms and beliefs, the altering practices would have no foundation and no orientation. From a hermeneutic perspective, it is this connection with the realm of tradition that renders our actions intelligible. The scope of intelligible practices is therefore essentially limited, and so is the scope of the practices of transforming resistance. It is not difficult to explain change and transformative practices within the framework of Gadamer's philosophy. But this is only true of specific forms of change and transformation, forms which one could call reformist (small, slow, and partial transformations). What Gadamer's philosophy cannot account for is radical and revolutionary transformation. Any radical transformative practice of resistance that distances itself from the existent conditions—and thereby detaches itself from the ground of tradition—would, according to Gadamer, lose its justification and its orientation. It would lose its intelligibility.

The communitarian thinker Michael Walzer assesses the role of tradition in a very similar way. According to his theory, we would be unable to explain the reasons and motivations for resistance without taking the actual existing values and the shared moral dispositions of the society in question into account.

According to Walzer, existing and shared norms and values are the source of resistance. Indignation—as a main motivation for resistance—results from a perceived discrepancy between concrete social conditions, practices and institutions on the one hand, and the acknowledged ideals and values on the other. Under these circumstances, practices of resistance aim to minimize the discrepancy by fighting for a society in which existing values are implemented more adequately. Walzer writes:

> What we do when we [criticize something] is to give an account of the actually existing morality. That morality is authoritative for us because it is only by virtue of its existence that we exist as the moral beings we are. Our categories, relationships, commitments, aspirations are all shaped by, expressed in terms of, the existing morality. [...] One might say that the moral world is authoritative for us because it provides us with everything we need to live a moral life—including the capacity for reflection and criticism.[6]

In Walzer's theory, practices of resistance have a transformative aspect. They intend to change or eliminate existing social conditions and practices. Nevertheless, their main aim is a conservative one: the existing moral structure at the basis of a society is to be preserved and realized in an improved way. Resistance always takes place in the name of an existing moral perspective. The existence of a received moral structure is a precondition for the possibility of resistance. This is the case because motivation, justification, and goal-orientation, which are in Walzer's opinion necessary for resistance, cannot be explained otherwise.

When regarding practices of resistance from a hermeneutic-communitarian vantage point, one has to take into account how intelligible practices are subjected to structural conservatism. Practices of preservation and transformation are conducted in the name of something which already exists in society. These practices shape our moral orientation, our interests, and hopes. Seen from the perspective of hermeneutics, every practice of resistance necessarily contains an element of preservation.

3. Resistance and Radical Transformation

Several theoretical approaches challenge the assumptions of structural conservatism. There are weaker and stronger versions of these objections. Proponents of the weaker version claim that the explanations given by Gadamer and Walzer are too restrictive, and that there are additional practices of resistance which draw on existing beliefs and values to a far lesser extent than the described practices. One can, for example, connect forms of resistance with other reference points and other sources of motivation than one's own tradition: for example, other cultures and other traditions. On the other hand, proponents who hold the stronger version of this objection maintain that practices which draw on existing traditions, beliefs, and values, altogether fail to be resistant in the proper sense of the word. This position assumes that the only practices that count are those that successfully escape tradition and the prevalent beliefs and values.

According to this position, the main criteria for assessing the resistance comes from the degree of distance between the practice and the existing circumstances. Resistance here is conceptualized as a more radical contestation of existing conditions. As a result, resistance cannot be achieved by reinterpreting and revising the individual elements of a tradition, as hermeneutic and communitarian theories might suggest. We have to be critical and willing to discard received values, understandings, and practices. If the aim is to counter the whole structure of existing conditions, rather than to merely counter some specific elements and individual interpretations of the tradition, it is then all the more important to consider more radical forms of resistance. It is especially important to consider such radical forms whenever existing conditions are regarded as so thoroughly problematic that any possible reformulation or interpretation of these practices becomes part of the problem, in other words, when these practices become the very conditions which they themselves were supposed to overcome. This is especially the case whenever the understanding, reasons, value systems, hopes, and aims of the resisting subjects are affected and determined by the circumstances against which the resistance is to be directed. One can think, for example, of the constellations portrayed in gloomy colours by Adorno and Horkheimer. The mechanisms of oppression and alienation, which are, necessarily, target of resistant practices, become so deeply embedded in the constitution of the culture, of rationality, and of subjectivity, that no effective critical distance towards them seems possible. Our thinking, our self-conception, our ordinary political or critical practices, and even our ideas of a better world, become accomplices of identity thinking and capitalist logic. They therefore appear not to modify the problematic conditions, but rather to cement and perpetuate them.[7]

Resistance can occur only when it establishes a greater distance to the existing conditions than seems to be possible from the structural-conservatist positions. In the following I want to examine such radical forms of resistance with regard to the theoretical models of Butler, Rorty, and Arendt. These philosophers each propose different forms of cultural change, which escape the limitations posed by structural conservatism. But before working through this step, I want to take as a starting point Heidegger's description of the historical and cultural world in "The Age of the World Picture," since the event-like revolutionary model of resistant practice will become clearer against this backdrop.[8]

In this text, Heidegger assumes that history takes a discontinuous course. In particular, he sees the transitions from antiquity to the Middle Ages and from the Middle Ages to the modern period as being characterized by vast changes affecting the whole culture. In both cases, radically new forms of being emerge after the ruptures. Heidegger characterizes these three periods as having fundamentally different metaphysical constellations; their ontological and epistemological properties are radically different. It is therefore impossible to compare the different periods with one another; to do so or to explain all three of them with one and the same method would be to involve oneself in an unjustifiable transfer of perspectives and models which can only be adopted meaningfully in the context of one of the given periods.

Thus Heidegger conceptualizes the phases of historical change as being more radical and more fundamental than they are in Gadamer's or Walzer's models of continuity and reformation. But the phases between these fundamental transformations—the actual historical periods or ages—are characterized by fewer changes. According to Heidegger, the fundamental metaphysical constellation remains stable and unchanged for centuries. All the reformist changes during a period are therefore seen, in principle, only as surface phenomena. Essentially they are an expression and an effect of a deep structure, which is basically static and unaltered.

Thus Heidegger postulates two fundamentally different forms of potential social and cultural change. Reformist alterations are superficial because they occur within a framework which remains fundamentally unchanged, and therefore continues to determine and regulate the moves of any practice.[9] In contrast, radical and revolutionary changes can also come about. This form appears when transformations happen to the framework itself, thus making new practices and moves possible. This form of change is radical and discontinuous. Moreover, it cannot be explained or legitimized with recourse to existing practices of justification because all rational and legitimate practices are, as such, characterized as reformatory. The very fact that a practice can be justified exposes it as inherent to the existing system. Accordingly, it takes on the form of being valid but not transgressive. Radical change, on the other hand, is not justifiable, and it is therefore always connected with aspects of irrationality and illegitimacy.

But such radical change is not something we can initiate or bring about. It is something that *happens*; or in Heidegger's terminology, it is an event. For Heidegger, social change is thus conceived of as a kind of destiny.[10]

For Butler, this description of the cultural and historical world is what generates the task of conceiving of a radical form of resistance in the first place. According to Heidegger and Foucault, it is the metaphysical or discursive constellation of a period that defines what is possible: it defines what is considered to be true, what is considered to be rational and intelligible, and even which forms of subjectivity are available. But what if resistance were to turn against the reasoning of a period and therefore against the possible ways of being a subject? What if an established order were able to be modified only by changing its fundamental metaphysical or discursive constellation? Heidegger barely gives a hint as to how it might be possible for subjects to influence their framing conditions in a way that would lead to a radical change that would open up fundamentally new forms of existence.

The theory of critical resistance put forward by Butler aims to explain how such forms of radical transformation are nevertheless possible. In her eyes, if subjects were unable to alter the discursive conditions that make their existence possible, human agency itself would dissipate. Agency, critique, and resistance all have the same meaning in Butler's theory. These terms refer to the possibility of altering the discursive framework of what is intelligible, thinkable, and liveable. It is a crucial part of her theory that no normal intelligible, conventional, and rational practices are able to alter one's discursive conditions. To indicate social injustices, to stress shared values, to demand political reforms, to imagine a better society, to take part in a protest march, or to argue with somebody about social matters—none of these practices is resistant in the strong sense, but (in the end) affirm and cement the existing discursive constellation. Actions which according to Butler's theory actually do have a potential of resistance are, so to speak, failures or disturbances in the discursive framework. Violations of discursive rules and conventions, nonconformist locutions and actions, recontextualizations and resignifications of concepts all lead to a shift in meaning and thus modify the structure of discourse altogether.

These actions are not fully justified within the framework of the existing order, nor do they aim at a specific outcome. One might say that they are world-disclosing: they are not moves in an already disclosed cultural space but rather open up new possibilities of thinking, acting, and living by confusing the existent discursive order. It is impossible to both act and foresee what the results of the action will be and what might be possible in the space the action opens up. The resisting action is therefore not performed with the view of achieving a specific result. Moreover, it is not performed in the name of a concretely envisioned social condition, it is performed in the name of "an open future of cultural possibilities."[11] The aim of the radical practices of resistance, conceived of in this manner, cannot be formulated in advance; the aim of these practices, one might say, is change for the sake of itself.

Rorty's analysis of radical social and cultural transformations follow a similar pattern. Rorty claims that these transformations come from the invention of new vocabularies, which, in turn, establish new orders of justification and thereby new worldviews, self-images, and life-forms. Rorty's theory of cultural change is heavily influenced by Thomas Kuhn's view of the structure of scientific revolutions. Kuhn states that in the natural sciences we can regularly find phases of change that cannot simply be described as developments or reforms, but that must, rather, be seen as revolutionary, systemic breaks from the former conditions. These changes, which Kuhn calls "paradigm shifts," are so radical that in the course of the transformation most elements crucial to a scientific discipline are modified. Essential beliefs, concepts, theoretical models, even empirical phenomena and data (because of the theory-ladenness of observation) are transformed in this process. Kuhn stresses that the holistic character of these revolutionary changes is the main feature distinguishing them from reformist changes in phases of so-called "normal science." Holism in this context means that the new elements cannot be integrated one by one into the existing scientific framework. Rather, one has to learn a whole new language game to understand the meaning of the new scientific theory. Only by learning the new concepts and practices as a whole does one gain a new perspective. This perspective can lead to such a radically different form from the old view that, as Kuhn says, it is as if the scientists before and the scientists after a paradigm shift lived in different worlds.

Rorty also emphasizes the relevance of Holism in his concept of vocabulary.[12] Different vocabularies can be conceived of as separate groups of concepts which are interrelated in a specific way. They can connect sentences and convictions in an argumentative way. The sentences of each type of vocabulary belong within the same system of justification. Everything that can be used to justify a sentence, and everything that a sentence can justify, belongs to the same vocabulary. By definition, sentences from different vocabularies cannot be connected in this way; they are, in light of other vocabularies, neither true nor false but are simply meaningless. Each vocabulary is characterized by specific practices, terms, and conventions that determine what is regarded as rational or irrational, true or false, interesting or uninteresting. Rorty does not allow for a practice of justification or a criterion to have validity across different vocabularies; to allow for this would lead to a sort of "meta-vocabulary," which could be used to compare different vocabularies. Because evaluation is possible only within a vocabulary, there is no external standpoint from which vocabularies can be evaluated as such. Rorty assumes, therefore, that different vocabularies and perspectives on the world are incommensurable and exist side by side.

According to Rorty, the invention of new vocabularies is a transformative practice which can lead to a radical break with existing practices. New vocabularies constitute new frameworks for action and thought. They make possible something which seemed impossible before. But as in Butler's theory, this transformative practice is neither rational nor justified from the moment of its employment. From the perspective of existing vocabularies, that is, from the perspective of what Rorty calls "normal discourse," the invention of new vocabularies appears to be meaningless. This is the case because the new vocabulary constitutes a new context of justification and cannot be justified within the old vocabularies. Also—and here is another parallel to Butler—the invention of a new vocabulary cannot be as intentional and goal-oriented as other actions are, because goals would have to be formulated in the very vocabulary that the new one is trying to overcome. A new field of possibilities is thus created without knowledge of the actual possibilities it will open up.[13]

Under these circumstances, what could possibly motivate the invention of a new vocabulary, and consequently a new worldview and form of life? If the practice of transformation is neither justified nor orientated towards specific goals, then there appears to be a lack of motivation to engage in the practice of transformation. In Kuhn's theory, a scientific revolution is always motivated by a crisis of the dominant paradigm. In contrast, innovative practices are always possible in Rorty's model, even without a crisis. The reason why Rorty thinks this is because, at least implicitly, he favours change over tradition. He considers it a characteristic of human beings to always create new images of the world, new self-conceptions and practices; and he regards it as a restriction on human potential if this capacity for innovation is not realized. Thus, he remarks, the aim of his philosophy is to avert the danger…

> …that some given vocabulary, some way in which people might come to think of themselves, will deceive them into thinking that from now on all discourse could be or should be normal discourse. The resulting freezing-over of culture would be […] the dehumanization of human beings.[14]

Accordingly, tradition and established social orders in general are a potential threat to human existence and human freedom. Rorty normatively favors change over stagnation, the new and unforeseen over the common and conventional.

Such a normative accentuation on change, and such an emphatic perspective on novelty, can also be found in the political thinking of Hannah Arendt.[15] Her perspective on the new stems from her conception of the nature of human beings. On her account, conventional stagnation and the petrification of cultural and societal conditions are also seen as threats to human potentiality and human freedom.[16] Stagnation and petrification limit the human ability to begin anew, which we possess simply by virtue of our being born inasmuch as birth must be conceived of as a new beginning.[17] Arendt understands the potential to begin anew in a radical way. Human beings are free agents because they can generate, undetermined by preceding conditions. "An act can only be called free," Arendt writes, "if it is not affected or caused by anything preceding it."[18] Free action, according to Arendt, is free only when it breaks with existing conditions. Free action therefore becomes contingent. It is not derived from the wishes, motives, beliefs, or intentions of the agent. It therefore seems to be disconnected from the history and the personal identity of the acting subject. Thereby free action becomes a kind of event, which bursts, so to say, from the outside, into the chronological order of the world.[19] (Arendt realizes very well that this is an apparently paradoxical description of action.)

> It is in the very nature of a beginning to carry with itself a measure of complete arbitrariness. Not only is it not bound into a reliable chain of cause and effect, a chain in which each effect immediately turns into the cause for future developments, the beginning has, as it were, nothing whatsoever to hold on to; it is as though it came out of nowhere in either time or space. For a moment, the moment of beginning, it is as though the beginner had abolished the sequence of temporality itself, or as though the actors were thrown out of the temporal order and its continuity.[20]

Political action, according to Arendt, must be free action in this sense. Other practices, such as labor and work, are determined by existing rules and circumstances, but political action is the kind of practice that allows agents to express their freedom. Therefore, it is a practice that leaves current conventions and conditions behind, bringing something completely new into the world. In *On Revolution*, it becomes clear that Arendt conceives of revolutions—the radical break with existing conditions—as a paradigmatic kind of political action. Similar to Butler, although against a different theoretical background,

Arendt thus amalgamates concepts such as freedom, action, revolution, politics, and critique, in such a way that each of the concepts can be explained in terms of the others. Political action is free action, and free action can in turn be understood as revolutionary action. Action, for Arendt, essentially means a break with the agent's present conditions, together with the agent's normative outlook, beliefs, and intentions. On this view, a moment of contingency lies at the heart of free action. And yet, practices are often explained and legitimized with regard to existing conditions by drawing on the current normative and epistemic orders. Since such actions can be explained with respect to preceding incidents and conditions, they are therefore not considered to be free. These backward-looking practices cannot, by definition, be seen as political, critical, or resistant practices.

4. On the Middle Ground

As I have outlined so far, contemporary discourse in critical theory and political philosophy exhibits a fundamental opposition between two disparate models of resistant practice, which differ with respect to the temporal structure of resistant action. Both positions deny that the other gives a cogent account of resistant, political, or critical action at all. One can outline the conflict as follows: From the perspective of each position, the other account fails to explain one of the necessary conditions for resistant action. In the event-like revolutionary account, the structural-conservative model of action cannot be understood as resistant or critical. On this view, structural-conservative action cannot be resistant because it lacks the necessary critical distance from its existing conditions due to its essential connection to intelligible and normative orders. Because they are normatively grounded, and are both rational and motivated, structural-conservative practices cement and perpetuate the existing cultural constellation. They are therefore part of the power structure against which resistant action has to take a stand. The objection against the structural-conservative model posed by the event-like revolutionary perspective is therefore that what it calls resistant practice is not in fact resistant at all.

Conversely, a structural-conservative position insists that an event-like revolutionary account cannot make clear in what sense resistant processes can be understood as actions or practices. Because they are conceived of as the irruption of "the new," as event-like breaks which are not derived from past conditions, we can view the processes of change as neither rational nor intentional. The structural-conservative account defines action as behaviour agents can give reasons for.[21] Such explanations only make sense in relation to current epistemic and normative frameworks, and hence action must draw on existing circumstances. Acts that are supposed to transcend or to overcome that framework cannot be rationally justified or normatively legitimated. Agents of event-like revolutionary action are not in a position to answer questions as to why they perform their resistant practices or take up their resistant stances.[22] Stated differently, the agent does not perform the actions in question from the standpoint of his or her current rational and normative identity.[23] What this account calls "resistant" would seem to be something one cannot *do* according to the common theories of action. Therefore, the objection of the structural-conservative position against the event-like revolutionary model amounts to the assertion that resistant practice is not really practice at all.

These are serious objections that a theory of resistant practice should be able to deal with. In light of the aforementioned objections, one can describe the requirements for a cogent theory of resistance as follows: the theory should take into account the aspects that make a resistant practice a practice, as well as the aspects that make this practice resistant. Furthermore, it should have the theoretical means to describe at least three different kinds of resistant practices: preserving practices, reformist and only slightly transformative practices, as well as revolutionary and strongly transformative practices (provided they can still be conceived of as practices). I think that hermeneutic philosophy is a good starting point for the development of a theory which can describe this wide range of resistant practices and stances. This is the case because I assume that drawing on current conventions, beliefs, and norms is a necessary condition for any human practice. There has to be, I would say, a structural conservative trait in every theory of action and practice. One has to take into account that resistant agents take a stance or participate in a practice because they have reasons to do so. It does not matter how radical the transformation is, or how hopeful people are for the new and for the rejection of the old; transformation still remains a result of a practice and thus it has to be understood as connected to the identity and the intention of the acting subject.[24] The hermeneutic account meets this requirement by placing the agent and the action in a normative, social, and historical context.

However, although one seems to have to accept a structural-conservative trait in the theory of resistant practices, the objections of the event-like revolutionary account have to be taken seriously. The structural conservatism should not be so strong that it undermines the possibility of strongly critical and transformative resistance. I am convinced that the hermeneutic account can be elaborated in such a manner by working out and intensifying some aspects that are already implicit in the theory and by supplementing the theory with some new insights. In the remaining part of this paper, I want to sketch four aspects of a hermeneutic theory of resistance that can explain both preserving and altering practices.

4.1 Action and frameworks of action

The view that intentional, justified, and motivated actions fail to be critical or transformative is connected with a certain conception of the relation between action and its enabling framework, or between practice and the social-historical context that enables it. Different theories suggest different candidates for such frameworks: the given fundamental metaphysical constellation (Heidegger), the existent normative and epistemic discursive order (Butler), or a particular vocabulary (Rorty). These framework conditions constitute an intelligible space of thinking, acting, and living. For event-like revolutionary thinkers, those actions which are performed within such frameworks cannot reach or affect the framework conditions themselves. On their view, rational and intentional actions actualize and perpetuate the given framework condition but they do not alter them. Change has to be initiated from the outside by something independent of the given conditions.[25] Real change therefore cannot be achieved through means at the disposal of rational agents in the intelligible framework. Contrary to this view, the hermeneutic account assumes that we can very well reach and affect the framework conditions by means of our rational and intentional actions and practices. There are possibilities for transforming the enabling conditions from the inside. The frame is just as dependent on our practice as our practice is dependent on the frame; each changes with the other. Therefore, it is possible to bring about changes in a rational and justified way; which are not merely cosmetic but can also alter the fundamental enabling deep structure. It *is* possible to bring about real changes that transform the intelligible space of thinking, acting, and living.

4.2 World-disclosing practices

From the viewpoint of event-like revolutionary theories, it can appear as if hermeneutic theories of resistant practice cannot take relevant innovations or transformations into account because they assume our actions only interpret— and thereby reproduce—our existing epistemic and normative order. But it is possible for a hermeneutic account to explicate a concept of practice that leaves room for the new and the different because it integrates aspects of creativity, imagination, and the unforeseeable. According to Gadamer, there is already a creative moment in the application of traditional norms and beliefs. Starting from the classical concept of practical knowledge, *phronesis*, Gadamer assumes that we do not have access to traditional knowledge in a way that would determine how to apply it in specific situations. In contrast to *techne* and *episteme*, the application in this case is irreducibly dependent on the individual agent's powers of judgment, imagination, and reasoning. The agent has to decide in which way tradition is to be applied in any concrete situation. What this means is that there is always room for interpretation and alteration in the process of applying traditional norms.[26] Furthermore, Gadamer's conception of dialogue shows that we are involved in practices that we cannot completely master or control and that the outcome of such practices always has the potential to surprise us. To enter into a real dialogue means that one cannot control the course of conversation. Nor can one reach, more or less instrumentally, an outcome one had in mind before the dialogue started. A dialogue can have surprising results, which none of the interlocutors had in mind before, and it also can change the beliefs and perspectives of the interlocutors in a significant way. Hermeneutic philosophy thus permits us to be rationally and intentionally involved in our practices which nevertheless remain beyond our control, and can therefore lead us to surprising results. Human practices as described by hermeneutics are not at all only mechanical or reproductive. They can be world-disclosing. They can open up new realms of thought and action.[27] They can do all of this even though they are not detached from tradition but connected with the given social and cultural context. We are familiar with these practices and we get involved with them intentionally and rationally. Even though being involved with these practices can change our perspective and our identity, we always, at least partly, assess these alterations in the light of existing norms, tasks, needs, and beliefs. This means that the concept of world-disclosure can be understood as part of our rational and intentional practices.

4.3 Contested tradition

The conservative orientation of the hermeneutic account follows from its emphasis on the importance of tradition. Tradition, and the inherited norms and beliefs which come along with it, shape our identities and the intelligible cultural space we inhabit. The degree of the structural conservatism that follows from this assumption depends partly on which concept of tradition one takes as a basis. Alasdair MacIntyre opposes thinkers who conceive of tradition as something "essentially conservative and essentially unitary."[28] According to his view, it is a mistake to think of tradition as a static and unified constellation of norms and beliefs that are re-actualized in the present and that determine the future. MacIntyre claims that tradition exists in the form of narratives, in the form of stories about history and past generations. But narrative tradition is not static; it is intrinsically dynamic and contested. There are different narrative interpretations of the tradition in question that are different in various respects. They differ concerning questions like these: What belongs to the tradition and what does not? Which elements are important and which are marginal? What are the most important present problems and future tasks?[29] As an example, MacIntyre notes how what it means to be a Jew or an American is something that remains disputed. To participate in a tradition means not to share a fixed set of values and beliefs with others, but to take part in a dynamic and ongoing debate about what the defining values and beliefs are, about how the past is to be narrated, what is conceived of as binding, and so on. This view suggests that differences, conflicts, and alternative perspectives are all an essential part of what tradition is. There are always causes and starting points for renewal and transformation within an existent tradition. Impulse for alteration, therefore, does not need to come from outside the tradition; it can come, instead, from the dynamic structure of the tradition. According to MacIntyre, it is even possible to conceive of revolutionary changes as described by Kuhn as continuations of tradition in the dynamic sense. When a narrative or an explanatory model falls into a crisis, it can be overcome by a revolutionary renewal. But such a revolution is not a radical break with the tradition, but is, of itself, a new interpretation of it. The new narrative can be understood as a continuation of the tradition because it integrates the old narrative, the causes of the crisis, and the process of renewal, into a new intelligible story.[30]

4.4 Discourse-analytical supplement

In hermeneutic philosophy, a critical and reflective stance is dependent on the articulation of other opinions and different perspectives. The alternative narrative of tradition has to be told, the other opinion brought forward, to fulfil the function of calling existing values, prejudices, and perspectives to mind and questioning them. This confrontation enables us to reflect on and critically assess elements of our normative and epistemic outlook, which would otherwise probably remain unnoticed and unexamined. But Gadamer's assumption concerning the possibilities of articulating different opinions and perspectives is perhaps too optimistic. A brief look at the role of women in our society over the past centuries makes it very clear that it is not always possible for everyone to articulate their view or be taken seriously by others. Therefore, a discourse-analytical supplement of the hermeneutic account seems to be required. From this perspective, one could analyze the power structures that shape the discursive constellations. The reason why this is important to do is because every discursive constellation is structured by rules that determine who is allowed to speak, who is to be taken seriously, and what counts as a relevant contribution. Such a discourse-analytical examination could make the given social conditions and normative limits of dialogue explicit and thus broaden our ability to articulate divergent views.[31]

Within the scope of a hermeneutic account, explicated and supplemented in the envisaged manner, it would be possible to develop a theory of resistance that could take into account different forms of resistant practices. This theory would still be structural-conservative in the way described above, but it would nevertheless allow for enough distance, critique, and innovation. It is, therefore, possible to integrate strongly transforming resistant practices into the hermeneutic account of resistance.

Notes

1 The significance of the temporal aspect of political action, and the complexity such temporal structures and constellations exhibit, are both dealt with in an exemplary fashion in Walter Benjamin's "Theses on the Philosophy of History." Briefly, this essay runs as follows: In the name of redemption, one has to get away from a teleological conception of historical progress, and to hope that a messianic revolution takes place instead. It is not within the power of man to bring about such a revolution, but it does not happen independently of human practices either. These practices are forceful, according to Benjamin, only when they are backward-looking, oriented towards the grief and suppression of previous generations; and not when they are forward-looking, oriented towards a better future. Walter Benjamin, "Theses on the Philosophy of History," in *Illuminations. Essays and Reflections* (New York: Schocken, 2012), 253–64. See also Oliver Marchart, "Time for a New Beginning. Arendt, Benjamin, and the Messianic Conception of Political Temporality," *Redescriptions: Yearbook of Political Thought and Conceptual History* vol. 10 (2006): 134–49.

2 For this see Jacques Rancière, "The Monument and its Confidences; or Deleuze and Art's Capacity of Resistance," in *Dissensus: On Politics and Aesthetics* (London: Continuum, 2010), 169.

3 Emil Angehrn, "Kultur zwischen Bewahrung und Veränderung. Eine hermeneutische Perspektive," in *Formen kulturellen Wandels*, ed. Stefan Deines et al. (Bielefeld: Transcript, 2012), 87–102.
4 Hans-Georg Gadamer, *Truth and Method* (London: Continuum, 2004), 282.
5 On various occasions, Habermas famously criticized Gadamer's theory as too conservative. For example, see his early paper on Gadamer in Karl-Otto Apel (ed.), *Hermeneutik und Ideologiekritik* (Frankfurt: Suhrkamp, 1971). See also on this debate Stefan Deines, "Der Spielraum reflexiver Praxis. Gadamer und die Kritische Theorie," in *Hermeneutics and the Humanities: Dialogues with Hans-Georg Gadamer*, ed. Madeleine Kasten et al. (Amsterdam: Amsterdam University Press, 2012), 110–32.
6 Michael Walzer, *Interpretation and Social Criticism* (Cambridge, MA: Harvard University Press, 1993), 20.
7 Adorno remarks along these lines: "There is no way out of entanglement." Theodor W. Adorno, *Minima Moralia: Reflections on a Damaged Life* (London: Verso, 2005), 27.
8 Martin Heidegger, "The Age of the World Picture," in *The Question Concerning Technology and other Essays* (New York: Harper, 1977), 115–54.
9 They are therefore not conceived of as real cultural changes at all.
10 "Human beings do not decide whether and how beings appear, whether and how God and the gods or history and nature come forward into the clearing of being, come to presence and depart. The advent of beings lies in the destiny of being." Martin Heidegger, "Letter on Humanism," in *Pathmarks* (Cambridge: Cambridge University Press, 1998), 252. It is fascinating to ask how Heidegger conceives of the conditions under which such radical changes can take place, for they do not seem to be completely independent of human practice. For example, Heidegger thought of his philosophy as a kind of preliminary laying of the ground for something to happen.
11 Judith Butler, *Gender Trouble: Feminism and the Subversion of Identity* (New York: Routledge, 1990), 93.
12 For the notion of vocabulary, see Richard Rorty, *Contingency, Irony, and Solidarity* (Cambridge: Cambridge University Press, 1989), especially Chapter 1.
13 David Hoy, *Critical Resistance: From Poststructuralism to Post-Critique* (Cambridge, MA: MIT Press, 2004), 11.
14 Richard Rorty, *Philosophy and the Mirror of Nature* (Princeton: Princeton University Press, 1979), 377.
15 For more on Hannah Arendt's conception of political action and the human ability to begin anew, see Oliver Marchart, *Neu beginnen. Hannah Arendt, die Revolution und die Globalisierung* (Vienna: Turia und Kant, 2005) and Linda Zerilli, "Castoriadis, Arendt, and the Problem of the New", *Constellations*, vol. 9 (2002): 540–53.
16 Hannah Arendt, "What is Freedom?," in *Between Past and Future: Six Exercises in Political Thought* (New York: Viking Press, 1961), 143–72.

17 "[The] idea that men are equipped for the logically paradoxical task of making a new beginning because they themselves are new beginnings and hence beginners, that the very capacity for beginning is rooted in natality, in the fact that human beings appear in the world by virtue of birth." Hannah Arendt, *On Revolution* (New York: Penguin, 2006), 203.

18 Hannah Arendt, *The Life of the Mind* (San Diego: Harcourt, 1981), 210.

19 Arendt speaks of "an unconnected new event breaking into the continuum, the sequence of chronological time." Arendt, *The Life of the Mind* , 210.

20 Arendt, *On Revolution*, 198.

21 According to Anscombe, an action is behavior the agent can give reasons for; he can give an answer to the question "Why?." Elizabeth Anscombe, *Intention* (Oxford: Basil Blackwell, 1957), § 5.

22 See for such concerns Hoy, *Critical Resistance*, 5f.; concerning the objection that resistant and critical action should be justified normatively cf. Nancy Fraser, "False Antitheses: A Response to Seyla Benhabib and Judith Butler," *Praxis International*, vol. 11 (1991): 166–77; Butler phrases the objection she is confronted with like this: "Now, one might wisely ask, what good is thinking otherwise, if we don't know in advance that thinking otherwise will produce a better world? If we do not have a moral framework in which to decide with knowingness that certain new possibilities or ways of thinking otherwise will bring forth that world whose betterness we can judge by sure and already established standards?" Judith Butler, in "What is critique? On Foucault's virtue," in *The Political*, ed. David Ingram (London: Basil Blackwell, 2002), 212–26.

23 In Butler's view, critical resistance demands "a willingness not to be" because the agent opposes and wants to overcome the very conditions that make his present identity possible. Judith Butler, *The Psychic Life of Power: Theories in Subjection* (Stanford: Stanford University Press, 1997), 130.

24 Naturally, not every change has to be the result of a human practice.

25 Foucault, for example, says that the beginning of something new—"probably begins with an erosion from outside, from that space which is, for thought, on the other side." Michel Foucault, *The Order of Things: An Archaeology of the Human Sciences* (London: Routledge, 1989), 56.

26 For the conception of phronesis, see Georgia Warnke, "Hermeneutics, Ethics, and Politics", in *The Cambridge Companion to Gadamer*, ed. Robert Dostal (Cambridge: Cambridge University Press 2006), 79–101.

27 Nikolas Kompridis shows that the process of world-disclosing is not opposed to human agency and practice. He points out that imagination and world-disclosing are not irrational but should be seen as part of our reasoning. Nikolas Kompridis, *Critique and Disclosure: Critical Theory Between Past and Future* (Cambridge, MA: MIT Press, 2006).

28 Alasdair MacIntyre, "Epistemological Crisis, Dramatic Narrative, and the Philosophy of Science", *The Monist*, vol. 60 (1977): 465.
29 Ibid., 471.
30 Furthermore, we have to take into account that traditions are not only contested internally but also externally, since we have to conceive of modern societies as pluralistic. Modern societies are shaped by a plurality of traditions, perspectives, values, and ideals. Resistant practices therefore always navigate a dynamic field of conflicting or communicating traditions.
31 Hans-Herbert Kögler suggests very convincingly such a discourse-analytical supplement of hermeneutics. Hans-Herbert Kögler, *The Power of Dialogue: Critical Hermeneutics after Gadamer and Foucault* (Cambridge, MA: MIT Press, 1999).

Bibliography

Adorno, Theodor. *Minima Moralia. Reflections on a Damaged Life.* London: Verso, 2005.
Angehrn, Emil. "Kultur zwischen Bewahrung und Veränderung. Eine hermeneutische Perspektive," in *Formen kulturellen Wandels,* edited by Stefan Deines et al., 87–102. Bielefeld: Transcript, 2012.
Anscombe, Elizabeth. *Intention.* Oxford: Basil Blackwell, 1957.
Arendt, Hannah. "What is Freedom?," in *Between Past and Future. Six Exercises in Political Thought.* New York: Viking Press, 1961, 143–72.
Arendt, Hannah. *On Revolution.* New York: Penguin, 2006.
Arendt, Hannah. *The Life of the Mind.* San Diego: Harcourt, 1981.
Benjamin, Walter. "Theses on the Philosophy of History," in *Illuminations. Essays and Reflections,* 253–64. New York: Schocken, 2012.
Butler, Judith. *Gender Trouble: Feminism and the Subversion of Identity.* New York: Routledge, 1990.
Butler, Judith. *The Psychic Life of Power: Theories in Subjection.* Stanford: Stanford University Press, 1997.
Butler, Judith. "What is critique? On Foucault's virtue," in *The Political*, edited by David Ingram, 212–26. London: Basil Blackwell, 2002.
Deines, Stefan. "Der Spielraum reflexiver Praxis. Gadamer und die Kritische Theorie", in *Hermeneutics and the Humanities: Dialogues with Hans-Georg Gadamer,* edited by Madeleine Kasten et al., 110–32. Amsterdam: Amsterdam University Press, 2012.
Foucault, Michel. *The Order of Things. An Archaeology of the Human Sciences.* London: Routledge, 1989.
Fraser, Nancy. "False Antitheses: A Response to Seyla Benhabib and Judith Butler." *Praxis International* vol. 11 (1991): 166–77.
Gadamer, Hans-Georg. *Truth and Method.* London: Continuum, 2004.

Habermas, Jürgen. "Zu Gadamers *Wahrheit und Methode*," in *Hermeneutik und Ideologiekritik*, edited by Karl-Otto Apel, 45–56. Frankfurt: Suhrkamp, 1971.

Heidegger, Martin. "The age of the world picture," in *The Question Concerning Technology and other Essays*. New York: Harper, 1977, 115–54.

Heidegger, Martin. "Letter on Humanism," in Pathmarks. Cambridge: Cambridge University Press, 1998.

Hoy, David. *Critical Resistance: From Poststructuralism to Post-Critique*. Cambridge/MA: MIT Press, 2004.

Kögler, Hans-Herbert. *The Power of Dialogue: Critical Hermeneutics after Gadamer and Foucault*. Cambridge, MA: MIT Press, 1999.

Kompridis, Nikolas. *Critique and Disclosure: Critical Theory between Past and Future*. Cambridge/MA: MIT Press, 2006.

MacIntyre, Alasdair. "Epistemological Crisis, Dramatic Narrative, and the Philosophy of Science." *The Monist* vol. 60 (1977): 453–72.

Marchart, Oliver. *Neu beginnen. Hannah Arendt, die Revolution und die Globalisierung*. Vienna: Turia und Kant, 2005.

Marchart, Oliver. "Time for a New Beginning. Arendt, Benjamin, and the Messianic Conception of Political Temporality." *Redescriptions. Yearbook of Political Thought and Conceptual History* vol. 10 (2006): 134–49.

Rancière, Jacques. "The Monument and its Confidences; or Deleuze and Art's Capacity of Resistance," in *Dissensus. On Politics and Aesthetics*, London: Continuum, 2010.

Rorty, Richard. *Philosophy and the Mirror of Nature*. Princeton: Princeton University Press, 1979.

Rorty, Richard. *Contingency, Irony, and Solidarity*, Cambridge: Cambridge University Press, 1989.

Walzer, Michael. *Interpretation and Social Criticism*. Cambridge, MA: Harvard University Press, 1993.

Warnke, Georgia. "Hermeneutics, Ethics, and Politics," in *The Cambridge Companion to Gadamer*, edited by Robert Dostal, 79–101. Cambridge: Cambridge University Press 2006.

Zerilli, Linda. "Castoriadis, Arendt, and the Problem of the New." *Constellations* vol. 9 (2002): 540–53.

5

Resistance and Social Transformation in Walter Benjamin's "On the Critique of Violence"[1]

Alexei Procyshyn

1. Introduction

Few of Walter Benjamin's essays have attracted and sustained as much attention as his "On the Critique of Violence." From Schmitt's early admiration to Derrida's and Agamben's more recent discussions, the work has consistently served as a philosophical well-spring.[2] With its historically anchored but speculative account of violence, along with its rich, suggestive discussion of myth, fate, and religion, the essay's appeal is evident. Most of us, however, seem to have been so taken with the surface effects of Benjamin's critique—with the frights and surprises awaiting us at each of its controlled stylistic swerves—that we often fail to identify their deeper causes. By and large, his essay has been treated as an occasion to exercise our own intellectual powers by offering keen descriptions of our responses to the small traumas Benjamin's essay produces, or by pointing out the rhetorical and grammatical nuances that render anything like a definitive interpretation well nigh impossible.

In this chapter, I take a different tack. I argue that this "violence-essay" offers an incisive critique of (post-)Kantian conceptions of practical action that emphasize the role played by institutions in shaping agents and their potentials for action. More precisely, I show that Benjamin provides us with a critique of, and alternative to Max Weber's theory of politics, as outlined in his 1919 lecture *Politics as Vocation*. Contra Weber, who examines the institutional and intersubjective preconditions of political action to emphasize the qualities and commitments involved in an individual's political engagement,[3] Benjamin reformulates such "objective" constraints so that certain forms of political action or resistance—e.g. the general strike—no longer entail the Faustian dilemmas, or related tragic structures (e.g. the "causality of fate") inherent to Weber's account, because practical action is no longer exhaustively specified by the basic structures purporting to mediate intersubjective, practical action.

As we will see, Benjamin's analysis of this "nonmediated" kind of action focuses on the manifestation of a collective political agent that in other accounts—such as Weber's—remains structurally obscured by its institutional context. This analysis involves (1) reconceptualizing violence such that it is no longer understood exclusively as a *means* for pursuing socio-historically determined ends, and (2) rejecting a theoretical focus upon individual agents and their means-ends ratios in favour of an account of collective action. These features, I will show, are crucial for understanding the "Critique of Violence." On the view presented here, the essay articulates a coherent, *inherently non-mystical* kind of social engagement in which "violence" denotes a limit-phenomenon separating distinct kinds of social agency.

2. Historical Situation

My suggestion that we read Benjamin's essay in counterpoint to Weber's work finds support in the immediate situation of Benjamin's published article. First, "Critique of Violence" appeared in the 1921 volume of Weber's journal, *Archiv für Sozialwissenschaft und Sozialpolitik* (which he edited until his death in 1920). So the allusions to Weber's work would not have been missed by his audience. Second, from 1919 to 1920, Benjamin was planning a book-length treatment of the problem of violence in politics. The planned work, as Tiedemann and Schweppenhäuser have reconstructed it,[4] was to include the essay "*Zur Kritik der Gewalt*," along with a shorter piece, entitled "*Leben und Gewalt*," which was written in April 1920. The rest of the project was to comprise a long, two-part essay: the first, which Benjamin had begun to write,[5] was to be entitled "*Der wahre Politiker*"; the second part was to be further subdivided into two sections entitled, respectively, "*Die Abbau der Gewalt*" and "*Teleologie ohne Endzweck*." Only "*Zur Kritik der Gewalt*" was ever published (1921), however, and the remaining pieces have all been lost.

The outline of Benjamin's project is instructive. In its timing and structure, it resonates with—and seeks to critically respond to—Max Weber's influential account of political action and practical reason in "*Politik als Beruf*,"[6] where he focuses primarily on describing the "true" politician, that is, the qualities and character that an *individual* who wishes to become a politician must possess ideally in order to endure political life and face the ethical problems and paradoxes engendered by what Weber takes to be the essence of all political deliberation and action: namely violence (*Gewaltsamkeit*). As Weber puts it, "the specific use of legitimate force as such in the hands of human organizations is what determines the particular ethical problems in politics."[7]

Weber's position is of course eminently understandable. The Great War, which he initially supported, had recently ended and international recriminations were in full swing. The socialist Kurt Eisner, who had made public the official documents detailing Germany's role in instigating the war, had gone on to become Prime Minister of Bavaria, and was assassinated by Count Arco-Valley on February 21, 1919. Several weeks prior, in the north of the country, the leaders of the Spartacist league, Karl Liebknecht and Rosa Luxemburg, instigated the so-called Berlin uprising of January 15, 1919, and were assassinated on January 25. These events prompted a brutal repression of both the Bavarian Soviet in Munich and the Spartacist movement in Berlin. In the midst of these international and national upheavals, Germany's acutest public intellectual and the father of the contemporary social sciences reluctantly agrees to give a lecture on "politics as vocation" to the Free Student Movement at Ludwigs-Maximilians Universität in München.[8] Weber's lecture concentrates on giving a *description* of the institutional and practical parameters of political engagement, and the orientations individuals may take towards them. His perspective is pragmatic and decidedly liberal: given the contemporary institutions of law, political organization, and the manner in which they structure rational behavior, successful political action requires its agents and avatars to have a specific qualities in order to negotiate and survive the ethical paradoxes that accrue to action in these contexts. Above all, this means that political action is everywhere mediated by institutions: by definition, *direct political action* is impossible, and the "true politicians" assume the functional roles determined by the basic structures of their situation. Weber thus remains faithful to the prevailing political and legal structures, while trying to avoid lapsing into an apology for the status quo. "Politics means a slow powerful drilling through hard boards with a mixture of passion and a sense of proportion."[9]

With its planned sections on the true politician and true politics, understood—as the references to the "dismantling of violence" and a "teleology without Telos" indicate—in terms critically opposed to Weber's, Benjamin's *Politics*-project would have thus responded to the Weberian "is" of political life with the counterfactual force of a possible world's "ought." This, at any rate, seems to have been Benjamin's plan, which at the very least provides the basis for a compelling reading of the only extant piece of the project, the "Critique of Violence" essay. We should not be surprised then to find that this essay *does* in fact challenge Weber's basic assumptions concerning rational action, violence, and the two basic orientations to politics he identifies. It even begins to suggest, albeit in rather metaphorical terms, an alternative to them, in a language inspired by Weber's own appeal to religious discourse.

Indeed, even Benjamin's metaphors turn on his opposition to Weber. For Weber's favorite figures for political action derive from *religious* and *mythical* motifs. From his allusions to Greek and Indian polytheisms (meant to capture the pluralism and relativity of our most basic values and value-orientations), and his discussion of the pitfalls of Christianity's absolutizing ethical standpoint (as evidenced by the Quakers' impotence to defend themselves), through to his invocation of the various attempts to rationalize and cope with the tragic nature of human action figured by the Indian doctrines of Karma and Dharma, the Persian dualisms of good and evil, or the Ancient Greeks' Dämon and Fate, etc., Weber's sociological text is shot through with religious language. What makes Benjamin's appeal to, and contrast of the Jewish story of Korah with the Greek legend of Niobe, so interesting is the fact that it lays bare a glaring absence or oversight in Weber's text, namely Judaism, which is one of the few religious orientations that Weber does *not* take up, or rather does not differentiate from the absolutizing ethic of Christianity (which he sees as including a "Jewish value-orientation"). On Benjamin's reading, however, a Jewish perspective on politics demonstrates the possibility for a *universal* value-orientation that escapes the vicissitudes of a teleological account of reason and the causality of fate that Weber's theory of action entails.

3. Weber, Rationality, Violence

To get a proper sense of the challenge Benjamin's essay poses to Weber's account of politics, we need to return to the details of "Politics as a Vocation." In this lecture, Weber offers an account of the conditions of possibility for politics in general, and then seeks to delineate the orientations (what Weber calls an ethic) that individuals may take towards specific problems, given these conditions. This involves, according to Weber, spelling out the relevant institutions that determine our contemporary political organizations and procedures, the personal qualities of the individuals who enter into these public spaces, the norms and values agents must embrace to undertake and endure a political career, and finally the deliberative tools to evaluate and discuss political engagement as such. Together, these features give us a theory of institutionally situated practical reason.

Now, as anyone familiar with the structure of Weber's lecture can attest, the basic qualities of a mature politician—i.e. commitment to a cause, a deep sense of responsibility, and the sense of proportion afforded by a detached or distanced relationship to people or things—are all attributes of a self-conscious, rational agent. Indeed, these features mark the point of insertion of Weber's well-rehearsed and tested theory of rationality, which allows him to *evaluate* political action by examining the aptness of means to ends by extrapolating the socially embedded values one recognizes and the basic materials available for undertaking a given course of action. "All serious reflection about the ultimate elements of meaningful human conduct," Weber writes in his explicitly methodological writings, "is oriented primarily in terms of the categories 'end' and 'means.'"[10] By understanding practical action as everywhere circumscribed by the ends an agent sets for herself and the specific means she may use to achieve them, Weber develops his account of practical reason, which he summarizes as follows:

> Inasmuch as we are able to determine [...] which means for the achievement of a proposed end are appropriate or inappropriate, we can [...] estimate the chances of attaining a certain end by certain available means. In this way we can indirectly criticize the setting of the end itself as practically meaningful (on the basis of the existing historical situation) or as meaningless with reference to existing conditions.[11]

The theoretical emphasis on the appropriateness of means to ends, relative to a specific historical context and a specific set of values (i.e., an ethic), allows Weber to understand an individual's actions and intentions as everywhere informed by her institutional setting. This also explains why he focuses on *violence* in "Politics as a Vocation." As Weber notes, an accurate description of political action cannot be given in terms of the *ends* being served. Rather, given the general structure of practical reason, an account of politics has to rely on the means specific to it. For what makes an action explicitly political (as opposed to say, economic, artistic, or scientific) can be specified only by the means unique to it. And, since Weber argues that the rationalization of politics amounts to a State's consolidation and centralization of the ability to act violently, he naturally takes "violence" to be the intrinsic means and determining factor of politics.[12]

For Weber, then, the sufficient condition for calling a given action "political" concerns the means employed: institutionally structured uses of violence or coercion. To the extent that Weber can clarify the relationship between violence and the existing political institutions (as a process of expropriation, centralization, and codification of the former by the latter), he can also specify the prerequisites that *individuals* must satisfy in order to wield these violent means *appropriately* within *properly political* arenas. This reflective perspective allows him to formulate what he takes to be the intrinsic problem associated with politics in general, and to insist on the qualities that *individual political agents* must have in order to *survive* their engagements. "It is entirely true and a fundamental fact of history," Weber explains, "that the ultimate product of political activity frequently, indeed, as a matter of course, fails utterly to do justice to its original purpose and may even be a travesty of it."[13] Political action, for Weber, is inherently *tragic*. And the ironies that politicians must be able to withstand turn out to be a consequence of his (and every other) teleological account of practical reason. Weber makes this connection explicit, by noting practical action's "affinity [*Verwandtschaft*] [...] with tragedy, in which all our activities are ensnared, political action above all."[14] Those who can legitimately claim politics as a vocation, Weber thus argues, are the individuals who can accept the opacity of rational action, take responsibility for its (unintended) consequences (or its counter-finalities, to talk like Sartre), and press on *notwithstanding*. But this "*notwithstanding*" marks the structure of tragedy.

Weber thus conceives of politics in terms of the institutional space in which violence is a legitimate means to an end (any end), and then describes "legitimacy" in relation to three features: the institutions and social organizations that structure concrete political action (i.e. determine what is objectively possible); the specific orientations that determine an individual's basic commitments, foreground specific concerns, and thereby identify the ends that individuals may pursue in relation to these social structures; and, finally, the teleological structure of rational deliberation, which selects the most appropriate means for achieving a goal relative to the objective possibilities of a given situation and the specific values of the deliberator. Weber's account thus marries a reflective, meta-critical account of deliberative action (what we might call a "quasi-transcendental" theory of rationality, after Habermas) with a historically grounded analysis of politics and political organization. Political engagement thus becomes a special case of rational action, to be subsumed under his general account of rationality itself. This subsumption, moreover, allows Weber to critically examine our concrete political engagements in terms of the *fitness* among *context*, *means*, *individual value-orientation*, and an action's *practical execution*.

What remains for Weber is to develop the basic value-orientations to political life. According to him, contemporary politicians tend to hold either an ethic of conviction (*Gesinnungsethik*) or an ethic of responsibility (*Verantwortungsethik*). More importantly, these two ethical orientations stand under two fundamentally opposed "maxims": the "*gesinnungsethische Maxime*,"[15] on the one hand, reads "The Christian does rightly and leaves the results with God,"[16] whereas the *verantwortungsethische* orientation holds "that you must answer for the (foreseeable) *consequences of your* actions."[17] Now, Weber takes the ethic of conviction to represent an incoherent orientation towards political action, which fails for precisely the same reasons that Hegel identifies when discussing the Beautiful Soul: "you must be a saint in *all* respects or at least want to be one; you must live like Jesus, the Apostles, St Francis, and their like, and *then* this ethic will make sense and be the expression of true dignity. But *not otherwise*."[18] Yet, with violence as its intrinsic *means*, the very structure of politics precludes such a value-orientation. If, as Weber contends, "legitimacy" is determined by the rational standards governing the "success" of a particular action relative to the values being upheld and the objective possibilities produced by a given historical situation, then it is *impossible* for an ethic of conviction to ever be legitimate. Conviction, in short, is never sufficient for success: the *Gesinnungspolitiker* can never live up to his ideals, because the ends he seeks to serve are structurally *precluded by* the very institutions he works within. "Anyone who wishes to act in accordance with the ethic of the Gospel should abstain from going on strike—for Strikes are a form of coercion [...]. Above all, such a person should not speak of 'revolution.'"[19]

4. Violence as Manifestation

This account of Weber's theory of politics and practical rationality should make the tensions between his position and Benjamin's palpable. For Benjamin, too, is concerned with how one's basic orientations towards political engagement are structured by one's historical position, and how the relationships between means and ends delineate successful political engagement. However, Benjamin's *terminus a quo* in the violence-essay is an intractable jurisprudential paradox underlying the relationship between means and ends—and hence teleological accounts of practical action more generally.

Unlike Weber, however, Benjamin does not take this to be a mere matter of value-orientation. That is, whereas Weber takes violence to be a fact of politics and then moves on to consider the ethical implications of this *datum* for individuals who are engaged politically, Benjamin focuses on the institutional structures that determine the legitimacy of violence *as* a political means.

Benjamin, in other words, is concerned with the *social ontology* underwriting practical action: what a situation's institutions afford specific social actors, or (in Weber's language) how the present institutions dictate a situation's objective possibilities (for subjectivation, action, etc.). This explains why Benjamin privileges the concepts of "right" and "justice." The latter categories allow him to make the commitments of Weber's theory of rational action explicit. His basic insight is that any discussion of law crucially involves being able to claim a right to something *and* to use that right *in order to* protect oneself against others. But the nature of the claim and the manner of its use are not strictly speaking a matter of value orientation. In Benjamin's terms, any claim concerning individual rights implies a moment of "law-positing" and "law-preserving" violence—but neither form of violence is actually interrogated by Weber's sociological account. What Benjamin will seek to show is that these two moments define our institutional settings and render some courses of action objectively impossible (invisible, unimaginable). To say that an action is objectively impossible, however, means simply that it is not consistent with the status quo, *not* that it is incoherent or unrealizeable. Furthermore, if undertaken, such an action would entail some (potentially significant) transformation of the social situation. Minimally, it would introduce new categories into our social ontology. If successful, Benjamin's critique of violence repudiates Weber's purposive or teleological conception of rationality and his account of violence as an *exclusively coercive means* that is constitutive of the political sphere.

The interpretative key to Benjamin's critique of Weber's "violence," and his essay as a whole, is his tantalizingly underdeveloped idea that *violence is expressive*. Although an agent can achieve her ends violently, the philosophical importance of "violence" lies in what this violent performance discloses, or makes manifest, rather than its aptness, qua means, to ends one seeks to achieve. "The nonmediate function of violence," Benjamin explains, "is not a means but a *manifestation*."[20] A violent performance, Benjamin explains, is the objective manifestation of an individual's character or essence:

> A function of violence that cannot be mediated[...] is illustrated by an everyday life-experience. As regards man, he is impelled by anger, for example, to the most visible outbursts of violence that is not related as a means to a preconceived end. It is not a means but a *manifestation*. Moreover, this violence has thoroughly objective manifestations in which it can be subjected to criticism.[21]

Benjamin's "manifestation" introduces a new critical vantage from which to consider violent action. For it shifts our theoretical focus from violence qua means to the distinctive character of a social actor—her values, context, and relations to others—disclosed in a violent performance.

The expressive role Benjamin assigns to "violence" connects the methodological and substantive strata of his essay. On the one hand, the idea that violence is disclosive shifts our theoretical focus from the intentions or ends informing violent action to who *manifests itself in* violence. As Benjamin notes, the shift introduces an alternative to Weber's evaluative practice of assessing the aptness of the means to ends, which underwrites (so Benjamin implies) accounts of both positive and natural law. Indeed, Benjamin opens his essay by identifying the unproductive opposition (almost antinomy, in the Kantian sense) between these two juridical frameworks: "Natural law attempts, by the justness of the ends, to 'justify' the means, positive law to 'guarantee' the justness of the ends through the justification of the means."[22] But from Benjamin's perspective, any attempt to understand "Right" in terms of legitimate means or just ends fails to account for what is truly at stake: namely *who is able to act*.

If specific kinds of violent performance are disclosive rather than instrumental, Benjamin can salvage precisely what Weber repudiated as an "absolutizing ethic of conviction": the ability to sanction engagements (e.g. a general strike) that go beyond the restricted scope of the "objective possibilities" of the situation in which such engagements occur. For, on a Benjaminian reading, these kinds of "violent" actions do not merely—or necessarily—exemplify a socially structured type of purposive action. Rather, they define the (collective) agent acting. Hence, it is possible to take up a coherent *revolutionary* stance against actual states of affairs without falling into the performative contradictions, bad faith, and general incoherence that, according to Weber, an ethic of conviction engenders in political life.

5. Benjamin *contra* Weber

Let us briefly recall the various threads we have been pursuing. For Weber, our social, political, and legal institutions are—by definition—the objective, "rationalized" counterpart of our subjective "rational" capacities. *Contra* Weber, Benjamin's opening discussion of law argues against evaluating the legitimacy of these objective structures by appeal to purposive rationality, whose means–ends ratios entail violence (in the political sphere). Indeed, means–ends thinking generates the central problem for Benjamin's critique of violence, namely that by aligning violence with instrumental reason and binding it to the category of means, we commit ourselves to an impoverished conception of the spaces and possibilities of political action. We also tether ourselves to a Weberian rational calculation of objective possibilities (constricted value orientations, institutionalized *means*, and sanctioned *ends*). The problem with such an account is that, to the extent that violence is a means, its legitimate deployment hinges on its *aptness* within actual social organization in which it is. Aptness, however, follows from the status quo. The problem here is simply that Weber's conditions for justifying an action and the conditions governing its legitimacy come apart in interesting ways that Weber cannot accommodate. For instance, it is hard to see how Weber could handle a conscientious objection to institutionalized injustice,[23] which relies upon an ethic of conviction (and the sentiment Weber mocks: "Not I, but the world is wrong"), and rejects the "live options" of a situation.

As the example of conscientious objection makes clear, Weber's definitions of politics, political action, and political agency are far too narrow to account for *political resistance*. Indeed, Weber's immediate historical context implies that the narrowness is by design. Because resisting agents must adopt an ethic of conviction, Weber is committed to saying that they do not "have what it takes" to be successful in political arenas. History offers a good number of counterexamples to Weber here—Ghandi, perhaps, Martin Luther King, Jr., or some of the student movements. Benjamin's expressive conception of violence, on the other hand, enables us to think through what Weber tries to define away. His theory of manifestation offers a non-instrumental evaluative perspective that promises to free our political engagements from the constraints Weber placed on the "ethic of conviction" by expanding the scope of possibilities beyond what is instrumentally available to agents within their respective social spaces.

From Benjamin's vantage, Weber's conception of politics as the *legitimate monopoly* on violence fails to account for the *legitimacy of violent action* (since it only specifies the *efficacity* of some such actions). This failure is the crux of Benjamin's discussion of law-instituting and law-preserving violence. In brief, Benjamin maintains that a law *recognizes* that certain ends have been successfully pursued by violent means. The recognition, which creates a legal precedent, licenses future uses of violence to achieve similar ends—so long as these pursuits do not threaten the basic structure one inhabits. Notice, however, that the legal recognition that some ends may be pursued violently *leverages* the instrumental successes of the past against functionally identical efforts in the present that challenge or attempt to change the status quo.

Notice also that Benjamin's dynamic of law-instituting violence and law-preserving violence reformulates the Weberian theories of purposive action and rationalization in order to highlight the deficiency just identified. On the one hand, Benjamin's description of law-instituting violence reproduces the pattern of purposive action, since it involves the assessment of means and ends, relative to specific values and historical circumstances. Law-instituting violence institutionalizes a specific pattern of action in which violence proves to be an effective means for pursing specific goods. It is therefore perfectly consistent with Weber's approach to rationality and political engagement. Indeed, it delineates a process of *rationalization*. On the other hand, Benjamin's "law-preserving violence" describes how rationalized patterns of action operate in order to *stabilize* the basic structure of society. What Benjamin's discussion of law-instituting and law-preserving violence shows, however, is that the processes of rationalization and stabilization smuggle in—rather than explain—the coercive elements. For the rationalizing process to be successful, i.e., to yield a stable basic structure, social actors must conform to the rationalized patterns of action. This conformity requires the introduction of a new coercive force whose sole justification is the survival of the status quo. In both law-instituting and law-preserving violence, then, the idea of *instrumental success stands in for the idea of right action*.

On Benjamin's behalf, we may say that the legal recognition of ends via precedent thus involves (illicitly) limiting what is possible to what remains consistent with our actual institutional states of affairs. Benjamin's discussion shows that the *fact of law*, as it were, is supposed to be sufficient to inquire into its legitimate application. But the *legitimacy of a particular law itself* is structurally excluded from consideration, since that would threaten the social stability these laws purport to achieve. Hence the opening salvo of Benjamin's essay: the proxy institutions of reason rely upon historically recognized *ends* to sanction and streamline specific *means*. What positive law recognizes, however, is that specific goals have in fact been successfully pursued with violence, but this recognition fails to address the rightness of the ends pursued, as well as the reasonableness of the means used. Furthermore, positive law treats "violence" as a brute fact, leaving the meaning and value of the notion entirely obscure.

From Benjamin's historico-philosophical perspective, Weberian approaches to practical action and rationalization render violence *rationally inaccessible*. Although *some* notion of violence flanks our legal deliberations and practical actions, it resists philosophical analysis because the basic interests of positive law orient us towards different concerns. Violence becomes a blind spot rather than an explicit problem. Even Weber, who defines politics in terms of the legitimate monopoly on violence and relies upon some notion of violence for the evaluation of a rationally pursued end, never gives an *account* of it. Making "violence" logically primitive brings us to a philosophical impasse, for it ensnares us in a cycle of law-instituting and law-preserving violence that merely perpetuates and intensifies the mythical character of practical action. Action is subject to the hidden forces of fate and to the tragic ironies of a finite perspective, because law is grounded in a violence that it fails to investigate and in the fear of retaliation.

6. Expressions of Reason

This brings us to the second phase of Benjamin's argument, which aims to secure an image of political engagement that is independent of the institutional bind that Weber and the Post-Kantian tradition find themselves in. This stage of his argument, as we will see, hinges on understanding "legitimacy" in terms of what a performance makes manifest. Hence, rather than trying to evaluate a specific course of action by appealing to a teleologically articulated notion of rational success that *we impute to it* on the basis of some set of features we have singled out, Benjamin connects an action's legitimacy to the agent undertaking it and who expresses or manifests itself in so acting.

Benjamin brings this point home by considering the different "expressive contents" of the political and general strikes. On his analysis, these acts fundamentally differ with regard to their reliance upon the *institutional situation*, the *convictions* underwriting them, and the *kind of subject* capable of acting. In a political strike, for instance, the collective striking body depends on and justifies its actions in terms of legally recognized ends. The ability of political strikers to act consciously and collectively as a unified body *is constituted* by the legal and institutional framework defining their social situation. A political strike therefore *depends on* and *reaffirms* the basic structure that makes it possible by recognizing it as a successful means and codifying its manner of implementation. In the case of a general strike, however, the wholesale rejection of the status quo expresses or manifests a collective agent whose existence does not rely on legally recognized ends. Indeed, as Benjamin points out, the general strike does not seek to actualize an institutionally framed objective possibility but to create new potentials for emancipatory political action. (Benjamin's account here is presciently accommodating of contemporary phenomena such as the decline of unions in post-industrial societies and the rise of "occupations.") This explains why Benjamin's essay turns on the problems and paradoxes involved in the legal codification of means–ends deliberation (i.e., rationalization), why "violence" becomes the fulcrum of his discussion, and why his conception of politics is unapologetically anarchistic.

Indeed, Weber's understanding of anarchy—"If no social institutions existed which knew the use of violence, then the concept of 'state' would be eliminated, and a condition would emerge that could be designated as 'anarchy,' in the specific sense of this word"[24]—is leveraged by Benjamin out of its counterfactual function as a boundary condition of political action. Weber, as we know, objects to an anarchic conception of political action for the same reasons that he rejects a pure ethic of conviction: anarchism appears to involve a basic category error, since the very idea of non-coercive communal action that remains unmediated by the basic structures of the state (or individual means–ends deliberations) is unthinkable on Weber's account. By contrast, Benjamin's aligns the Weberian sense of anarchy with his conception of violence as manifestation. So understood, there is in fact a real possibility for non-coercive, institutionally unmediated political action whose main act would be the wholesale refusal of current socio-economic relations.

Benjamin's argument here offers something like an existence proof for the possibility of an alternative conception of political action whose paradigmatic case is the *general strike*. What makes the general strike exceptional, what differentiates it from the common *political strike*, Benjamin insists, is the fact that the general strike is fundamentally free from coercive and instrumental calculations.[25] The difference between these two modes of comportment may be summarized as follows: in a general strike, individuals simply cease to comport themselves according to the relations and objective possibilities that define their social situation. In this radical cessation of "reasonable" action, they actualize a distinctive possibility that seemed initially inaccessible to the contemporary configuration of their social spaces. The political strike, by contrast, takes advantage of this configuration by *legally sanctioned extortion*, and thus remains thoroughly consistent with the present state of affairs, which it merely serves to entrench.

The general strike allows Benjamin to anchor his anarchic ideal of political engagement in the actual world by showing how the collective subject it manifests can abandon the institutional relations and objective possibilities constituting a given historical situation and open up a new space of possibilities that would otherwise remain inaccessible to individual agents. Benjamin's argument here is characteristically dense, and interwoven with suggestive remarks concerning war, pacifism, and "childish" forms of anarchism. But this intricate tapestry of concerns nevertheless aims to demonstrate a single point: the criteria we derive from teleological accounts of practical reason and apply to straightforwardly instrumental cases of violence (e.g., punishing criminals, going to war for resources, coercive techniques for collective bargaining) *cannot be used* to evaluate the violence involved in a general strike, because the latter simply has no *end*. Or, perhaps more precisely, a general strike does not serve an end in any classical sense, and hence we cannot approach it in the same way we would more conventional, instrumental, forms of action.

Ultimately, the general strike's legitimacy is bound up with its expressive content—i.e. its manifestation of what I have been referring to as a "collective subject." However, before addressing this idea of a collective subject, which rounds out Benjamin's account of violence, we need to see *why and how* the possibility of a general strike—and hence the possibility of non-instrumental rational activity—vitiates Weber's (and post-Kantianism's) account of practical action and politics. Again, Benjamin's basic claim concerning the historical recognition of legal ends turns out to be decisive. For, on the one hand, the absence of a natural or legal end makes it impossible to institutionalize or rationalize a general strike. The difference between the instrumental violence of the political strike and the "pure violence" of the general strike is ultimately the difference between *Macht* (power) and *Gewalt* (violence), which Benjamin develops by transposing his political categories into the figurative registers of myth and religion. With their taste for tragedy, Greeks and Germans alike opt for a conception of rational action that relies on the *power (Macht) involved in setting limits* to human action, whereas the Jewish conception of God's ability to expiate human limitations (institutional or otherwise) provides us with a model for understanding *Gewalt*.

As Benjamin's discussion of mythic violence makes clear, the cycle of law-positing and law-preserving violence provides the basic structure for every legend of trespass and retribution (as well as struggle for recognition). The narrative logic of myth crucially depends upon the *ability* to enforce and to recognize limitations. The violence inflicted by trespass, for instance, is the manifestation of an individual's *power*. So understood, this mythic conception of violence, which Benjamin finds exemplified in the legend of Niobe, is structurally identical to his account of positive law. Recall that Niobe was punished for failing to respect a higher authority: at a ceremony honouring Leto, Niobe boasted about her large family and mocked Leto for having only two offspring (Apollo and Artemis). For this trespass against her station, Leto had Niobe's children murdered. In shock, Niobe retreated to Mount Siplylon, where her grief overtook her and she turned to stone—"as a boundary stone on the frontier between men and gods."[26] The story of Korah, on the other hand, expunges precisely this power narrative. Korah is Weber's true politician: he is a proponent of positive law and a champion of an ethic of responsibility. According to the book of Exodus, Korah opposed the Mosaic law on the grounds that these commandments did not come from God, but from Moses himself and that the Law benefited only Moses and his kin. Korah's opposition (was) ended in violence: he and his followers, together with all their possessions, were swallowed up by the earth such that no trace of them was left behind. What the divine violence of the Jewish story illustrates, however, is not an individual's power to institute or preserve the historical institutions and boundaries of positive law, but rather a transpersonal ability to generate a fuller spectrum of possibilities than what fits the present state of affairs. This is why divine violence appears as a miracle. In its transformation of the status quo, something appears that was hitherto thought impossible, because it was structurally excluded from the situation. Benjamin's *divine violence* thus brings into relief three ideas: first, that *political resistance* can operate independently of the "properly political" institutional frameworks which define a given situation and give rise to the mythic cycle of fate qua instituting and preserving violence. Second, it shows how a new, collective subject can manifest itself in these acts of resistance: insofar as "divine violence" is coextensive with the general strike's refusal to accept a situation's social relations as binding or determining, it expresses the constitutive values of a group (or body politic) and is therefore non-instrumental. Finally, this positive sense of resistance has historical import in that it provides a point of origin in Benjamin's sense: it separates the "before" and "after" in terms of the emergence of a previously unknown collective subject.

    The story of Korah, which marks the *emergence* of Judaism and its separation from the *prehistory* of the Israelite exile, exemplifies the historical import that Benjamin accords political resistance qua divine violence. Had Korah not been swallowed up, the very idea of Judaism would have never become intelligible. Moreover, this story helps Benjamin to distinguish between *power* and *violence*. The kind of resistance exemplified in these biblical events is fundamentally at odds with the Greek story of Niobe, Benjamin maintains, because the *violence* of the former is expressive and constitutive rather than purposive (i.e., instrumental, driven by consequences). While Niobe's fate cannot be understood independently of her infraction and the instrumental use of power, the same considerations are completely out of place in the Jewish context.[27] The decisive difference between power and violence turns on *who* acts: power (*Macht*) is always exercised by an individual agent *within* a well-defined, institutionally determined situation; violence (*Gewalt*) announces a collective subject capable of transforming this situation but that cannot be explained exclusively in terms of the institutional coordination or mediation of the constituent actions of individual participants.

By aligning the Jewish story of Korah with the *communal, decentralized* character of the general strike, Benjamin rejects Weber's *polytheism* of value and value-orientation in favour of a *value-monotheism* that is in fact more "responsible" in the face of what could and ought to be than any contractual ethics. If, as I have been arguing, Korah is a proponent of positive law rather than the Mosaic Law, then his *paganism* is as resolutely rejected by divine violence as his politics. Benjamin's discussion of this biblical story thus seeks to salvage an ethic of conviction from Weber's critique by showing that a *shared conviction is constitutive* of a group and of collective agency and that such a conviction—rather than map onto the objective possibilities of a historical situation—can utterly transform the situation that purports to exclude it. Benjamin's essay thus moves from a consideration of the status of an individual's actions, which are determined by a given historical situation, to a consideration of a collective subject that expresses itself in its *opposition* to this social situation. This opposition, as we saw, has its source in a collectively held conviction, which becomes manifest in "universal" acts of resistance, like a general strike or divine violence, that cannot be reinscribed within Weber's ethic of responsibility. For in focusing on the constitution of a collective subject, Benjamin shows that violence is not merely a means (to be) used by individuals in their pursuit of various political ends, but that this very conception of political action is derivative in relation to the basic values (convictions) that are constitutive of collective political agency and action. More forcefully put, what is manifest in the *pure violence* (or expression) of a collective is not a datum for instrumental calculation.

Benjamin's violence-essay thus shows that we can conceive of political action in terms of the constitution of a collective subject that is independent of its social situation, and that *value monism* is just as possible as an ethical orientation in and to politics as Weber's value pluralism, with its sense of tragedy and fateful resignation. Benjamin's account challenges Weber's insistence that political action is inherently *individual action* undertaken within the institutional structures defining a particular historical situation. It also challenges his liberal understanding of political action as the exercise of one's legitimate power(s), and replaces it with a conception of politics as an exercise in resistance. For what "divine" or "pure" violence means is that historical limits *can* be changed, that the objective possibilities immanent in a given social situation are neither definitive nor exhaustive of what we can do. History is not a series of precedents, but rather a long string of miracles.[28]

Notes

1 This chapter is an updated version of my previously published article, "Manifest Reason: Walter Benjamin on Violence and Collective Agency." *Constellations: An International Journal of Critical and Democratic Theory* vol. 21, no. 3 (2014).
2 See Drucilla Cornell, Michel Rosenfeld, and David Gray Carlson (eds), *Deconstruction and the Possibility of Justice* (New York: Routledge, 1992). Giorgio Agamben, *State of Exception*, trans. Kevin Attell (Chicago: University of Chicago Press, 2005). Mathias Fritch, *The Promise of Memory: History and Politics in Marx, Benjamin and Derrida* (New York: SUNY Press, 2005). Anselm Haverkamp (ed.), *Gewalt und Gerechtigkeit: Derrida-Benjamin* (Frankfurt am Main: Suhrkamp, 1994).
3 In this sense, Weber's account of politics and political action is prescient of Pippin's more recent reading of Hegel's practical philosophy. See Robert B. Pippin, *Hegel's Practical Philosophy: Rational Agency as Ethical Life* (Cambridge: Cambridge University Press, 2008).
4 *GS* II: 943.
5 *Briefe,* 227.
6 For a dissenting interpretation, see Peter Fenves, *The Messianic Reduction*, 187–226. Fenves reads Benjamin's "Critique of Violence" as an implicit critique of Kant's *Metaphysics of Morals*. This interpretation is grounded in the well-documented fact that Benjamin was familiar with Kant's tract (his essay "Goethes Wahlverwandtschaften" quotes it, and his original dissertation project on Kant's concept of history would have also made reference to this text). According to Fenves, Benjamin's critique involves opposing the category of justice to Kant's category of right. The Violence-essay, Fenves contends, "is unlike any other text that Benjamin published in terms of the directness with which it confronts the category of justice" (*The Messianic Reduction,* 208). I do not share Fenves' assessment of Benjamin's essay. Although *Gerechtigkeit* and its cognates appear some fourteen or fifteen times in the first two paragraphs of the essay, it is completely absent from the bulk of Benjamin's analysis, reappearing only in the final three pages, where Benjamin concludes by restating the basic paradox of jurisprudence with which the essay began.

The whole point of Benjamin's essay is that justice is emphatically not something that can be confronted directly, for any such direct, *thematic* engagement would place it in the service of mythic violence and instrumental reason as *justifying* a course of action. If Benjamin brackets the concept of justice (for this is what his call, in the fourth paragraph of the essay, for bracketing any consideration of the criteria for "justice" amounts to), he cannot then oppose the bracketed notion to Kant's conception of Right. That would be an utterly incoherent strategy—and whatever else we may think of Benjamin's essay, it is not incoherent. To the extent that Fenves' account insists on the centrality of "justice," it yields paradoxical results. His interpretation fails, in sum, because he misunderstands the opening sentence of Benjamin's essay: "The task of a critique of violence can be characterized as the presentation [*Darstellung*] of its relationship to Right and Justice" (*GS* II: 179/ *SW* 1: 236). On the reading on offer here, Benjamin's opening gambit is to make violence a limit-phenomenon, which differentiates *between* Right and Justice. And this involves, as Benjamin shows, delineating a specific kind of practical agency that is no longer bound up with the teleological structure of Reason, in which violence can only be rationalized—justified—as right. Insofar as Benjamin's strategy is to show what violence manifests, it would seem strange to think that he *opposes* the notion of right to the notion of justice.

7   Max Weber, "Politik als Beruf," 245; Max Weber, "Politics as a Vocation," 89.
8   See Tracy B. Strong and David Owen's Introduction to *The Vocation Lectures*, xxxiv. The bulk of my remarks above follow their reconstruction of the historical context of Weber's lecture. Max Weber, "Politics as a Vocation." in *The Vocation Lectures*. ed. David Owen and Tracy B. Strong. trans. Rodney Livingstone (Indianapolis: Hackett Publishing, 2004), xxxiv.
9   Max Weber, "Politik als Beruf," 250–2; Max Weber, "Politics as a Vocation," 93.
10 Max Weber, "Objectivity in Social Science and Social Policy," in *The Methodology of the Social Sciences,* ed. Edward A. Shils and Henry A. Finch. trans. Henry A Finch (Glencoe: The Free Press, 1949), 50–112.
11 Ibid.
12 Weber, "Politik als Beruf," 158; Weber, "Politics as a Vocation," 33.
13 Weber, "Politik als Beruf," 230; Weber, "Politics as a Vocation," 78.
14 *PB* 229/*PV* 78, translation modified.
15 Weber, "Politik als Beruf," 237; Weber, "Politics as a Vocation," 83.
16 Ibid.
17 Ibid.
18 Weber, "Politik als Beruf," 235; Weber, "Politics as a Vocation," 82.
19 Ibid.
20 *SW* 1: 248, emphasis added
21 *GS* II: 196–7; *SW* 1: 248, emphasis added.
22 *GS* II: 180/*SW* 1: 237.
23 Weber's own attempt to address the problem—by appeal to the process of rationalization itself—is reminiscent of Kant's attempt to deduce "Right" from an "original acquisition" by relying on the idea of a *lex permissiva* (see §§11–18 of the *Doctrine of Right* [Ak. VI: 260-71]). Whatever the origins of our historical situation, the institutionalization of specific legal codes is somehow supposed to lead to a just form of deliberation and action. But the basic problem still remains: to the extent that we evaluate political action by the criteria we extrapolate from purposive reason, we subordinate "legitimacy" to some notion of aptness among value-orientation, a situation's objective possibilities, and an action's practical execution.

Any form of engagement that does not recognize the institutionalization of what is possible, in a given historical situation, or does not accept a pre-formed value-orientation is by definition *illegitimate*, because the criteria for evaluating such engagement are bound up with the very institutions being challenged.

24 Weber, "Politics as a Vocation," 78.
25 *SW* 1: 245f.
26 *SW* 1: 248.
27 In fact, Korah's opposition to the Mosaic law was calculated, and hinged on his oracular view of the future: he had already foretold that his bloodline would live on, and thought that this divination secured his survival. In contrast again to the story of Niobe, God's divine violence did not wipe out Korah's children.
28 As recent general strikes have shown, *collective resistance* can transform our basic institutional structures and generate new potentials for practical, intersubjective action. I need only refer here to the 2000 general strike in Cochabamba, Bolivia, over the privatization of the water distribution system (and again more recently, in 2005, in El Alto, Bolivia). The complete cessation of work, coupled with mass demonstrations, resulted in the Bolivian government announcing a state of emergency. The ensuing violence led both government officials and the corporations involved in the privatization plan to go first into hiding and then, when the police and military could no longer guarantee their safety, to flee the country. This shows how spontaneous mass organization can overcome state violence or coercion and institute popular governance. For a journalist's account of these events, see Benjamin Dangl, *The Price of Fire: Resource Wars and Social Movements in Bolivia* (Oakland: AK Press, 2007). For a participant's account, see Tom Lewis and Oscar Olivera, ¡*Cochabamba! Water War in Bolivia*. Foreword by Vandana Shiva (Cambridge, MA: South End Press, 2004).

Bibliography

Agamben, Giorgio. *State of Exception*, trans. Kevin Attell. Chicago: University of Chicago University Press, 2005.

Benjamin, Walter. *Walter Benjamin: Gesammelte Schriften*. 7 Vols. in 14 Parts, ed. Rolf Tiedemann and Hermann Schweppenhäuser. Frankfurt am Main: Suhrkamp, 1991.

Benjamin, Walter. *Walter Benjamin: Selected Works*. Vol 1., ed. Marcus Bullock and Michael W. Jennings. Cambridge, MA: The Belknap Press of Harvard University Press, 1996.

Benjamin, Walter. *Walter Benjamins Briefe*. 2 Vols. ed. G. Scholem and Th. W. Adorno. (Frankfurt am Main: Suhrkamp, 1991).

Cornell, Drucilla., Michel Rosenfeld, and David Gray Carlson, eds. *Deconstruction and the Possibility of Justice*. New York: Routledge, 1992.

Dangl, Benjamin. *The Price of Fire: Resource Wars and Social Movements in Bolivia.* Oakland: AK Press, 2007.

Fritch, Mathias. *The Promise of Memory: History and Politics in Marx, Benjamin and Derrida.* New York: SUNY Press, 2005.

Haverkamp, Anselm, ed. *Gewalt und Gerechtigkeit: Derrida-Benjamin.* Frankfurt am Main: Suhrkamp, 1994.

Kant, Immanuel., *Metaphysics of Morals*, ed. Mary McGregor. Cambridge: Cambridge University Press, 2000.

Lewis, Tom, and Oscar Olivera. ¡*Cochabamba! Water War in Bolivia.* Foreword by Vandana Shiva. Cambridge, MA: South End Press, 2004.

Pippin, Robert B. *Hegel's Practical Philosophy: Rational Agency as Ethical Life.* Cambridge: Cambridge University Press, 2008).

Procyshyn, Alexei. "Manifest Reason: Walter Benjamin on Violence and Collective Agency," *Constellations: An International Journal of Critical and Democratic Theory,* 21.3 (2014): 390–400.

Weber, Max. "Objectivity in Social Science and Social Policy," in *The Methodology of the Social Sciences,* edited by Edward A. Shils and Henry A. Finch. trans. Henry A Finch, 50–112. Glencoe: The Free Press, 1949.

Weber, Max. "Politik als Beruf," in *Max Weber: Gesamtausgabe.* Vol. 17, Book 1., edited by Horst Baier et al. Tübingen: JCB Mohr (Paul Siebeck), 1992.

Weber, Max. "Politics as a Vocation," in *The Vocation Lectures*, edited by David Owen and Tracy B. Strong. trans. Rodney Livingstone, 32–94. Indianapolis: Hackett Publishing, 2004.

6

Passive Resistance: A Daoist Approach

Mario Wenning

1. Introduction

In the fourth-century BC classic *Art of War*, the legendary Chinese philosopher-general Sun Tzu 孫子 (541–482 BC) states: "In the practical art of war (…) to fight and conquer in all your battles is not supreme excellence; supreme excellence consists in breaking the enemy's resistance without fighting."[1] There is no doubt that both winning without fighting and the image of a world in which attacks and resistance are no longer needed have an appeal. However, Sun Tzu, who has been commonly associated with philosophical Daoism based on the later classification of philosophical schools in the Book of Han 漢書 (completed in 111 AD), is not advocating a refusal to engage in war. The philosopher-general was no pacifist and did not—or at least not unconditionally—reject the use of violence. The aim of military strategy is, for him, to "break" the enemy's capacity for resistance without wasting energy in unnecessary confrontations.[2] Instead of proposing direct attacks, he propagates a dynamic strategy of evasion and surprise that refuses direct engagement. He aims to resolve the destructive logic of escalating confrontations. While the enemy is left pursuing actions that normally provoke adverse responses, refusing to engage those responses changes the rules of the game in favor of the party that avoids such predictable patterns of action. Those who are skilled in the art of nonresistance manage to cultivate and preserve vital energy, while the enemies' actions fail to reach their intended target. Rather than accepting the inherited practices of warfare and engaging the enemy in conventional war, Sun Tzu's stratagem aims to outplay potential conflicts by dissolving them at the right time, ideally already before they even arise and manifest themselves in destructive ways. It is no surprise that this ancient guerilla manifesto influenced the military strategies of Mao Zedong (毛澤東) and continues to serve as a reference to highlight the difference between the unpredictable strategy rooted in classical Chinese philosophical tradition and conventional Western tactics.

The strategy of evading confrontation is not restricted to military conflicts but can be applied to the domains of economics, management, or political supra-planning. Due to their polysemantic character and adaptability to diverse contexts, classical Chinese stratagems have not failed to generate interest at a global level. They present lessons how to outsmart one's opponents in complex situations, i.e., situations that prevent ordinary tactics of cost–benefit calculations and instrumental planning. When the level of complexity is high, risks multiply beyond control and the actors are increasingly unlikely to achieve a previously determined goal.[3] The general's stratagems reduce complexity by focusing on how to take oneself back.

One common distinction in classical Chinese strategic thinking is that between *shih* (勢), the increase of one's influence and power by tangible as well as intangible factors such as the hearts and minds of the people, and *li* (利), the increase of benefits rooted in material self-interest, but also the capacity to crush the enemy's forces. While there was a preference for the former over the latter, skilled strategists were always capable of changing the *shih* strategy to the more assertive *li* when necessary. Ultimately, shih-strategy was premised on sustaining a harmonious relationship with the cosmic dao (道).[4] Comparing the classical Chinese dynamic approach with the modern Western tactics of confrontation, Henry Kissinger remarks: "Western strategists test their maxims by victories in battles; Sun Tzu tests by victories where battles have become unnecessary."[5] In all fairness, it must be acknowledged that warring states—as well as modern—China has experienced countless battles. Many of these battles have been extremely brutal. Acts of extreme violence in self-administered justice are also common throughout Chinese history and a common reference in Chinese pop culture. Conflicts take on different culturally shaped forms from those in the West, though. In the Confucian tradition, with its emphasis on filial piety, it has been common to distinguish between local targets of anger or revenge and the distant emperor imagined as a loving grand patriarch who will be appealed to as a potential source of remedy.[6] At the same time, despite the focus on strategic action, passivity is considered to be a core component of strategic thinking in Western thought as is illustrated by the Prussian general and theoretician of war, Carl von Clausewitz. Known for his definition of war according to which "war is simply a continuation of political intercourse, with the addition of other means."[7], Clausewitz also emphasizes the importance of strategic waiting and withdrawal. He distinguishes various modes of defense, including a strategy of retreat. A besieged army "can withdraw to the interior of the country and resist there." Clausewitz continues: "The purpose of this withdrawal is to weaken the attacker to such an extent that one can wait for him to break off his advance of his own accord, or, at least, be too weak to overcome the resistance with which he will eventually be confronted."[8] This passage demonstrates that, despite Clausewitz's insight that "the most passive kind of defense is the strongest," defensive strategies are complemented by a focus on preparing for an attack. This primacy of attack constitutes a core difference from Chinese conceptions of passive resistance that aim to reduce the enemy's resistance without fighting. Clausewitz writes: "there is no contradiction in saying that one is able to resist more effectively in a strong and suitably entrenched position, and that, after the enemy has wasted half his strength on it, a counter-attack will be that much more effective."[9] In contrast to Sun Tzu, Clausewitz does thus not embrace a primacy of strategies of subversive evasion, but only a calculated retreat to a "strong and suitably entrenched position." A strategic retreat buys an army time and allows for a counterattack at the right moment, namely when the enemy's capacity for resistance has been minimized. A calculated retreat is thus accepted only to prepare for a more effective counterattack when the enemy's capacity for resistance has been reduced. The radically subversive notion of a primacy of passivity and retreat we find in classical Daoism causes us to rethink what it means to resist well. Rather than conceiving of resistance exclusively as a defensive strategy, for the Daoists passivity was, paradoxically, itself a form of more efficacious practice. This insight is not restricted to the Chinese context. It has been a prominent feature in transcultural movements of resistance.

2. Transcultural Resistance

Resistance movements East and West are frequently influenced by culturally distant models, including the classical Chinese art of winning without fighting. Ancient or culturally distinctive models seem new in a cultural context where they are unfamiliar and serve as sources of inspiration. Transcultural references become important especially during periods of deep social and political unrest.[10] When ordinary strategies taken from one's familiar strategic reservoir no longer seem to work, it is time to expand one's scope of reference in the realm of tactical know-how. When experiencing radical civilizational crises and the old forms of protest are outdated, it is particularly tempting to reach beyond one's cultural reservoir when articulating and practicing resistance. It is well known that passive resistance movements have been inspired by Gandhi's ethics of nonviolent civil resistance. Gandhi himself was influenced by Christian ethics as well as the deeply rooted tradition of non-violence (*ahimsa*) in ancient Jainism, Buddhism, and Hinduism. Similarly, Martin Luther King, Jr. and the American Civil Rights Movement drew on culturally heterodox paradigms that combined elements from African and European, especially classical Greek and Christian, traditions. While radical at the time, their emphasis on nonviolence and civility now belongs to the familiar cultural reservoir of resistance movements.

The potentials of Chinese (and especially Daoist) sources and historical experiences for articulating distinctive perspectives on as well as practices of resistance has been explored to a lesser extent.[11] Especially in the Western imaginary, Chinese culture tends to be portrayed as cultivating obedient subjects who blindly follow their collective. At first sight, the association of Chinese culture with passive resistance may thus strike the reader as misplaced for at least two reasons. First, Chinese mentality is often portrayed as obedient to the point of cultivating submissiveness that corresponds to a specific kind of "oriental despotism." As Montesquieu has already argued, "China is a despotic state whose principle is fear."[12] The stereotype of oriental despotism has been influential throughout modern political history. As an extension of this stereotype, Chinese people have been conceived as forming obedient and homogeneous masses of servile subjects who do not dare to question and resist authority, be it in the family context that is governed by filial piety or the political domain in which absolute loyalty is expected while dissent is frowned upon and penalized severely. Furthermore, the emphasis on passivity contradicts the stereotype according to which a specifically Chinese work ethics privileges activity and hard work over passivity. Thus, the paradigmatic Spanish expression "*un trabajo de chinos*," a task done by a Chinese person, refers to tasks that require significant effort, diligence, and patience. It is usually applied to workers who can endure hardship and keep going even under difficult conditions. The Chinese work ethic is commonly imagined as emphasizing highly strenuous and tedious tasks that are performed in an unreflective and uncritical spirit. Confucianism in particular is identified as the ideological foundation for obedience and a work ethics that emphasizes inner-worldly success through a concerted and ritualized effort that stretches over generations.[13] Evaluated from a Western perspective that emphasizes individual human rights and the capacity for critique, the flipside of the emphasis on communal values in China is that individuals sacrifice their goals and unreflectively subordinate themselves to an alleged greater good. While this image of China stood for traditionalism and stagnation, the recent shift in geopolitical dynamics suggests that Confucian work ethics that emphases hard work to advance one's family's and one's nation's greater good seems to excel compared to its aging Protestant rival as the most dynamic motor of twenty-first-century global capitalism. Capitalism with Protestant characteristics is on the decline and those who remain committed to it are undergoing an identity crisis, while the capitalism with Confucian characteristics flourishes and presents itself as hypermodern.

3. Adaptations of Daoist Resistance

The briefly summarized stereotypical assumption of a homogeneous culture of obedient and hard-working people hardly does justice to the diversity of historical and contemporary trends in the People's Republic of China. China has not only given rise to (and is represented by) a collectivist work ethic, but it is also historical home of religious and philosophical traditions that emphasize individual acts of defiance, traditions that have evolved even under authoritarian rule as is documented by an increase of labor rights movements and protest on social media over the last decades. A capacity for subtle protest is also exercised by religious groups that are navigating the gray zone within and beyond the state control of religious freedoms.[14] Even more invisible is the group of those who may appear to be obedient, but, upon closer observation, reveal signs of discontent and engage in subtle practices of dissent. These traditions often fall outside the radar screen of research on resistance since they manifest themselves in unusual forms of dissent, ranging from sleep-ins to ironic forms of displaying fake obedience. Daoism in particular has not cherished collective conformism, but subversive practices of individual and group resistance. In this chapter I will explore how far the tradition of Daoism has inspired resistance movements by offering spiritual inspiration as well as conceptual resources to motivate practices of passive revolt. I start by recalling two forms of drawing on these sources to legitimate resistance—a heroic form of subversion and a fluid form of evasion—before turning to contemporary applications.

The Daoist canon has inspired resistance fighters in different context and for various motifs ever since the yellow turban rebellion (184–205 AD). It continues to have an impact, in addition to mainstream conceptions of resistance in the liberal tradition, up until current phenomena such as the umbrella movement in Hong Kong or the counterculture resistance movement of cultivating low desires known as "lying flat" (*Tangping* 躺平) who are transgressing against an increasingly exploitative labor market with inhumane working hours (referred to as 996 since the work schedule is from 9 AM to 9 PM, 6 days of the week) in the PRC. The subversive promise of cultivating passive competences, such as low desires and inertia, was not only the potential of gaining peace by abandoning an economy that emphasizes ambition, but the accomplishment of significant practical and political tasks without in the process wasting energy in what is perceived as pointless struggles.

The reception of conceptions and practices of passivity from the East has taken on different—and sometimes contrary—forms. At the risk of oversimplification, one can distinguish a heroic from a non-heroic version of cultivating passivity. Both forms of resistance, while drawing their inspiration from Daoist ideas, are not limited to China. This can be demonstrated with examples from the resistance movement against Nazi Germany: the call to heroic resistance by the resistance fighters of the "The White Rose" movement and the account of subversive evasion presented by the Marxist poet Bertolt Brecht.

At the end of their second leaflet aimed at waking up the German people, the members of the White Rose cite Chapters 58 and 29 from the classic *Daodejing* (道德經). Chapter 29 is particularly relevant in our context since it presents, in poetic outline, the ethos of taking no action. For the authors of the pamphlet, it is intended to serve as a critique of the tendency by authoritarian governments to advocate activism and the drive towards domination that served as the psychopolitical basis of the Nazi attempt to establish a Third Reich. The following passage from the Daoist classic *Daodejing* is cited in the pamphlet:

> "He who attempts to control the empire and to design in according to his arbitrary will; I do not see him reach his goal; that is all."
>
> "The empire is a living organism; it cannot be made, truly! He who wants to manipulate it, spoils it, he who wants to dominate it, loses it."
>
> Thus: "The high human being therefore lets go of excessiveness, lets go of arrogance, lets go of assaults."[15]

In James Legge's translation, the passage from the *Daodejing* reads:

> "If anyone should wish to get the kingdom for himself, and to effect this by what he does, I see that he will not succeed. The kingdom is a spirit-like thing, and cannot be got by active doing. He who would so win it destroys it; he who would hold it in his grasp loses it. (…) Hence the sage puts away excessive effort, extravagance, and easy indulgence."

> 將欲取天下而為之，吾見其不得已。天下神器，不可為也，為者敗之，執者失之。故物或行或隨；或歔或吹；或強或羸；或挫或隳。是以聖人去甚，去奢，去泰。

The Daoist critique of the drive to control was a prominent point of reference for those persecuted by the Nazi regime. For the members of the underground student group that called itself The White Rose after Bruno Traven's novel by the same name, the intended purpose of distributing underground leaflets in Munich, one of the centers of the Nazi movement, was to "enlighten from human to human (...) without rest until the last one will be convinced of the most extreme necessity of his fight against this system." To motivate the citizens to revolt against the tyrannical and inhumane Nazi regime, the student resistance movement drew on the ancient Daoist strategies of resistance. They intended to overcome the complacency of German bystanders and motivate them to join the underground movement. The readers were supposed to transcend their political apathy and overthrow the totalitarian regime that, according to the analysis offered by the Hans and Sophie Scholl, had initially deceived the population before then revealing its true, despotic character. One commentator interprets the turn to Eastern wisdom traditions to justify the White Rose's call to resistance as follows:

> The quotes from Lao Tse Tung repeat many of the leaflet's thoughts in a more philosophical language. (...) They serve the purpose of justifying the idea of protesting an unjust regime by putting it into a larger cultural context. Whereas Goethe and Schiller had provided national examples, Lao Tse Tung widens the sphere into the cosmopolitan discourse. While laudable as a strategic move, the introduction of the Chinese thinker is also problematic as it would be difficult to evaluate how many readers felt directly addressed by his works; certainly very few outside the Bildungsbourgeoisie. The reference reinforces the impression of a superior distance set by the leaflet's authors between themselves and the general German public.[16]

The appeal to Daoist insights in a radically different cultural and historical context from that of ancient China may seem like a problematic form of cultural exoticism. As the commentator notes, it is elitist in introducing a reference that would only be recognized by highly educated cosmopolitan citizens. At the same time, it is an effective tool of transcultural critique. The transhistorical as well as transcultural reference appeals to a cosmopolitan moral code of what it means to be human that is being violated by the Nazis. Referring to an ancient wisdom extracted from a culturally and historically foreign cultural sphere allows to criticize the authoritarian regime as inherently unjust and its mode of operation doomed to fail, both historically and on moral grounds. In concrete terms, the pamphlet aims to expose the rule by "arbitrariness" (*Willkür*). The passage suggests that morally mature people—true "high humans"—do not claim to be superior men, as the Nazis had alleged. Rather, a morally upright person lets go of (*läßt ab*) excessiveness (*Übertriebenheit*), arrogance (*Überhebung*), and assaults (*Übergriffen*). In hindsight we know that the hope associated with the pamphlets, namely the triggering of a popular uprising against the Nazi regime's hubris of mastery, would come to nothing. The resistance fighters were betrayed, publicly condemned in a show trial, and executed. The siblings Hans and Sophie Scholl, the most prominent members of the resistance group, have become martyrs for their bravery in fighting a totalitarian regime. Their resistance was at least in part inspired by Daoism and was carried out against all odds. They were not motivated primarily by short-term successes, but by doing what was right, even in the face of a potential death sentence. Their resistance can be described as heroic, because they were fighting for a higher ideal by undertaking extreme personal risks. It is due to this heroism that they attained significant posthumous status as martyred resistance fighters.

Rather than generating calls to heroic resistance against a totalitarian regime as in the case of the White Rose, Daoism has also been a reference point for articulating a "soft", nonheroic form of resistance. This is exemplified by another case of an effective transcultural adaptation of Daoism. During his exile from Nazi Germany, the Marxist poet Bertolt Brecht carried a painting with him that depicted Laozi (老子), the legendary author of the *Daodejing*, riding a water buffalo toward the western border of the Middle Kingdom. Brecht's poem about the "Legend of the Origin of the Book Daodejing on Laozi's Road into Exile" does not call to heroic resistance and a popular uprising as the White Rose had done. Instead, the core of the sage's wisdom is being expressed as follows: "he learnt that soft water, by way of movement over the years, will grind strong rocks away. In other words: that hardness succumbs."[17] Drawing on the example of Laozi and the Daoist imagery of the subversive force of water, the poem suggests that an exodus may not be a sign of cowardice and escapism, but rather a legitimate strategy of resistance when the political conditions are so rotten that they do not allow for other forms of meaningful dissent.

In contrast to the popular uprising intended against all odds by the White Rose, Brecht does not call for ordinary political action, but joins the motifs of exodus and the subversive force of water. Rather than, for example, drawing on the culturally more familiar exodus narratives inspired by the Old Testament to justify a culture of protest and confrontation, Brecht alludes to classical Daoist imagery of subversive fluidity. The poem thereby combines the theme of exodus and the hope in ultimately overcoming the seemingly invincible totalitarian regime. Applying his conception of artistic estrangement, the Marxist poet draws on the ancient Chinese myth of Laozi´s escape to reinterpret a seemingly hopeless situation as giving reasons for hope. The intended meaning could also be rendered with the "Western" proverb, "with persistence a drop of water hollows out the stone." However, by drawing on the ancient Chinese imagery as the members of the White Rose had done, Brecht adds a transhistorical truth to it. Instead of calling for a public uprising in a heroic mode, Brecht's Laozi takes leave and relies on transformations in the grand scheme of time in which seeming strength can turn out to be a weakness and vice versa.[18] The transcultural appeal provides the poem a force for believing that what may seem like a hopeless form of escape and surrender could indeed turn out to be a fruitful form of resistance. Indeed, the support of poets who were lucky enough to escape such as Brecht or Thomas Mann as part of the resistance against Nazi Germany during their exile turned out to be important. It motivated others to join resistance movements and represents—then and to this day—a different Germany from that of the German bystanders and perpetrators cheering to the Führer. Brecht's poem emphasizes that the seeming retreat into exile of the sage simultaneously marks the origin of the classic *Daodejing* and thereby the tradition of passing down subversive Daoist wisdom over generations. Furthermore, the poem adds in a subtle ending that this creative resistance in the spirit of a philosophical escape is not only due to the sage. The escape is possible due to the work of others: the ox that carries the sage, the child who accompanies and speaks for the silent sage, and the border official who demanded a written summary of the sage's teaching before letting him leave the Middle Kingdom. Their usually invisible contributions that are revealed by the poem is in line with the tendency of the element of water to remain translucent.

    The two examples of drawing on Daoist ideas in an effort to reinvent seemingly impossible forms of resistance under the Nazi regime present distinctive versions of transcultural appropriation. They seem to motivate opposing forms of resistance: heroic resistance as documented by the White Rose aims for an active struggle against the system, while Brecht's poetic adaptation of Laozi's escape presents a conception of resistance that is rooted in a sense of trust in the power of time to subvert and overcome the most reified political circumstances just as water has the capacity to overcome stone.

    The two examples illustrate that, due to their polysemantic density and idiosyncratic nature, Daoist texts offer motifs that allow for justifying differing practices of subversion in different cultural and temporal contexts. It is partially the appeal of being spatially remote and, at the same time, an ancient form of wisdom praxis that allows Daoism to resurface in and be adapted to radically different contexts. In line with this malleability and adaptability, Daoist "soft power," symbolically expressed in the capacity of water to overcome the greatest obstacles, has become a common trope of resistance fighters globally. The force of soft or liquid resistance presents an alternative notion of praxis from that of heroic resistance as it has become representative of protest movements and the figures representing such movements.

4. *Wuwei* as Subversive Practice

The core concept of Daoism that is relevant when rethinking resistance is that of *wuwei* 無為, customarily translated as non-doing or non-action. Other dimensions include naturalness, spontaneity, non-competition, and non-striving. The concept serves to denote practices that present an alternative to ordinary strategic action that aims to achieve a certain end by way of engaging one's effort to pursue—usually higher and distant—goals. It is no exaggeration to state that *wuwei* is the most prominent and the most frequently interpreted concept in Daoist philosophy. Interpreters have highlighted the paradox of trying to not try while largely ignoring the subversive dimensions of *wuwei* as inspiring practices of resistance. The term appears repeatedly in the *Daodejing* and the other Daoist classic *Zhuangzi* (as well as in other classical Chinese texts, including those associated to belong to the Confucian canon).

In the remaining part of this chapter, I will not add to the abundant exegetical literature that aims to tease out the historical meanings of this concept of *wuwei* and the practices it denotes together with related concepts such as that of self-forgetfulness;[19] nor do I present *wuwei* as an esoteric therapy that promises special capacities or peace of mind in a crazy world. Instead, I pursue the question in which way *wuwei* may be considered to refer to practices that have the potential to be considered acts of resistance in radically different socio-political contexts from ancient China or the resistance against Nazi Germany. I shall turn to *wuwei* in the context of navigating within today's neoliberal economy and culture of ambition. In contrast to the concept of active resistance understood as the purposeful and ambitious striving towards accomplishing a goal, *wuwei* denotes forms of practices that are performed in a manner that negate or avoid (*wu*) purposeful, instrumental, or ambitious action (*wei*). *Wuwei*-like actions resemble water and its seemingly contradictory attributes: still and raging, soft and hard, invisible and muddy, destructive and nourishing life.[20] The effectiveness of an absence of struggle and a critique of forms of action that prioritize means–ends calculations according to fixed notions of what constitutes usefulness and an ethos of striving for ulterior goals represents a Daoist counter-strategy, a strategy that breaks with the assumptions underlying usual strategic forms of strategic thinking and action.

At first sight, one may be tempted to think that passive resistance and *wuwei* denote different and largely unrelated phenomena. Resistance is typically associated with struggle against social political phenomena that are perceived to be unjust, unfree, or otherwise debilitating and in need of change towards creating better positions. Positively stated, acts of resistance strive for conditions that a more just, free or in other ways attractive. In contrast, the practice of *wuwei* does not emphasize the need for overthrowing problematic conditions or contribute to a change towards justice. Rather it unmasks such strategies as often pointless or self-contradictory, especially in highly complex settings. Sometimes, *wuwei* is taken to be a mere survival strategy. According to this interpretation, staying out of harm's way allows preserving peace of mind or, at the very least, extend one's existence by remaining as invisible as possible and thereby evade the risks associated with action. For critics, *wuwei* is at best a strategy of avoiding conflict at all costs; at worst, practitioners of *wuwei* embrace conformism, the art of going along, a strategy of avoiding the waste of energy in risky struggles for distant goals that are core features of heroic notions of action in general and resistance struggles more specifically. As we have seen, the combination of an aesthetically appealing ease that mimics the often still, but sometimes raging force of water promises fulfillment has been attractive especially during periods of crises, including radical crises that undermine the very conditions of possibility of meaningful forms of political dissent, times that fetishize greatness and domination.

This raises the question what relevance does the concept have for conceptualizing resistance today? How can the concept be reinterpreted to avoid a conformist form of going along with the flow and of quietism that amounts to a conformist adaptation to less than ideal conditions? Admittedly, *wuwei* understood as inaction does not—or at least not necessarily—imply resistance. Many people are inactive without thereby revolting against pathological conditions. However, some forms of resistance may express themselves in a *wuwei*-like manner. For example, a refusal to think, speak, and act along the established forms of manifesting one's values may not express implicit consent, but can amount to resistance especially in contexts where typical forms of resistance are unavailable or have become coopted by what they are aiming to remedy.

5. Resistance-in-place

In her book *How to Do Nothing*, the artist Jenny Odell turns to the story of "The Useless Tree" from the Daoist classic *Zhuangzi* (莊子). This story depicts a tree that manages to survive throughout the ages while generations of other "straight" trees have been cut down. A carpenter passes by and leaves the tree standing, because it is deemed useless due to (what is perceived as) its deformation. The tree justifies its "life philosophy" in a dream to Carpenter Shi:

> "What do you want to compare me to, one of those cultivated trees? The hawthorn, the pear, the orange, the rest of those fructiferous trees and shrubs— when their fruit is ripe they get plucked, and that is an insult. Their large branches are bent; their small branches are pruned. Thus do their abilities embitter their lives. That is why they die young, failing to fully live out their natural life spans. They batter themselves with the vulgar conventions of the world— and all other creatures do the same. As for me, I've been working on being useless for a long time. It almost killed me, but I've finally managed it—and it is of great use to me! If I were useful, do you think I could have grown to be so great?"
>
> "Moreover, you and I are both [members of the same class, namely], beings —is either of us in a position to classify and evaluate the other? How could a worthless man with one foot in the grave know what is or isn't a worthless tree?"[21]

The story of the useless tree calls into question conventional notions of use and staying alive. In a typical Daoist manner, the tree's survival strategy plays on a number of paradoxes: the usefulness of being useless, being imperfect as a way of staying alive, a speechless tree that speaks to a human in a dream etc. Odell interprets the story as offering a form of what she calls "resistance-in-place" that she considers particularly promising under current socio-political pressures to conform to fixed standards of usefulness:

> the tree provides me with an image of "resistance-in-place." To resist in place is to make oneself into a shape that cannot so easily be appropriated by a capitalist value system. To do this means refusing the frame of reference: in this case, a frame of reference in which value is determined by productivity, the strength of one's career, and individual entrepreneurship. It means embracing and trying to inhabit somewhat fuzzier or blobbier ideas: of maintenance as productivity, of the importance of nonverbal communication, and of the mere experience of life as the highest goal. It means recognizing and celebrating a form of the self that changes over time, exceeds algorithmic description, and whose identity doesn't always stop at the boundary of the individual.[22]

For Odell, the "deformed" tree's "lesson" consists in escaping from the crippling impact of having to succeed in the current economic regime and thereby rediscover a new "highest goal": the experience of having a place and, ultimately, of life itself. It is thus not simply a refusal, but an existential affirmation of accepting imperfection as not only crippling but also as enabling that is being embodied by the tree. Yet, the focus on staying-in-place, while attractive, may not reflect the classical Daoist cosmo-ontology that highlights the inescapable "natural" power of transformation. The tree is not only imperfect, but has been undergoing countless processes of change throughout the years and the seasons. What distinguishes the tree is not that it decides to remain where it is and what it is; a tree is always a tree. What distinguishes this specific imperfect tree is that it is left unharmed due to its imperfections and that it has learned to see these unique features not as deformations. The tree is neither merely a raw material to be used for ulterior ends, such as chairs and tables made out of "straight" wood. The major difference between this tree and its more valuable neighbors is that it has lived long enough to enjoy its imperfect existence.

The story of the useless tree does have one important twist that may be at odds with the proposed ethics of getting back into place that Odell is proposing. The tree does not only criticize adhering to conventional standards of what is considered useful; it also turns against the practice of giving lessons to be learned or models to be emulated that is very typical of humans aiming at or claiming perfection. This tree is, in a word, anti-educational and anti-moralizing.[23] Even though the tree is "surrounded by marveling sightseers" and the carpenter's apprentice asks how it can value uselessness if the people admiring it have built a shrine around it, the carpenter responds that:

> "In fact, the tree considers it a great disgrace to be surrounded by this uncomprehending crowd. If they hadn't made it a shrine, they could easily have gone the other way and started carving away at it. What it values is not what they value. Is it not absurd to judge it by whether it does what is or is not called for by its position, by what role it happens to play?"[24]

In the final paradoxical twist, then, the carpenter has learned the lesson that giving lessons about use and uselessness as well as the search for models to be followed is out of place. The tree's "message" lies in not trying to live up to any standards and accepting that this is just fine. The tree is an individual rather than a merely useful exemplar of the species tree. She frowns upon those crowd-followers who continue to need such an education.

6. Conclusion

For the purpose of precision, one can summarize at least four dimensions of resistance that have emerged in this and related stories from the Daoist canon: 1) the refusal to conform to established practices or standards of usefulness; 2) escape or staying where one is as a strategy of avoiding energy in pointless struggles and pursuits; 3) remaining an individual without a need to prove oneself or teach others; and 4) bearing one's imperfections gracefully. Passive resistance in a Daoist spirit presents a subversive combination of these dimensions and is, in contrast to other forms of passive resistance, not motivated primarily by preventing violence from occurring and escalating or creating a better—a just—society, even if it may do this indirectly as well.

This chapter has introduced a passive resistance that is a genuine form of subversive praxis of dissent. In contrast to the ethics of non-violent or civil resistance pioneered in Gandhi's anti-colonial struggle or the civil rights movement associated with Martin Luther King, Jr.'s political activism, it is not necessarily non-violent even if it may seek to avoid pointless confrontations. For the classical Chinese philosophers, violence was an inescapable part of natural as well as human reality. In a more radical form, they called into question the very focus on ambition and instrumental activity that underlies ordinary modes of strategic thinking in peace and war.

An updated version of the notion of *wuwei* also serves as an antidote to forms of instrumental action in economies of ambition, but also breaks with the mainstream discourse on resistance that has dominated the imaginary of what it means to resist well. While passivity may also have the benefit of increasing one's lifespan (as in the story of the "useless" tree), it is not primarily a life-saving strategy, which would be another instrumental pursuit, but represents a philosophy of accepting difference and reacting differently. Paradoxically, the Chinese insight into the power of passivity could be subversive precisely at a moment where East-West relations have returned to being marked by increasing strategic activism, mutual suspicion, fear, and anger.[25]

The adaptation of Daoist ideas by the White Rose, Bertolt Brecht and, in today's context, activists such as Odell may reflect the perspective of highly educated Western citizens who refer to Daoism in a mode of transcultural exoticism. It would be a mistake, though, to consider the ancient Chinese wisdom concerning the subversive power of water and passivity, including the capacity to resist the pressure to resist actively, to be exclusively an upper middle-class ideology or a form of anti-political escapism. This form of counter-strategy is neither civil nor disobedient. The imperfect tree prefers to remain invisible. She does not want to teach, lead, or follow. What she does achieve is to remain stubborn in resisting the all too human tendency of trying to become better.

Notes

1 Sun Tzu, *Art of War*, trans. Ralph D. Sawyer, Ch. 3, Planning Offensives (Boulder, CO: Westview, 1994), 175–9, 177.
2 In *All-under-heaven: The Tianxia System for a Possible World Order*, trans. Joseph E. Harroff (Berkeley: University of California Press, 2021), Zhao Tingyang argues that traditional Chinese thought is not motivated by the friend–enemy distinction that, according to him, is common to Western rationality epitomized by Carl Schmitt. Instead, Chinese strategy aims to transform enemies into friends and thereby preserve cosmic harmony. Interestingly, the underlying binary distinction between friends and enemies is common to classical Chinese as well as modern strategists of war.
3 Harro von Senger, *The 36 Stratagems for Business: Achieve your Objectives through Hidden and Unconventional Strategies and Tactics* (London: Cyan Communications, 2005).
4 William H. Mott and Jae Chang Kim, *The Philosophy of Chinese Military Culture: Shih vs. Li* (New York: Palgrave, 2006).
5 Henry Kissinger, *On China* (London: Penguin, 2012), 26.
6 Ho-fung Hung, *Protest with Chinese Characteristics: Demonstrations, Riots, and Petitions* (New York: Columbia University Press, 2013). The prevalence of this form of local resistance, including violent acts of self-administered justice, paired with a trust in the highest representatives of government, has been a common theme in Jia Zhangke's films. See, for example, *A Touch of Sin* 天註定 (2013).
7 Carl von Clausewitz, *On War* (Oxford: Oxford University Press, 2007), 252.
8 Carl von Clausewitz, *On War* (Oxford: Oxford University Press, 2007), 172.
9 von Clausewitz, *On War*, 174.
10 Eric Hayout presents a critical reconstruction of notions of a distinctive form of "Chineseness" that one finds, for example, in contemporary Western science fiction. A transhistorical Chinese identity is constructed as, while trying to evade open conflict, presupposing the assumption of a constant state of war. Cf. "Chineseness: A Prehistory of Its Future", in Eric Hayout, Haun Saussy, and Steven G. Yao, *Sinographies: Writing China* (Minneapolis: University of Minnesota Press, 2008), 3–33.
11 William E. Scheuerman remarks, "Non-violent lawbreaking demanded in reality more discipline and self-control than violent political action, with both King and Gandhi regularly suggesting that it was not passive but instead "active"—and for them correspondingly 'manly.'" *Civil Disobedience* (Medford, MA: Polity, 2018), 21.

Gandhi initially spoke of "passive resistance" and then, later, of civil resistance to distinguish it from Thoreau's conception of civil disobedience. According to Gandhi, Thoreau's conception was not sufficiently non-violent. In contrast to the concern for masculinity expressed in both Gandhi's and King's conception of resistance, Daoists focus on the subversive force of passivity that is frequently associated with the "feminine" or the mother. Moreover, the classical Daoists do not idealize non-violence unconditionally. See chapters 8 and 9 by Ellen Zheng in Ping-cheung Lo and Sumner B. Twiss (eds), *Chinese Just War Ethics* (London: Routledge, 2015).

12 Montesquieu, *The Spirit of the Laws* (Cambridge: Cambridge University Press, 1989), 128.

13 The classical account of this conception is developed by Max Weber, *The Religion of China: Confucianism and Taoism*, trans. Hans H. Gerth (Glencoe: The Free Press, 1951).

14 Isaac Manfred Elfstrom, *Workers and change in China: resistance, repression, responsiveness* (Cambridge: Cambridge University Press, 2021). See also Keping Wu, "Buddhist and Protestant Philanthropies in Contemporary Southeast China: Negotiating the 'Grey Zone,'" in Philip Fountain, Robin Bush, R. Michael Feener (eds), *Religion and the Politics of Development* (New York: Palgrave Macmillan, 2015), 129–53.

15 Accessed on June 13, 2022, in the White Rose Archives available at https://www.weisse-rose-stiftung.de/white-rose-resistance-group/leaflets-of-the-white-rose/.

16 Corina L. Petrescu, *Against All Odds: Models of Subversive Spaces in National Socialist Germany* (Frankfurt: Peter Lang, 2009), 130.

17 Bertolt Brecht. "Dass das weiche Wasser in Bewegung/ Mit der Zeit den maechtigen Stein besiegt. / Du verstehst, das Harte unterliegt." See also the study by Heinrich Detering, *Bertolt Brecht und Laotse* (Göttingen: Wallstein, 2008).

18 For Walter Benjamin, Brecht's poem highlights the humane force of friendliness even in the midst of historical catastrophe as a core element of Daoist wisdom. Benjamin establishes a parallel between the revolutionary aspects of messianism and the "revolutionary softness" of Daoism. See Walter Benjamin, "Kommentare zu Gedichten von Brecht", in *Schriften II* (Frankfurt: Suhrkamp, 1955). See also Fabian Heubel, *Gewundene Wege nach China: Heidegger—Daoismus—Adorno* (Frankfurt: Klostermann 2020), 162–7. A related interpretation of Daoist stories as suggesting a critique of established patterns of usefulness is presented by Heidegger in his Daoist-inspired "Evening Conversation." However, in contrast to the image presented in Benjamin's and Heidegger's interpretation, the Daoist stories do not emphasize waiting, nor do they presuppose a messianic conception of history or revolutionary agency.

19 Studies that focus on *wuwei* include Edward Slingerland, *Effortless Action: Wu-wei As Conceptual Metaphor and Spiritual Ideal in Early China* (Oxford: Oxford University Press, 2007); Danesh Singh, "*Wuwei*, and the Necessity of Living Naturally: A Reply to Xunzi´s Objection," *Asian Philosophy*, vol. 24 (2014): 212–26; Nickolas Knightly, "The Paradox of Wuwei? Yes (and No)", *Asian Philosophy*, vol. 23 (2013), no. 2,

115–36; Yijun Xing and David Sims, "Leadership, Daoist Wu Wei and Reflexivity: Flow, Self-protection and Excuse in Chinese Bank Managers' Leadership Practice," in *Management Learning* vol. 43, no. 1 (2011): 97–112.
20 Sarah Allan, *The Way of Water and Sprouts of Virtue* (Albany: SUNY Press, 1999).
21 Zhuangzi, *The Essential Writings with Selections from Traditional Commentaries*, trans. Brook Ziporyn (Indianapolis: Hackett, 2009), 4:17.
22 Jenny Odell, *How to Do Nothing: Resisting the Attention Economy*, Brooklyn: Melville House 2019, XVI.
23 On this interpretation see Hans-Georg Moeller and Paul J. D'Ambrosio, *Genuine Pretending: On the Philosophy of the Zhuangzi*, New York: Columbia University Press, 2017.
24 Zhuangzi, *The Essential Writings*, 4:17.
25 See for example Evan Osnos' article, "Angry Youth: The New Generation's Neocon Nationalists," *The New Yorker*, July 28, 2008. Available online at: https://www.newyorker.com/magazine/2008/07/28/angry-youth

Bibliography

Allan, Sarah. *The Way of Water and Sprouts of Virtue*. Albany: SUNY Press, 1999.
Clausewitz, Carl von. *On War*. Oxford: Oxford University Press, 2007.
Detering, Heinrich. *Bertolt Brecht und Laotse*. Göttingen: Wallstein, 2008.
Elfstrom, Isaac Manfred. *Workers and Change in China: Resistance, Repression, Responsiveness*. Cambridge: Cambridge University Press, 2021.
Hayout, Eric. "Chineseness: A Prehistory of Its Future,", in *Sinographies: Writing China*, edited by Eric Hayout, Haun Saussy, and Steven G. Yao, 3–33. Minneapolis: University of Minnesota Press, 2008.
Heubel. *Gewundene Wege nach China: Heidegger—Daoismus—Adorno*. Frankfurt: Klostermann 2020.
Hung, Ho-fung. *Protest with Chinese Characteristics: Demonstrations, Riots, and Petitions*. New York: Columbia University Press, 2013.
Kissinger, Henry. *On China*. London: Penguin, 2012.
Knightly, Nickolas. "The Paradox of Wuwei? Yes (and No)." *Asian Philosophy*, vol. 23 (2013), no. 2, 115–36.
Moeller, Hans Georg, and Paul J. D'Ambrosio. *Genuine Pretending: On the Philosophy of the Zhuangzi*. New York: Columbia University Press, 2017.
Montesquieu. *The Spirit of the Laws*. Cambridge: Cambridge University Press, 1989.
Mott, William H., and Jae Chang Kim. *The Philosophy of Chinese Military Culture: Shih vs. Li*. New York: Palgrave, 2006.
Odell, Jenny. *How to Do Nothing: Resisting the Attention Economy*, Brooklyn: Melville House 2019, XVI.

Osnos, Evan. "Angry Youth: The New Generation's Neocon Nationalists," *The New Yorker*, July 28, 2008. Available online at https://www.newyorker.com/magazine/2008/07/28/angry-youth, accessed on July 11th, 2022.

Petrescu, Corina L. *Against All Odds: Models of Subversive Spaces in National Socialist Germany*. Frankfurt: Peter Lang, 2009.

Scheuermann, William E. *Civil Disobedience*. Medford, MA: Polity, 2018.

Singh, Danesh. "*Wuwei*, and the Necessity of Living Naturally: A Reply to Xunzi´s Objection." *Asian Philosophy*, vol. 24 (2014): 212–26.

Sun Tzu. *Art of War*, trans. Ralph D. Sawyer. Boulder, CO: Westview, 1994.

Slingerland, Edward. *Effortless Action: Wu-wei As Conceptual Metaphor and Spiritual Ideal in Early China*. Oxford: Oxford University Press, 2007.

Weber, Max. *The Religion of China: Confucianism and Taoism*, trans. Hans H. Gerth. Glencoe: The Free Press, 1951.

White Rose Archives available at https://www.weisse-rose-stiftung.de/white-rose-resistance-group/leaflets-of-the-white-rose/.

Wu, Keping. "Buddhist and Protestant Philanthropies in Contemporary Southeast China: Negotiating the "Grey Zone," in *Religion and the Politics of Development*, edited by Philip Fountain, Robin Bush, and R. Michael Feener, 129–53. New York: Palgrave Macmillan, 2015.

Xing, Yijun, and David Sims. "Leadership, Daoist Wu Wei and Reflexivity: Flow, Self-protection and Excuse in Chinese Bank Managers' Leadership Practice." *Management Learning* vol. 43, no. 1 (2011): 97–112.

Zhao Tingyang. *All-under-heaven: The Tianxia System for a Possible World Order*, trans. Joseph E. Harroff. Berkeley: University of California Press, 2021.

Zheng, Ellen, Ping-cheung Lo, and Sumner B. Twiss, eds. *Chinese Just War Ethics*. London: Routledge, 2015.

Zhuangzi. *The Essential Writings with Selections from Traditional Commentaries*, trans. Brook Ziporyn. Indianapolis: Hackett, 2009.

7
Resistance through Transformation: Spiritual Practices as a Pedagogy of Unlearning and Becoming

Jinting Wu

1. Introduction

To write about spirituality and resistance in the same breath may seem paradoxical. After all, spiritual practices have largely focused on the inner landscape and prioritized the notions of acceptance, non-judgment, and transcendental interpretation of external circumstances. Spiritual aspirants of various backgrounds generally adhere to the principles of nonviolence, benevolence, and common humanity in handling societal and personal challenges. Resistance, on the other hand, is often theorized as *oppositional* acts through which individuals and groups confront external circumstances in order to enact change. The emerging resistance studies scholarship, though disagreeing on the specific articulations of resistance, seems to converge on the idea that conflict and struggle, whether they are hidden in everyday tactics or manifested in open revolts, are central to how people work to challenge power.[1] Practices that differ from hegemonic understandings of resistance tend to be neglected. This chapter thus asks: is it possible to think about resistance through the lens of spirituality? What insights on contemporary human conditions may be gained by interrogating spirituality as a form of resistance, rather than as a contrasting social practice?

In the first two decades of the twenty-first century, we find ourselves at the threshold of a new consciousness whereby more and more people search for meaning through spiritual practices outside religious frameworks and dogmatic beliefs. While spirituality has become a popular concept in public discourse around the globe, and while research studies in disciplines such as neuroscience, psychology, social work, nursing, and education have led to a new understanding of spiritual well-being as a vital element of human existence,[2] spirituality is ofttimes misconstrued as esoteric, eccentric, and irrational. The various approaches to spirituality across cultures and traditions further render the concept vague and notoriously hard to define. This chapter locates spirituality primarily in the Eastern tradition. Independent of ritualized belief systems of religions, spirituality as approached in this writing entails a set of practical exercises (such as meditation, contemplation, journaling, and the like) to achieve existential goals, including the transcendence of the self towards a cosmic Being of oneness, living fully in the present moment, appreciating the interconnectedness of all life forms, and quest for meaning and a higher reality. Spiritual techniques, such as meditation and contemplation, are shared across wisdom traditions as an important aspect of personal flourishing, yet are rarely, if ever, discussed within the resistance studies literature. They are regarded as lifestyle or self-care matters at best. The reason for this omission can perhaps be attributed to spiritual practitioners' general attitude of acceptance, inner peace, and resilience in the face of suffering and adversity. Their apparent lack of resistance behaviors, such as rejection, denial, and hostility, conceals the fundamental ways in which external circumstances can be radically re-narrated in micro-level human experience through the subject's own transformation.

Taking up the role of spirituality in self-(trans)formation and the ongoing reconstruction of the world, this chapter engages with three analytical steps. First, it briefly reviews the literature on "everyday resistance" to develop a baseline understanding of this relatively elusive concept. Second, it examines the rise of spirituality in contemporary world to discuss the limits of resistance studies in addressing the transformation of subjectivity and human flourishing. Third, it discusses spirituality as a site of pedagogical resistance and transformation in school settings. As I will demonstrate, spiritual practices are oriented towards the radical re-mapping of subjectivity, through which the practitioners transcend external circumstances and partake in ushering in a new collective consciousness. Resistance viewed in this light differs significantly from the traditional forms of civil disobedience or subversion targeted at institutions and macro-structures, and takes on a distinctly powerful form of transformation from within.

2. Resistance in Everyday Life

The concept of resistance has increasingly populated social science publications in recent decades.[3] Its prolific appearances against the backdrop of social sciences' fascination with the study of power, seem to confirm the well-known remark by Michel Foucault that "[w]here there is power, there is resistance."[4] While there are ongoing debates and ever increasing complexities of definition of what counts as resistance, sociological literature has approached the question of resistance through two primary modes: namely, the study of macropolitical struggles, and the more recent shift towards everyday forms of resistance. Macropolitical analyses of resistance focus on visible, collective struggles, such as revolutionary upheavals in the classical definition, and the more widespread articulations of social movements and identity politics.[5] Everyday resistance, meanwhile, concerns how people act in day-to-day lives in ways that may undermine power, which suggests that resistance is a continuum between dramatic confrontations and mundane life events.[6] As a recurrent social phenomenon, everyday resistance exists as a *normal* part of life whereby subaltern groups engage in invisible and dispersed tactics to survive repressive situations.

In their often-cited review, Hollander and Einwohner identify two major propositions in the uses of the term "resistance" in social science literature: that resistance involves an *action*, and it is *oppositional*.[7] In what follows, I will draw from two major figures to elaborate the ways in which everyday resistance is understood as oppositional (James Scott) and an activity (Michel de Certeau). I then turn to Michel Foucault's work on the "aesthetics of existence" or the "care of the self" to offer a critique of the insufficient understanding of power and self in the conceptual territory of everyday existence.

The concept of everyday resistance is typically attributed to James Scott and his classic study of peasant rebellions in a small village in Malaysia. Scott looks at the persistent forms of cultural resistance and non-cooperation in rural settings to argue that oppression and resistance are in constant flux;[8] the subtle, uncoordinated, everyday forms of resistance, such as sarcasm, theft, disloyalty, sabotage, and foot-dragging, deserve our attention as much as visible historical events such as organized rebellions. These common tactics of oppressed groups, despite being dispersed, hidden, and politically invisible, play a crucial role in helping people survive and undermine domination. Scott terms such micro maneuvers as "infrapolitics" in which individuals contest established orders (what he calls "public transcript") without directly confronting elite norms and power hierarchies.

The political efficacy of everyday techniques, according to Scott,[9] lies in the *oppositional intention* of the subalterns, through small-scale, relatively safe, often unpronounced ways that nonetheless promise instrumental gains for those practicing them. Although not openly contesting norms and order, these practical techniques are still pregnant with political consequences, capable of creating "a political and economic barrier reef of their own" to overturn the ship of the state, just as acts of open confrontations.[10] Such resistance is particularly effective in situations where open revolts are impossible or risky, and its effect lies somewhere between structure and agency: "Most of the political life of subordinate groups is to be found neither in the over collective defiance of powerholders nor in complete hegemonic compliance, but in the vast territory between these two opposites."[11]

Despite the enormous influence of Scott's formulation of everyday resistance and the numerous empirical studies on subaltern conditions it continues to inspire,[12] it seems to create an unnecessary dichotomy between two forms of resistance—while their difference seems to be only a matter of scale, rather than essence—thus inadvertently equating the subaltern politics with the invisible forms of resistance, and neglecting the fact that they do employ more open and collective actions.[13]

Besides James Scott, Michel de Certeau also approaches everyday resistance as protracted uses of invisible and small actions by the dominated group in society. While Scott approaches everyday class struggles in repressive contexts from the perspectives of anthropology and political science, de Certeau examines the creative everyday practices in liberal-democratic settings through the lenses of postmodern cultural studies.[14] The everyday life presents countless ways for the dominated groups to use, or in de Certeau's terminology, "consume" languages, symbols, and artifacts of the dominant culture. For de Certeau, ordinary ways of operating or doing things within a given culture—such as cooking, walking, and talking—should not be considered as passive social activity and obedience towards normative schemes of actions. Rather, practical activity of social actors allows them to both employ the elements of the imposed system and exercise their agency as users and interpreters of culture. For de Certeau, everyday resistance is about the "*way of using* imposed system" through artful tactics that offer loosely regulated, improvised ways for individuals to turn order of things to serve personal aims.[15]

De Certeau draws from Swiss structural linguist Ferdinand de Saussure's distinction between language (*langue*) and speech (*parole*) in his conceptualization of everyday practice as resistance.[16] A cultural norm or social structure is comparable to language, and the way humans interpret and employ the normative structure in daily life is comparable to the speech act of enunciation in Saussurean linguistics. Therefore, in his semiotic understanding of culture and power, de Certeau proposes that practical activity of human agents should be the focus of investigation, because it is the act of enunciation (*parole*) that endows the structure (*langue*) with human intentionality and interpretations. Resistance through everyday tactics is often invisible within a culture's normative spaces, and exists in the interstices between enunciation (*parole*) and structure (*langue*). A notable feature of such everyday resistance is "the productive openness and individualizing potential created by the gap between *langue* and *parole*" that allows social actors to "construe their culture from the point of view of their self-preservation and self-presentation, and creatively bend it to the conditions of daily life."[17]

The practical act of consumption, for instance, occupies a core analytical space in de Certeau's formulation of resistance. The everyday consumption practices of watching TV, reading a health magazine, shopping in a supermarket, and the like, constitute a particular process of cultural production characterized by fragmentation and quasi-invisibility. Individuals use/consume the customs, laws, symbols, and products diffused by the elites but make something else out of them—not by rejecting them but by the many different ways of using and interpreting them to serve the individuals' own ends. For instance, consumers of health magazines may make sense of what they read and draw up subsequent actions in very different ways, which may nor may not be aligned with the intention of the market producers. Such everyday tactics places power outside the totalizing logic of the market, and shifts the locus of resistance from structural change to the day-to-day ways of operating (or signification, in Saussure's terminology) that enable the ordinary persons to reclaim some autonomy from the all-pervasive structural forces.

While Scott conceives of "weapons of the weak" as a miniature and hidden version of macropolitical struggles, de Certeau speaks about everyday tactic as "an art of the weak ... within the enemy's field of vision ... [that] operates in isolated actions, blow by blow" without a proper locus.[18] While Scott's vision of power is very much in line with the macro structure, de Certeau views power through the poststructural lens of discourse, symbols, and norms. As important as their studies of everyday resistance have been, their conceptual repertoires leave little room for critical resistance as self-formation. I will now turn to Foucault's work on the "aesthetics of existence" to discuss how a shift of attention to the subject, the self, can open up a new dimension in the conceptual territory of resistance studies. As we have seen, struggle is intrinsic to the constitution of power which is fundamentally negative, à la Scott; whereas ways of consuming and operating, per de Certeau, constitute the tactical resistance of those under the sway of power's domination. The key move that Foucault makes in conceiving of power so as to account for practices of self-formation is "his shift from *force* as the operative concept of power to *conduct*" through the term "governmentality."[19]

Governmentality is broadly defined as "conduct of conduct" that shapes desirable behaviors not through direct forms of state control and bureaucratic regulations, but through a field of more or less open possibilities that allows individuals to carry out independent acts in accordance with these options and trajectories.[20] In such a formulation, Foucault considers freedom, rather than resistance, as the condition for the exercise of power: the governmental model of power presupposes the individual's freedom (however minimal) to choose amongst a range of structured options as the necessary prerequisite for power to exist and have an effect. For instance, the global neoliberal condition has forged particular governing techniques based on self-regulation and accountability, and produced industrious, self-reliant, docile individuals who engage in calculative choice of a market type.[21] Thus the contemporary regime of governmentality produces particular type of subjects by shaping individual conducts from within, and by forging dispositions whereby individuals strive for success while reproducing, knowingly or unknowingly, the neoliberal agenda. The governmental mode of power is thus enabled through the technologies of subjectivity, and can be only "resisted" by the emergence of a different subjectivity, and by recreating ourselves otherwise.

Therefore, Foucault's understanding of resistance fundamentally departs from the (infra)political and tactical conceptions advanced by James Scott and Michel de Certeau. Resistance is neither merely the intended sabotaging of the dominant agenda, nor the daily enactment of the dominant script for personal ends, but rather that whose aim is to "promote new forms of subjectivity through the refusal of the type of individuality that has been imposed on us for several centuries."[22] That is, to forge new forms of subjectivity through the historical technique of self-formation, through work *on* and *of* the self, which Foucault refers to as an "aesthetic of existence."

Foucault's appeal to reconstitute the self in ever new ways resonates historically with the Socratic injunction to "care for oneself" as the way to obtain truth, and the Kantian definition of critique as fundamentally in service to the task of self-formation and enlightenment.[23] Such an aesthetic of existence aims not simply to develop resistance against power—this would be merely reactive—but more crucially to reclaim the task of forging autonomous forms of life so as to live, act, and be otherwise, which is creative and transformative. This type of resistance through self-(trans)formation constitutes a certain slippage within the dominant power structure, and calls for a new mode of existence as not only an ethical imagination, but our obligation as well.

3. Spiritual Pursuits as a Form of Resistance

Foucault's urge to foster a new mode of existence and achieve mastery of the self resonates remarkably with the ethos of spiritual practices concerned in this chapter. Spiritual practices offer a method of training, as well as a lifestyle, for people to transform themselves so as to experience the world anew. While the literature on resistance has largely focused on the economic, political, and sociocultural dimensions, it has paid relatively little attention to how the affective elements of consciousness and spirituality can also be sites of resistance where our intentions, motivations, behavioral and mental tendencies are fine-tuned as a way to reshape the human experience of external crises and collective social issues. In our contemporary societies, spiritual practices constantly find their ways into diverse social, psychotherapeutic, and educational domains and become a new aspiration for inner peace, compassion, and deeper fulfillment. According to the National Center for Health Statistics,[24] the practice of yoga and meditation increased significantly from 2012 to 2017 for adults and children in the United States. The World Health Organization is increasingly pressured by international communities to recognize spirituality as an integral part of a holistic approach to health and well-being.[25]

Overcoming material inequalities and structural vulnerability, the paramount goal in the Marxist line of thinking regarding resistance, is insufficient to eliminate human suffering, because human flourishing lies far beyond material conditions. Traditional resistance theories have to confront a simple fact that "capitalism has continually transformed itself to the point that we no longer have a viable alternative to it."[26] Therefore, it is absolutely crucial to acknowledge that social change is not simply a matter of altering outside circumstances, but requires simultaneously changing the inner landscape and experimenting new modes of subjectivity by which to experience the world anew.

Foucault's later work offers insight on the conditions and possibilities of the subject's transformation through the Greek notion "care of the self." In his lectures at the Collège de France, Foucault traces the Delphic notion "know yourself" (*gnothi seauton*), which occupies a central position in the history of Western thought, to an early philosophical formulation of "care of the self" (*epimeleia heautou*). Foucault deftly argues that "know yourself" is subordinate to the imperative of "care of the self," because knowledge alone is not sufficient for the subject to access the truth: "[A] subject could not have access to the truth if he did not first operate upon himself a certain work that would make him susceptible to knowing the truth."[27]

Foucault describes this work performed upon oneself through the lens of spirituality, which he defines as "the search, practice, and experience through which the subject carries about the necessary transformations on himself in order to have access to the truth."[28] According to Foucault, *epimeleia heautou*, which is a general form of spirituality, concerns, first, "an attitude towards the self, others, and the world;" second, "a certain way of attending to what we think and what takes place in our thoughts;" and third, "a number of actions exercised on the self by the self ... by which one changes, purifies, transforms, and transfigures oneself, [such as] techniques of meditation, of memorization of the past, of examination of conscience, of checking representations which appear in the mind, and so on."[29] In this formulation, spirituality (i.e. the transformation of the being of the subject by his care/work on himself) is the condition of possibility for the philosophical quest for the truth.

Foucault further observes that entering the modern age, this transformative potential of truth was gradually lost when care of the self was replaced by the principle of knowing yourself, and when the condition for the access to the truth became knowledge and knowledge alone. In what he calls the "Cartesian moment," the world assumes the "thereness" of evidential truth awaiting for the discovery by the individuals, whose only reward is the indefinite development and accumulation of knowledge. But such truth cannot have the effect of enlightenment, because the condition of knowing no longer falls under spirituality and requires nothing in terms of the knower's transformation of his being as subject.[30] Such Cartesian type of knowledge postulates a self-world division in that truth is external and accessible through development of knowledge by the knowing subject, but such truth can hardly "save the subject" as truth is relegated to the scientific domain of knowledge and entails no necessity for the subject's work upon himself, thus no possibility of enlightenment and transformation.

Contemporary resistance studies are also caught up in the modern relationship to the truth, which is limited to intellectual explanation about forms of power and subversion, rather than transforming the lives of individuals and providing them with a practical art of living that requires nothing less than the metamorphosis of subjectivity. The problems plaguing a growing number of people in contemporary world, regardless of their economic status, are increasingly emotional and spiritual in form that "concern our relations with others, our sense of meaninglessness, our addictions and our mental health."[31] Abolishing material inequalities alone can hardly provide the much-needed answer to global well-being. In fact, unchecked material growth has set in motion discursive practices of individualism, greed, and competition in which all are implicated with the growing distress of mental health and psychological crises.[32]

In post-scarcity contexts where material need is no longer the primary concern, it is more and more difficult to identify a single social bloc or class enemy to resist. Power assumes a dispersed character instead of a zero-sum game. In this light, the negative connotation of resistance that assumes the solution to social problems lies in the abolishing of something, is tasked with the need for constructing new dimension of human experience. In order to comprehend this new existential dimension, the enduring structure–agency dichotomy that dominates much of social science thinking about resistance, rooted in the foundational self/world dualism,[33] needs to be radically reconsidered. As well, the theoretical repertoire of resistance studies needs a new paradigm that invites a meditation on the world as coterminous with, rather than independent of, the self, thus breaking the hyphen separating structure and agency.

Spiritual and mystic traditions around the world have long acknowledged that the self plays a creative, world-manifesting role; the self is one with the world. As James Allen proclaims in his famous essay "As a Man Thinketh," the world is but the looking-glass of one's interior circumstances.[34] Allen maintains that one's thinking has influence on her/his character and holds the key to life's conditions, and by working diligently on purifying one's thought thus ennobling one's self, one remakes the condition, environment, and destiny. The key to changing one's circumstances is through self mastery, Allen advises, which comes from a calm, settled mind as a result of the spiritual practice of meditation, giving rise to "the flowering of life, the fruitage of the soul."[35]

Kabir, the fifteenth-century Indian mystic poet, once says, "There is a Secret One inside us; the planets in all the galaxies pass through his hands like beads."[36] The Secret One that Kabir refers to, that connects all, that is both inside us and in all the galaxies, is the Infinite, the Divine, that is nowhere but everywhere. The mystical wisdom illuminates our search for well-being as fundamentally a search for wholeness in an apparently fragmented world. It is a vision of reality that each being is both part of the world and contains the whole of it. Such spiritual wisdom challenges the self-world dualism, which has led to impulses of fear and control as we see in contemporary social and environmental crises.

The radical interdependence of self and world is also upheld by Buddhist philosophy. Reality, in the Buddhist principle of interdependent co-arising, is neither just out there nor inside the mind. It is one in which all existence is relational, and all things are interdependent and co-arising in interaction.[37] This oneness of reality can only be experienced by the approach of subtraction, of letting go, of detaching from "mistaken ideas, outdated horizons of experience, and the very calcifications of self" to arrive at what the Buddhists call the absolute nothingness of reality.[38] The nothingness does not mean lack or void in the usual pejorative sense, but is understood paradoxically as a ceaseless flux of universal energy in all things in which *nothing is lacking*. [39]

The First Noble Truth of Buddhism holds that life is suffering and transient, and the primary cause of suffering is the ego's attachment to things impermanent, which leads to delusion and separation from the oneness of reality.[40] Individuals then derive knowledge through "binaristically constructed concepts of self, gender, race, and a host of other categories with which they then identify and to which they become deeply attached at the same time that they assign the oppositional terms to others."[41] It is precisely such binaries that underpin our global dysfunctions today, and that are the target of our "resistance" effort through transforming ourselves towards a higher consciousness of unity.

In Buddhist teaching, the spiritual technique of meditation plays a particularly decisive role in facilitating the Eightfold Path towards self-transformation, described in the Fourth Noble Truth as Right Understanding, Right Thought, Right Speech, Right Action, Right Livelihood, Right Effort, Right Mindfulness, and Right Concentration.[42] In meditation, one learns to suspend the dualistic mind by observing thoughts with nonreactive equanimity, and move to intuition, feeling, and heartfelt responses to the totality of experience without judgments. In this sense, a spiritual aspirant seeks not to resist or reject life's many ups and downs, but works upon her/himself towards obtaining what is called transsubjectivity in Zen Buddhism, in which the usual self identification and self–world separation fades away and a cosmic consciousness emerges to embrace all existences as one in essence.

This transsubjectivity cannot be obtained through cognitive knowing—which, if obtained as such, will leave the self unaltered. To illustrate how meditation facilitates the work upon the self so as to see the world in a new way, a seasoned Zen meditation practitioner (given the pseudonym of Linda) is quoted below.

> **Linda** There is a sense of being in this present world. Thoughts and emotions come up just like the rest of your life, but you settle in and quiet down. Things that are on my mind do come up. Come, and go. Then after that, you're just sitting in the present. An alert, awake, calm state ... I don't know if I can put it into words. This OKness, this "natural" condition, I don't know how to put that into words. You see how everything takes care of itself, naturally ... I had been

sitting and it became clear to me that, though I was sitting still, I was at the same time not separated from any activity. In "stillness," people were riding bicycles, washing, catching fish, and cooking. It was all going on at the same time. No differences between stillness and activity in zazen [zen meditation]. Very free feeling...

...

Interviewer   You are saying that you are feeling that I or other objects are as much you as you are? That your subjectivity and mine are exactly the same?

Linda   There is something to be said, and as you can see, I don't know "who" is saying it. I have to sort of ignore your questions, because in those terms, I can't answer. I don't know. You sit, and you'll feel it. "You" stops [sic], and "that's it".[43]

The nurturing of presence, oneness, and an observing attitude is a central theme in Linda's narrative. Despite the ebbs and flows of her thoughts and emotions, she was able to achieve a relaxed alertness, what she calls "the natural condition" in which "everything takes care of itself, naturally." Such a sense of acceptance and assurance ("Okness") comes from her inner stillness, cultivated through years of meditative practice, which by putting the calculating mind to rest, gradually returns the self to its original state of no-self ["You" stops [sic], and "that's it"] in which all imbibes the same essence of reality. There is a strong indication that language is insufficient to describe her experience authentically ("I don't know if I can put it into words"), precisely because language is intrinsically structural and binary (between the signifier and the signified, *langue* and *parole*). In meditation, however, even the distinction between the apparently opposite states of stillness and activity collapses ("In 'stillness,' people were riding bicycles, washing, catching fish, and cooking. It was all going on at the same time"). Just like the eye of the storm or the center of a fast moving wheel, at the core of an activity there is stillness; and in stillness, expansion and movement becomes possible. Detaching from categorical, judgmental worldview, Linda imbibes a sense of freedom ("very free feeling") and union between the material life and a higher form of reality.

Meditation has proven efficacious in fine-tuning the subtle, habitual aspects of lived experience that are otherwise inaccessible to consciousness, by cultivating "a particular way of paying attention, one that gives rise to a moment-to-moment, non-judging awareness."[44]

Through meditation, resistance against external circumstances morphs into "resisting" the ego-self that secures its self identification through categorization and that interprets the world as a source of frustration to its desires and entitlements, and the result of such "resisting" is nothing but ongoing transformation.

4. Spirituality as Pedagogical Resistance and Transformation

In this final section, I will discuss the role of spirituality as a site of pedagogical resistance in school settings. The rising interest in spirituality in the new millennium has been reflected in recent education literature as well.[45] A small number of empirical studies have focused on connecting spirituality with diversity and equity concerns in the classrooms, and interrogated the ways spiritual expressions constitute anti-oppressive pedagogies and can precipitate social change through transforming human consciousness.[46] Spirituality provides an inward, alternative space from which to cultivate new forms of behaviors and attitudes, which has strong implications for transformative experience to take place in the learning journey. Meanwhile, the mind-privileging academic framework adopts a view of reality predicated on structural terms and identity politics, and reproduces its own logic of domination in teaching and learning.[47]

Spiritually minded scholars have turned to mindfulness, meditation, and other contemplative techniques to approach teaching and learning as a spiritual paradigm, which involves a holistic human ontology, instead of merely a mental process reinforced by the mind/body duality. The broader "postsecular turn"[48] and "contemplative turn"[49] in education is a response to the ongoing pedagogical crises around the globe: the reduction of learning to testing, hidden inequity of tracking and discrimination, incessant demands for standards and competition, violence, and microaggression, and a host of psycho-social challenges students face. In response to these crises, there is an increasing recognition of non-Western philosophical and spiritual traditions, such as Daoism, Buddhism, and African Ubuntu, which offer radically different paradigms of education compared to the functionalist view of education as knowledge acquisition. While the knowledge system of the secular academy achieves very little in terms of social change besides intellectual understanding, spiritual epistemology shifts teaching and learning from an intellectual exercise to an embodied experience, indeed, an invitation to live, act, and be otherwise.

The Kyoto School of Philosophy, for instance, proposes a unique form of "negative education" through the Buddhist philosophy of "nothingness." Rather than a process of knowledge acquisition and socialization, education centered on the idea of negativity is characterized by "a *negative* movement of *subtraction*."[50] Here negativity is not understood pejoratively, but as a fundamental way in which the human being becomes human, through a process of unlearning. Sevilla explains subtraction thus:

> [B]y letting go of self, of the attachment to the subject (and its duality from the object), of its adherence to the one-sidedness of life vs. death, or good vs. evil.... the self is able to open up to reality in its fundamentally paradoxical nature, and at the same time, is able to awaken to its own authenticity—its "no-self" nature.[51]

While learning in school settings is generally regarded as an additive process that leads to a solidification of the self, the process of subtraction entails untangling oneself from implicit thought patterns, tendencies, and conceptual strictures deeply embedded in one's consciousness. Drawing on Nishitani Keiji, a key figure in the Kyoto School of Philosophy, Sevilla further introduces the idea of non-self as the condition for the deepest form of negative learning.[52] According to the Buddhist philosophy, the transformation from ego-self that "[grasps] itself and the world by reducing the complexity of reality to more simple conceptual structures," towards non-self, the standpoint of emptiness that responses to the world with malleability, indeterminacy, and detachment, constitutes a radical pedagogy of resistance through human transformation.[53]

The "negative" view of education sees the learner as opening up to reality by losing the self so as to become what Nishitani calls "the very things we are looking at" and allow a dynamic, open-ended response to the others "in their suchness."[54] This sharply contrasts with the conventional "positive" approach to education where mastery of knowledge so as to control reality is a predominant mode of learning and leaves the knower unaltered as "the point of departure from which everything else may be considered."[55] A negative pedagogy is a pedagogy towards nothingness/emptiness whereby "reality goes beyond definability ... above the categories of universal as well as particular ... [not] regarded as contentless and void in its relative sense ... [but] on the contrary, fullness of things, containing all possibilities."[56]

A negative pedagogy offers a radically different point of departure to engage anti-oppressive, social justice education. Too often discussions of equity and diversity issues in K–12 and university classrooms are reduced to conceptual categories of race, class, gender, sexuality, and the like. Such discussions, though helpful in establishing intellectual understanding of oppression and privilege, often do not engage the learner's noncognitive self, nor focus on what connects all as oneness beyond socially constructed identity categories. Through a negative movement towards unlearning, facilitated by experiential techniques such as meditation and contemplation, spirituality opens up a transformative space in the secular-rational classrooms, where curriculum becomes a meditative inquiry,[57] and learning becomes "an exercise of oneself in the activity of thought to get free of oneself".[58] This getting free of oneself through the meditative practice of detaching from perceptions and judgments, resonates with Foucault's urge to reconstruct subjectivity in order to access the truth, and is fundamentally an ethical endeavor.

The role of spirituality in pedagogical transformation is further illustrated by Miller's study of incorporating meditation in a teacher education program at a university setting. Shifting the curriculum focus from the intellect to the whole person, the study proves meditation to be a crucial part of a holistic education for pre- and in-service teachers.[59] Quoted below are reflective summaries from several study participants regarding their personal and professional transformation:

> I feel a deep resonance within myself and with colleagues, and this helps me notice and appreciate each encounter more fully. The most interesting and amazing impact for me is the change I notice in other people especially teachers on my staff. Every day I encounter people who treat me differently from the way they have treated me since I came to the school a year and a half ago. I do not believe that they have all changed. I have changed one aspect of my life. I have taken time to be in a state of pure awareness each day.[60]

> You can get really frustrated with these kids because these kids get really angry and frustrated because they can't read, and your first response is to be an authoritarian, when actuality they just need to be hugged and loved. So it (the meditation) really helps me to step back and look at what really is going on.[61]

> I'm a very active kind of teacher, and I have everybody doing different things ... But I'm sure it's meditation, I can't prove it, but I'm sure it's that thing that brings us together. And it connects—you connect on a different level, you know not just the intellectual. But you connect on a spiritual level and when we were like that in our classroom the supply teacher would notice: this is a very calm classroom.[62]

Regular meditation repositions behavioral, emotional, and mental tendencies, and allows the practitioner to perceive and experience the world anew. As noted in the first quote, the vice-principal observed a change in fellow teachers' attitude towards him, and attributed this to his own internal shift (towards "a state of pure awareness"). The external world may remain the same ("I do not believe that they have all changed"), but he has transformed from a us/them duality to a consciousness of oneness ("I feel a deep resonance within myself and with colleagues"). With this transformed/expanded consciousness, the world is no longer mired in the mind's conceptions, but is experienced in its ineluctable essence of togetherness.

In the second quote, a female teacher shifted from the impulse to be authoritarian in face of unruly, angry students, to an attitude of love and understanding ("they just need to be hugged and loved"). While it was easy to define students' behaviors as a classroom disciplinary issue, the teacher approached it by going beyond the apparent right or wrong, and shifting from the categorical mind to the compassionate heart whereby she took hold of reality differently ("to step back and look at what really is going on").

In the third episode, the teacher went a step further to introduce meditation to the students. Meditation had become a routine for her class, such that students would insist on doing it and not missing a day. This collective practice fostered a deeper connection ("I'm sure it's that thing that brings us together"), in which class members came to relate to each other beyond the intellectual realm, on a spiritual level. Because of meditation, the class always appeared very calm despite the active engagement in different learning tasks.

The above quoted teachers all went beyond the functionalist educational framework that emphasized tests and efficiency, to foster a consciousness of peace, harmony, and togetherness in their pedagogical roles. Through their practice of meditation, they strived to incorporate a spiritually guided consciousness into education which engaged not just the intellect but the whole person. With the realization that inner transformation is the catalyst for outer change, in a way, these teachers engaged in a kind of micro, everyday "educational resistance" through working upon themselves whereby transforming their pedagogical relations and outcomes. This kind of resistance is a silent inner journey, has little to do with civil disobedience or outer revolts, yet is a profound remapping of subjectivity that "liberates" one from the world filtered by one's looking-glass, through the meditative "act of pure observation—without analysis or judgment—that provides an existential entry into one's innermost recesses."[63] This kind of resistance requires ongoing work upon the self, rather than through intellectual knowledge to be mastered once and for all. Viewing subjectivity as capable of being unmade as made, emphasizing the role of spiritual practices in such (un)making, this form of resistance has broader pedagogical and ethical implications of the ongoing reconstruction of self and world.

5. Taking Stock, Looking Forward: A Personal Reflection

The significance of spirituality as a pedagogy of unlearning and becoming has become apparent to me over the past five years in my role as a student of the

Heartfulness system of meditation. In the fall of 2015 during my employment at the University of Macau, I accidentally stumbled upon Heartfulness through a campus meditation workshop. At that point, I had spent years searching in vain for a method that could help settle my constantly hectic mind. An aspiring early career scholar, I lived my intellectual persona fully, but while academic pursuits provided nourishment to the mind, they were unable to quench the innermost yearning of the heart. Occasionally, doubts surfaced as to the real impact of our work in higher education, as Nietzsche poignantly observes that universities "simply teach a critique of words by the means of other words," rather than enabling the transformation of the subject.[64] With a hankering for spirituality, I intuitively felt that to transform, one must look beyond intellectual means. And as serendipity would have it, the meditation workshop became a turning point in my personal transformation. I became a regular in the campus Heartfulness community, attending weekly cleaning sittings and group sessions held in the English Department, which was two buildings away from my office at that time. Bit by bit, without my knowing, my inner condition was silently shifting.

In retrospect, the cleaning method unique to the Heartfulness system was akin to the Kyoto school of "negative pedagogy." Based upon a profound understanding of the formation of impressions, the cleaning technique removes the daily accumulation of impressions, which are the emotional contents of our experiences and which, if unattended, remain dormant to the conscious mind, lead to the formation of our tendencies, and drive our action from moment to moment.[65] By removing impressions, one transcends the "I-ness" of the ego and gradually returns to a state of purity and simplicity. It is this condition of purity and simplicity, otherwise described as nothingness, that allows freedom to drawn and that transforms one from living a life of the mind to letting the heart blossom in the subtlest essence of reality. Through Heartfulness, my many roles as an academic, child, sibling, spouse, parent, and so on integrate into one single role of a spiritual aspirant, on a never-ending journey of unlearning and becoming. Through writing this chapter, I wish to share the spiritual gift with my readers in the hope that individual transformation, one heart at a time, will bring forth a new collective consciousness the world sorely needs today.

With spiritual practices such as meditation, the constant orientation towards the external environment is arced back towards the self; and the self becomes a dynamic site of resistance, "not by removing problems or by shutting them out, but by transforming us from the inside out so that we see the world in a new way, without the filters of our limitations."[66] While spiritual practices seek to enact change through reinventing the self and the (re)making of subjectivity, they can provide valuable alternatives to solving structural material problems. Only when we reach a collective consciousness that true, lasting well-being can be only cultivated from within oneself, and that one's well-being is intimately dependent on the well-being of all, can there be a consensual and sustainable way towards global justice.

Notes

1 James C. Scott, *Weapons of the Weak: Everyday Forms of Peasant Resistance* (New Haven, CT: Yale University Press, 1985); Michel de Certeau, *The Practice of Everyday Life* (Berkeley: University of California Press, 1984); Stellan Vinthagen and Anna Johansson, "'Everyday Resistance': Exploration of a Concept and its Theories," *Resistance Studies Magazine* vol. 1(2013): 1–46.
2 Jacqueline Watson, Marian de Souza, and Ann Trousdale (eds). *Global Perspectives on Spirituality and Education.* New York: Routledge, 2014; Cheryl Delgado, "A Discussion of the Concept of Spirituality," *Nursing Science Quarterly* vol. 18, no. 2 (2005): 157–62; James Gould, "Becoming Good: The Role of Spiritual Practice," *Philosophical Practice* vol. 1, no. 3 (2005): 135–47; Deborah Orr, "The Uses of Mindfulness in Anti-Oppressive Pedagogies: Philosophy and Praxis," *Canadian Journal of Education* vol. 27, no. 4 (2002): 477–97.
3 Jocelyn A. Hollander and Rachel L. Einwohner, "Conceptualising Resistance," *Sociological Forum* vol. 19, no. 4 (2004): 533–54.
4 Michel Foucault, *The History of Sexuality. Vol. 1: An Introduction* (New York: Random House, 1978).
5 Maria Hynes, "Reconceptualizing Resistance: Sociology and the Affective Dimension of Resistance," *The British Journal of Sociology* vol. 64, no. 4 (2013): 559–77.
6 Stellan Vinthagen and Anna Johansson, "'Everyday Resistance': Exploration of a Concept and its Theories," *Resistance Studies Magazine* vol. 1(2013): 1–46.
7 Jocelyn A. Hollander and Rachel L. Einwohner, "Conceptualising Resistance," 533–54.
8 James C. Scott. *Weapons of the Weak: Everyday Forms of Peasant Resistance.*
9 Ibid.
10 James C. Scott. "Everyday Forms of Resistance," *Copenhagen Papers* vol. 4 (1989): 33–62.
11 James C. Scott. *Weapons of the Weak: Everyday Forms of Peasant Resistance*, 136.
12 K. Sivaramakrishnan. "Some Intellectual Genealogies for the Concept of Everyday Resistance," *American Anthropologist* vol. 107, no. 3 (2005): 346–55.
13 Stellan Vinthagen and Anna Johansson, "'Everyday Resistance': Exploration of a Concept and its Theories," *Resistance Studies Magazine* vol. 1 (2013): 1–46.

14 Michel de Certeau, *The Practice of Everyday Life* (Berkeley: University of California Press, 1984).
15 Michel de Certeau, *The Practice of Everyday Life*, 18.
16 Ferdinand de Saussure., P. Meisel, and H. Saussy (eds), *Course in General Linguistics*, trans. Wade. Baskin (New York: Columbia University Press, [1916] 2011).
17 Gabrielle M. Spiegel, *Practicing History: New Directions in Historical Writing after the Linguistic Turn* (New York: Routledge, 2005), 7.
18 Michel de Certeau, *The Practice of Everyday Life* (Berkeley: University of California Press, 1984), 37.
19 Kevin Thompson, "Forms of Resistance: Foucault on Tactical Reversal and Self-Formation," *Continental Philosophy Review* vol. 36 (2003): 113–38.
20 Michel Foucault, *The Essential Works of Foucault: 1954–1984, Volume III* (New York: The New Press, 1997), 341–2.
21 Stephen J. Collier and Aihwa Ong, "Global Assemblages, Anthropological Problems," in A. Ong and S. Collier (eds), *Global Assemblages: Technology, Politics, and Ethics as Anthropological Problems* (Malden, MA: Blackwell Publishing, 2005), 13.
22 Michel Foucault, *The Essential Works of Foucault: 1954–1984, Volume III* (New York: The New Press, 1997), 336.
23 Kevin Thompson. "Forms of Resistance: Foucault on Tactical Reversal and Self-Formation." *Continental Philosophy Review* vol. 36 (2003): 129.
24 National Center for Health Statistics, "Use of Yoga and Meditation Becoming More Popular in U.S." (2018). Available online: https://www.cdc.gov/nchs/pressroom/nchs_press_releases/2018/201811_Yoga_Meditation.htm (accessed January 25, 2021).
25 Francesco Chirico, "Spiritual Well-Being in the 21st Century: It is Time to Review the Current WHO's Health Definition," *Journal of Health and Social Sciences* vol. 1, no. 1 (2016): 1–16.
26 Chris Barker, *Making Sense of Cultural Studies: Central Problems and Critical Debates* (London: Sage, 2002), 175.
27 Michel Foucault, *Essential Works of Foucault, Vol. 1: Ethics* (Harmondsworth: Penguin, 2000), 278.
28 Michel Foucault, *The Hermeneutics of the Subject: Lectures at the Collège de France, 1981–1982* (New York: Picador, 2005), 15
29 Foucault, *The Hermeneutics of the Subject,* 10–11.
30 Foucault, *The Hermeneutics of the Subject,* 29.
31 Chris Barker, *Making Sense of Cultural Studies: Central Problems and Critical Debates* (London: Sage, 2002), 20.
32 Li Zhang, "Cultivating Happiness: Psychotherapy, Spirituality, and Well-Being in a Transforming Urban China", in P. V. de Veer (ed.), *Handbook of Religion and the Asian City: Aspiration and Urbanization in the Twenty-First Century* (Berkeley, CA:

University of California Press, 2015), 315–32; Luka Zevnik, "Towards a New Perspective in Cultural Studies: Emotional and Spiritual Problems and Happiness in Contemporary Western Societies," *International Journal of Cultural Studies* vol. 13, no. 4 (2010): 391–408.

33 The separation of self from that which it observes has long been a guiding epistemological viewpoint in Western philosophy. Classical empiricists hold that the world is unquestionably out there and provides a stage of stimuli to our perceptions. It registers its data on our senses and allows us to know the reality which lies externally. On the other side of the debate are subjectivist idealists, who view external phenomena not as independent of the perceiver, but rather, as projections of the mind. Both are equally one-sided and reinforce the division between subject and object, between the thinking mind and the mechanical world.

34 James Allen, *As a Man Thinketh* (New York: St. Martin's Press, [1903] 2019).

35 James Allen, *As a Man Thinketh*, 20.

36 Joanna Macy, *World as Lover, World as Self: Courage for Global Justice and Ecological Renewal* (Berkeley, CA: Parallax Press, 2007), 27.

37 Joanna Macy, *World as Lover, World as Self: Courage for Global Justice and Ecological Renewal*, 38–9.

38 Anton Luis Sevilla, "Education and Empty Relationality: Thoughts on Education and the Kyoto School of Philosophy," *Journal of Philosophy of Education* vol. 30, no. 4 (2016): 639–54.

39 Greg Dubs, "Psycho-Spiritual Development in Zen Buddhism: A Study of Resistance in Meditation," *The Journal of Transpersonal Psychology* vol. 19, no. 1 (1987): 19–86.

40 Greg Dubs, "Psycho-Spiritual Development in Zen Buddhism," 20–1.

41 Deborah Orr, "The Uses of Mindfulness in Anti-Oppressive Pedagogies: Philosophy and Praxis," *Canadian Journal of Education* vol. 27, no. (2002): 477–97; see also p. 491.

42 Greg Dubs, "Psycho-Spiritual Development in Zen Buddhism," 21–2.

43 Greg Dubs, "Psycho-Spiritual Development in Zen Buddhism," 26.

44 Ashwani Kumar, *Curriculum as Meditative Inquiry* (New York: Palgrave Macmillan, 2013), 230.

45 Deborah Orr, "The Uses of Mindfulness in Anti-Oppressive Pedagogies: Philosophy and Praxis," *Canadian Journal of Education* vol. 27, no. 4 (2002): 477–97; Edward J. Tisdell, "In the New Millennium: The Role of Spirituality and the Cultural Imagination in Dealing with Diversity and Equity in the Higher Education Classroom," *Teachers College Record* vol. 109, no. 3 (2007): 531–60; Riyad Ahmed Shahjahan, "The Role of Spirituality in the Anti-Oppressive Higher-Education Classroom," *Teaching in Higher Education* vol. 14, no. 2 (2009): 121–31; Ashwani Kumar, *Curriculum as Meditative Inquiry* (New York: Palgrave Macmillan, 2013).

46 Riyad Ahmed Shahjahan, "The Role of Spirituality in the Anti-Oppressive Higher-Education Classroom," 121–31; Edward J. Tisdell, "In the New Millennium: The Role of Spirituality and the Cultural Imagination in Dealing with Diversity and Equity in the Higher Education Classroom," 531–60; Cynthia B. Dillard, Daa'Iyah Abdur-Rashid, and Cynthia A. Tyson, "My Soul is a Witness: Affirming Pedagogies of the Spirit," *International Journal of Qualitative Studies in Education* vol. 13, no. 5 (2000): 447–62.

47 Deborah Orr, "The Uses of Mindfulness in Anti-Oppressive Pedagogies: Philosophy and Praxis," 477–97.

48 Wu Jinting and Mario Wenning, "The Postsecular Turn in Education: Lessons from the Mindfulness Movement and the Revival of Confucian Academies," *Studies in Philosophy and Education* vol. 35 (2016): 551–71.

49 Oren Ergas, "A Contemplative Turn in Education: Charting a Curricular-Pedagogical Countermovement," *Pedagogy, Culture & Society* vol. 27, no. 2 (2019): 251–70.

50 Anton Luis Sevilla, "Education and Empty Relationality: Thoughts on Education and the Kyoto School of Philosophy," *Journal of Philosophy of Education* vol. 30, no. 4 (2016): 639–54. 643.

51 Anton Luis Sevilla, "Education and Empty Relationality," 639–54. 643.

52 Anton Luis Sevilla, "Education and Empty Relationality," 643.

53 Anton Luis Sevilla. "Education and Empty Relationality," 645–6.

54 Keiji Nishitani, *Religion and Nothingness* (Berkeley, CA: University of California Press, 1982), 9, 128.

55 Keiji Nishitani. *Religion and Nothingness*, 13.

56 Daisetsu Teitaro Suzuki, "The Buddhist Conception of Reality," *The Eastern Buddhist* vol. 7, no. 2 (1974): 1–21.14.

57 Ashwani Kumar, *Curriculum as Meditative Inquiry* (New York: Palgrave Macmillan, 2013).

58 Ilse Geerinck, Jan Masschelein, and Maarten Simons, "Teaching and Knowledge: A Necessary Combination? An Elaboration of Forms of Teachers' Reflexivity," *Studies in Philosophy and Education* vol. 29, no. 4 (2010): 379–93, 390.

59 John P. Miller and Aya Nozawa, "Meditating Teachers: A Qualitative Study," *Journal of In-Service Education* vol. 28, no. 1 (2002): 179–92.

60 John P. Miller and Aya Nozawa. "Meditating Teachers," 183.

61 John P. Miller and Aya Nozawa.. "Meditating Teachers," 187.

62 John P. Miller and Aya Nozawa. "Meditating Teachers," 188.

63 Ashwani Kumar, *Curriculum as Meditative Inquiry* , 10–11.

64 Timothy O'Leary, *Foucault and the Art of Ethics* (London: Continuum, 2002), 174.

65 Kamlesh D. Patel and Joshua Pollock, *The Heartfulness Way: Heart-Based Meditations for Spiritual Transformation* (Oakland, CA: Reveal Press, 2018), 105–10.

66 Kamlesh D. Patel and Joshua Pollock, *The Heartfulness Way: Heart-Based Meditations for Spiritual Transformation*, x.

Bibliography

Allen, James. *As a Man Thinketh.* New York: St. Martin's Press, [1903] 2019.
Barker, Chris. *Making Sense of Cultural Studies: Central Problems and Critical Debates.* London: Sage, 2002.
Chirico, Francesco. "Spiritual Well-Being in the 21st Century: It is Time to Review the Current WHO's Health Definition." *Journal of Health and Social Sciences* vol. 1, no. 1 (2016): 1–16.
Collier, Stephen J., and Aihwa Ong. "Global Assemblages, Anthropological Problems", in *Global Assemblages: Technology, Politics, and Ethics as Anthropological Problems,* edited by A. Ong and S. Collier, 3–21. Malden, MA: Blackwell Publishing, 2005.
Certeau, Michel de. *The Practice of Everyday Life.* Berkeley: University of California Press, 1984.
Delgado, Cheryl. "A Discussion of the Concept of Spirituality." *Nursing Science Quarterly* vol. 18, no. 2 (2005): 157–62.
Dillard, Cynthia B., D. Abdur-Rashid, and C. A. Tyson. "My soul is a Witness: Affirming Pedagogies of the Spirit." *International Journal of Qualitative Studies in Education* vol. 13, no. 5 (2000): 447–62.
Dubs, Greg. "Psycho-Spiritual Development in Zen Buddhism: A Study of Resistance in Meditation." *The Journal of Transpersonal Psychology* vol. 19, no. 1 (1987): 19–86.
Ergas, Oren. "A Contemplative Turn in Education: Charting a Curricular-Pedagogical Countermovement." *Pedagogy, Culture & Society* vol. 27, no. 2 (2019): 251–70.
Foucault, Michel. *The History of Sexuality. Vol. 1: An Introduction.* New York: Random House, 1978.
Foucault, Michel. *The Essential Works of Foucault: 1954–1984, Volume III.* New York: The New Press, 1997.
Foucault, Michel. *Essential Works of Foucault, Vol. 1: Ethics.* Harmondsworth: Penguin, 2000.
Foucault, Michel. *The Hermeneutics of the Subject: Lectures at the Collège de France, 1981–1982.* New York: Picador, 2005.
Geerinck, Ilse, Jan Masschelein, and Maarten Simons. "Teaching and Knowledge: A Necessary Combination? An Elaboration of Forms of Teachers' Reflexivity." *Studies in Philosophy and Education* vol. 29, no. 4 (2010): 379–93.
Gould, James. "Becoming Good: The Role of Spiritual Practice." *Philosophical Practice* vol. 1, no. 3 (2005): 135–47.
Hollander, Jocelyn A., and Rachel L. Einwohner. "Conceptualising Resistance." *Sociological Forum* vol. 19, no. 4 (2004): 533–54.
Hynes, Maria. "Reconceptualizing Resistance: Sociology and the Affective Dimension of Resistance." *The British Journal of Sociology* vol. 64, no. 4 (2013): 559–77.
Kabat-Zinn, Jon. "Indra's Net at Work: The Mainstreaming of Dharma Practice in Society," in *The Psychology Awakening: Buddhism, Science, and Our Day-to-Day Lives,*

edited by G. Watson, S. Batchelor, and G. Claxton, 225–49. York Beach: Samuel Weiser, Inc, 2000.

Kumar, Ashwani. *Curriculum as Meditative Inquiry.* New York: Palgrave Macmillan, 2013.

Macy, Joanna. *World as Lover, World as Self: Courage for Global Justice and Ecological Renewal.* Berkeley, CA: Parallax Press, 2007.

Miller, John P., and Aya Nozawa. "Meditating Teachers: A Qualitative Study." *Journal of In-Service Education* vol. 28, no. 1 (2002): 179–92.

Nishitani, Keiji. *Religion and Nothingness.* Berkeley, CA: University of California Press, 1982.

O'Leary, Timothy. *Foucault and the Art of Ethics.* London: Continuum, 2002.

Orr, Deborah. "The Uses of Mindfulness in Anti-Oppressive Pedagogies: Philosophy and Praxis." *Canadian Journal of Education* vol. 27, no. 4 (2002): 477–97.

Patel, Kamlesh D., and Joshua Pollock. *The Heartfulness Way: Heart-Based Meditations for Spiritual Transformation.* Oakland, CA: Reveal Press, 2018.

Saussure, Ferdinand de., P. Meisel, and H. Saussy, eds. *Course in General Linguistics*, trans. Wade Baskin. New York: Columbia University Press, [1916] 2011.

Scott, James C. *Weapons of the Weak: Everyday Forms of Peasant Resistance.* New Haven, CT: Yale University Press, 1985.

Scott, James C. "Everyday Forms of Resistance." *Copenhagen Papers* vol. 4 (1989): 33–62.

Sevilla, Anton Luis. "Education and Empty Relationality: Thoughts on Education and the Kyoto School of Philosophy." *Journal of Philosophy of Education* vol. 30, no. 4 (2016): 639–54.

Shahjahan, Riyad Ahmed. "The Role of Spirituality in the Anti-Oppressive Higher-Education Classroom." *Teaching in Higher Education* vol. 14, no. 2 (2009): 121–31.

Sivaramakrishnan, K. "Some Intellectual Genealogies for the Concept of Everyday Resistance." *American Anthropologist* vol. 107, no. 3 (2005): 346–55.

Spiegel, Gabrielle M. *Practicing History: New Directions in Historical Writing after the Linguistic Turn.* New York: Routledge, 2005.

Suzuki, Daisetsu Teitaro. "The Buddhist Conception of Reality." *The Eastern Buddhist* vol. 7, no. 2 (1974): 1–21.

Thompson, Kevin. "Forms of Resistance: Foucault on Tactical Reversal and Self-Formation." *Continental Philosophy Review* vol. 36 (2003): 113–38.

Tisdell, Edward J. "In the New Millennium: The Role of Spirituality and the Cultural Imagination in Dealing with Diversity and Equity in the Higher Education Classroom." *Teachers College Record* vol. 109, no. 3 (2007): 531–60.

Vinthagen, Stellan, and Anna Johansson. "'Everyday Resistance': Exploration of a Concept and its Theories." *Resistance Studies Magazine* vol. 1 (2013): 1–46.

Watson, Jacqueline., Marian de Souza, and Ann Trousdale (eds). *Global Perspectives on Spirituality and Education.* New York: Routledge, 2014.

Wu, Jinting, and Mario Wenning. "The Postsecular Turn in Education: Lessons from the Mindfulness Movement and the Revival of Confucian Academies." *Studies in Philosophy and Education* vol. 35 (2016): 551–71.

Zevnik, Luka. "Towards a New Perspective in Cultural Studies: Emotional and Spiritual Problems and Happiness in Contemporary Western Societies." *International Journal of Cultural Studies* vol. 13, no. 4 (2010): 391–408.

Zhang, Li. "Cultivating Happiness: Psychotherapy, Spirituality, and Well-Being in a Transforming Urban China", in *Handbook of Religion and the Asian City: Aspiration and Urbanization in the Twenty-First Century*, edited by P. V. de Veer, 315–32. Oakland, CA: University of California Press, 2015.

Part Three

Resistance in the Media, the Arts, and Religion

Network Resistance in China

Shih-Diing Liu and Lin Song

1. Rethinking "Depoliticized Politics"

In his article "Depoliticized Politics," Wang Hui provides a detailed intricate historical explanation for the decline of political culture and democratic participation in the twentieth century, especially after the 1960s.[1] He reflects upon the radical thought and political practice of the Cultural Revolution as a precursor to the "totalizing de-revolutionary process"[2] characterized by the following: the bureaucratization of the party-state in the 1950s, and the anti-bureaucratizing power degrading into internal power struggles and violence; concepts of class in the middle and later periods of the Cultural Revolution became degraded as tools for factional struggle; the state devolved from a space for political debate into a machine for governance; society's trend toward marketization following the reform, and its consequent crony capitalism, social inequality, and uneven development; the political party gradually deteriorated from an organization that represents specific political values and ideology to bureaucratic mechanisms for power distribution; the workers and farmers were excluded from the leadership and decision-making circles of the party-state machine; the market economy infinitely expanded toward the political and cultural fields, but the economic development process excluded necessary political discussions; the state took coercive measures to suppress social conflict; and the cooptation of social movements by the state apparatus. Wang believes that these depoliticizing trends do occur in China, but can also effectively explain the general crisis of democracy faced by the world. He points out that the core problem of contemporary politics is that when the parliament and political parties change from the public sphere of democratic politics into bureaucratic apparatus that only seeks to maintain stability, the space for political discussion also shrinks. However, his analysis fails to take into consideration how the trajectory of neoliberal depoliticization may entail different forms of resistance, culture, subjectivity, and political practice.

In an age where communication, creativity, and cooperation are increasingly central to the formation of popular political activities, we are especially concerned with how resistance is connected to and brought into existence by broad social controversy and struggle. Wang Hui's nostalgic discussions imply that the possibility of a "true" politics no longer exists because of the disappearance of the early practices of the Cultural Revolution. However, it has been clear that over the past two decades—and against the background of official control of discursive rights of the people—Internet-based communication, creativity, and cooperation have opened up new spaces for struggle. We refer to such Internet-based resistance as "network resistance". Compared to traditional mainstream media, Internet communication could empower people in myriad ways. Netizen engagement in this new ethical-political space can no longer be overlooked, and this social energy creates conditions of new political subjectivity.[3] The pervasive usage of communication networks such as the Internet and mobile devices not only provides citizen-subjects with limited yet crucial opportunities to create ad hoc communities, but also reveals the possibility of subverting existing power/knowledge regimes. Interaction, dialogue, and cooperation in communication networks are deployed to construct peculiar forms of resistance subjectivity. Importantly, though, while some theorists see netizens as "post-national subjects,"[4] we think this view is far from convincing. It is not just the state continues to play an indispensable sovereign role in international politics, but in the constitution of public discourse, the state remains an important subject-producing apparatus. In what follows, we probe into various arenas of Internet-based struggle and resistance, including popular mobilizations surrounding problems of survival, formation of communication networks that influence government decisions, and online contentions around international relations and diplomacy. By doing so, we make a case for Internet resistance as the expression of people's sovereignty under neoliberal depoliticization, while also highlighting its close interactions with—instead of a simple opposition to—state power.

2. Reclaiming the Right to Know and the Right to Life

Since the end of the 1990s, network resistance has increasingly spread to various terrains of daily life, creating a public space for reclaiming the right to know (*Zhi Qing Quan*) and other social rights. Compared to the model of labor-capital disputes in the traditional industrial era, social conflict in the network age seems to be gradually evolving into the right to control the flow of information. New forms of conflict are increasingly determined by the ability for rapid dissemination of information and self-organization. Several major events since 2007 have marked turning points in the rise of network resistance. For instance, after the news about Sanlu's infamous poisonous milk powder broke in 2008, the Internet quickly became the main platform where people could exchange information, express dissatisfaction, and organize boycotts. In a similar vein, a significant number of network struggles are focused on problems surrounding survival, such as pollution of the ecology and environment, official corruption, land grabbing, cultural preservation, public policy, social morality, dignity, and public safety. These struggles intervene in the deteriorating life forms created by political decisions and economic development. In terms of organizational forms, they do not have stable and fixed leadership structures, but tend to display or use remote self-organization, instantaneous communication, rapid assembly, and flexible responses. These autonomous mobilizations tend to be loosely structured, and do not seek to take over state power.

The recent coronavirus crisis in the city of Wuhan offers a good example. The city was abruptly put into lockdown as part of the government's containment efforts after early missteps. With public transit suspended, the city, home to 11 million residents, was paralyzed; there was a shortage of medical supplies and people were stranded at home. Under these circumstances, netizens transformed the social media platform Weibo into a space of self-organization. Because of its instantaneous nature, Weibo enabled Wuhan hospitals to appeal for donations online, to which netizens responded by sourcing and mailing medical supplies such as masks and protective suits from all over the world. Weibo also functioned as a temporary carpool platform as car owners volunteered to drive medical staff to work.[5] Moreover, through the creative use of hashtags and reposts, netizens gathered and shared information on Weibo to help those in need, including COVID-19 patients who had been refused hospital care, people with chronic diseases in need of medication, and elderly people living alone. Such self-organization responds to the need of social self-protection, and directly pertains to the question of state governance. Although many cases of mobilization do not appear to be related to the state directly, if they are interpreted in the broader context of political and social development, they are actually alternative resistance to the control by the party state. In a system in which the freedom of self-expression and organization is stringently limited, appearing as a non-organization becomes a necessary strategy. This NGNO (non-government-non-organization) culture is unique to China, and is more disperse and lacking in a fixed leadership compared to NGOs in the West. NGNOs can function as powerful mechanisms of resistance.[6] During the Wuhan coronavirus outbreak, state-backed charity Wuhan Red Cross, one of the few channels allowed to handle and distribute public donations, came under fire after netizens found out that medical staff in the city faced a severe shortage of protective gear despite huge public donations. Using "human search engines," a form of NGNO where netizens use communicative networks to autonomously and cooperatively uncover information about the figures or scandals they care about,[7] netizens soon found out and revealed on Weibo that while the local warehouse of the Red Cross was filled with donated medical supplies, only a fraction had been distributed.[8] They also reported that boxes of masks were taken by a vehicle registered to government officials, raising concerns of corruption.[9] Amidst outpouring criticism online, the Red Cross issued a public apology on its Weibo page and ended its de facto monopoly by allowing hospitals to handle public donations themselves. As the Red Cross case shows, NGNO mobilizations can focus on any issue, person, group, and institution, and can self-organize and coordinate. Participants search, collect, and publish background information and details of the past activities of those involved as a means of reclaiming their right to know. The issues vary from unfair judicial judgments and official corruption to patriotic loyalty or animal abuse. NGNOs such as human search engines have redefined the relationship between knowledge and power. But such informal, spontaneous, and carnivalesque mobilizations typically exist within the limit of official tolerance, and would not directly touch upon politically sensitive issues with regard to state power. For instance, regarding the mishandling of resources, netizens focused mainly on the integrity of local Red Cross officials, overlooking the deeper factors such as the organization's connection with state power and its long-existing problems of corruption and lack of transparency. Since NGNO mobilizations do not touch on deep structural problems or offer alternatives for change, they might easily be co-opted by the regime.

Chinese netizens' use of communicative networks such as forums, microblogs, and instant messaging applications not only challenges existing power/knowledge relationships, but also engenders a network of political communication influencing government decisions. An example worth mentioning is the recent exposure of a system of corruption and fraud in the *gaokao*, China's college admission exam, regarded as the most important exam for many people in China given that it plays a decisive role in shaping a student's future. In June 2020, Chinese media reported that a 36-year-old woman from Shandong province, Chen Chunxiu, had had her identity stolen sixteen years ago by someone who attended and graduated from college in her place. The imposter confessed that she had purchased Chen's identity through an agent, leaving Chen to believe that she had not scored highly enough to go to college; she ended up as a migrant worker. The news sparked robust discussion on Weibo. Many netizens questioned how Chen's identity had been stolen and suspected deep-seated corruption in local institutions.[10] Concerns escalated when another local newspaper revealed that, based on publicly available information, there had been a total of 242 incidents of student-identity theft in fourteen of Shandong's universities between 2002 and 2009.[11] Within days, the report went viral on Weibo through hashtags—trending topics on the platform—attracting 590 million reviews and uniting Weibo users in demanding a thorough investigation.[12] Under public pressure, the university in question re-admitted Chen in an attempt to make up for their past mistake. Shandong authorities launched an investigation into the case and punished forty-six people for their involvment. They also put in place new processes to ensure such incidents would not happen again, including a more rigorous identity-verification mechanism and the publication of university-acceptance results online.[13] Moreover, the case was discussed during a standing committee session of the country's top legislature, the National People's Congress, where lawmakers started discussing including identity theft for college admissions into criminal law.[14] The incident demonstrated how people's use of the political communication network could exert considerable influence over government decisions and policies.

3. In the Shadow of the State

As network resistance has gradually influenced the setting of the official media agenda, the government has done all it can to suppress its power. The heavy-handed response to the too feminist movement is exemplary here. After first coming to prominence in the United States during 2017, the too movement arrived in Chinese university campuses the following year when two women, Luo Xixi and Huang Xueqin, used the hashtag on Weibo to come out as victims of sexual harassment and accused two prominent university professors of sexual assault. Their stories led to an online outpouring of women's accounts of sexual harassment on Chinese university campuses, and eventually resulted in the sacking of the two professors in question as well as an announcement from China's Ministry of Education vowing to strengthen and improve the development of teachers' ethics.[15] The movement then continued to grow, moving from the academic arena to charitable organizations, the media, and religious institutions, effectively amounting to a moment of collective empowerment for Chinese women.[16] However, this campaign was also overshadowed close surveillance and censorship by authorities from the very start. As Fincher reports,[17] apart from deleting victim's petitions immediately after they were posted on Weibo and WeChat, the Chinese media was warned not to report on relevant petition incidents in order to maintain social stability. In the face of these obstacles, the too movement failed to expand to other sectors or make progress in the rule of the law.[18] In December 2019, the authorities arrested Huang, one of the pioneers of the movement, under the vague charge of "picking quarrels and provoking trouble," an act widely regarded as an attempt to silence dissenting voices. Despite the massive social pressure it put on the authorities, the Chinese too movement did not take off as a large-scale, national movement in the face of state suppression.

As large-scale, centralized forms of radical politics have been erased, network resistance has assumed a prominent role in reconfiguring state–society relations. Yet the real problem may be that these dispersed and ad hoc mobilizations do not go on to form a stronger and more consistent force to negotiate state power. Since these practices are generally based on single events or issues, they are fragmented and highly issue-based. A lack of consistent goals and solidarity also means that these diverse mobilizations are unable to propose alternative visions that differ from the dominant social imaginary. Even though some moments of network resistance provide rare opportunities for social connectivity and intervention, can those carnivalesque video clips and memes really challenge the dominant power structure, other than subverting official narratives? We observe that any long-term planning becomes extremely difficult in this kind of cyberculture. Network resistance may allow people to express their anger and promote autonomous social connectivity, but it is yet to become a radical alternative to the dominant social program.

4. The Appearance of Sovereign People

In *Empire*, Hardt and Negri formulate a critique of state theory by arguing that the discussion of sovereignty remains overly focused on the state,[19] while sovereignty is actually dualist:

> Sovereign power is not an autonomous substance and it is never absolute but rather consists of a relationship between rulers and ruled, between protection and obedience, between rights and obligations. Wherever tyrants have tried to

make sovereignty into something unilateral, the ruled have always eventually revolted and restored the two-sided nature of the relationship. Those who obey are no less essential to the concept and the functioning of sovereignty than the one who commands. Sovereignty is thus, necessarily, a dual system of power.[20]

In other words, the people—as a constitutive power of the state—are the foundation of any legitimate government, and are also the source of political authority. In order to maintain its rule, the state must continuously adjust to the demands of the people. The duality of sovereignty provides the current network resistance with the possibility of intervening in both domestic and international affairs through the concrete and immediate collective presence of sovereign people. The netizens' collective action mobilizes the fragments of sovereign individuals-collectives, and sutures the gap between "present" and "absent" sovereign people.

Within the nation, Chinese netizens often employ a rhetoric of representativeness as the means of rightful resistance and struggle for political change.[21] Posing a sharp contrast to some conflicts in Europe and America that resist representation by the state as a whole, Chinese protesters generally demand a more effective and just representation by political authorities, expecting the sovereign power to recognize their existence and to change the way of being governed. As a collective force, they aim to recover what they consider to be their legitimate rights. Network communication platforms such as social media play a crucial role for the struggle over representation. Not only do they enable protestors to share experiences, information, and formulate strategies, they also empower them to set the agenda by directly appealing to the public through first-hand contents such as protest scenes, police measures, and demands. These powerful visual documentations help amplify the protest events and often elicit follow-up reports by mainstream news media. Once an event becomes widely circulated and discussed in cyberspace, political authorities will be under more pressure to take measures to prevent regime legitimacy from being damaged. One example is the Wukan protests in September 2011. Villagers from the costal fishing village located in Guangdong Province started peaceful protests against corruption and illegal land seizure. Villagers claimed that more than 400 hectares of collectivized land had been stolen and that corrupt officials had scammed over 110 million US dollars from commercial land sale. Events escalated when protesters clashed with the riot police. Initially, local government officials were quick to offer to investigate the land-seizure allegations and promised a local election for impartial representatives to act in future land negotiations; as a result, villagers temporarily suspended their protests. However, just a few weeks later, in early December, three members of Wukan's elected representatives were arrested, and one died mysteriously in police custody. The death intensified the protests, and villagers forcefully evicted local Party officials and police. They also began holding daily protest meetings and requested intervention from the central government. In late December, senior provincial officials intervened by acknowledging villagers' basic demands. They agreed to make financial records public, to dismiss and investigate two local officials, and to redistribute land previously confiscated by the local government. Network communication played a central role in the protests. As Hess observes, Wukan's case was very much an "information struggle" as protesters fought to appeal to the public and sympathetic senior officials through media. Although mainstream media remained silent during the event, protesters tried to circulate their story sporadically through microblogging sites and search engines such as Weibo and Baidu.[22] When web censors worked more aggressively to prevent their publicity, Wukan residents turned to foreign correspondents who managed to enter the village in December, and even established a news center to coordinate their efforts. The extraordinary level of attention from international media enhanced the profile of the protest within China, where Weibo users circulated screenshots of print newspapers and foreign websites.[23] Notably, Wukan villagers explicitly framed their protests as *not* against the central government but against the local official. Eventually, even state-owned media, such as *People's Daily* and *Global Times*, reported positively on the villagers' demands and hailed Wukan as an example of democracy. The Wukan protests showcase the mediated practice of rightful resistance,[24] where the sovereign people act as a collective force to demand their rights by mobilizing a discourse of state representativeness and accountability visa social media. In this way, the people were able to claim sovereign power as a source of their political authority.

In the arena of international politics, network resistance is intensely reshaping the relationship between the people, state, and diplomacy. As the foundational source of legitimacy for modern states to rule, the sovereign people were generally "absent present" in state diplomacy decisions and in the process of exercising sovereignty to foreign countries as abstract a priori categories, until the network struggle allows a segment of the sovereign people to exercise sovereignty on their own. In the age of network communication, the "sovereign people" are no longer an abstract concept but begin using the network to make themselves "present" and intervene in the realm of international politics.[25] In some cases of international tensions, the distinction between the people-netizens and the state is also blurring—the exercise of national sovereignty increasingly relies on public expression by the governed, networked subjects. In the past, Western discourse has tended to see such collective actions as having been manipulated by the government, and a result of top–down official propaganda and thus lacking real autonomy. The hypothesis in this perspective is the absolute monopoly of the state, and that Chinese people lack the ability to think independently. However, unlike the rigid dualist perspectives of state versus society, Chinese netizens strategically appropriate official discourse to legitimize the general will of the people.

The latest wave of networked protests against Western hegemony follow the nationalist currents that began in the late 1990s, and seek primarily to defend the sovereign rights and dignity of the nation-state. From the 1999 protest against the American bombing of the Chinese embassy in Yugoslavia to the 2008 protests against the Olympic Torch disruption and what was perceived as biased reporting by the Western media, it becomes increasingly clear that the people are not a completely passive and manipulated population, but have the potential to become radical political subjects (even though this is only appears ephemerally). The series of network struggles brought new opportunities and challenges to China's diplomacy. These rallies demonstrate that the sovereign people remain the source of political power, which can generate sufficient authority to affect international politics. The now well-known practice of the "Diba Expedition" (*Diba Chuzheng*) is illuminating here. An online forum originally dedicated to a Chinese soccer player, Diba, first gained international attention in 2016 when a large number of its members self-organized to bypass China's Great Firewall and waged a "cross-strait meme war" on Facebook upon Taiwan's election of the pro-independence leader Tsai Ing-Wen. These netizens bombarded the comment section on Tsai's Facebook page with anti-independence memes referring to Tsai as a "provincial governor" and warning her that "If you dare declare Taiwan's independence, I will come over and enforce the law."[26] Showcasing a skillful maneuvering of technology and a swarm-style organization, Diba members posted over 70,000 comments in less than twenty-four hours and flooded the Facebook pages of Taiwanese pro-independence media outlets such as Apple Daily and Sanli News.[27] Wang comments that although the name and format of the Diba Expedition evoke an impression that a commander is in charge, the "expedition" is actually a collective action through which participants construct a patriotic subject that is admired and affirmed by all the participants.[28] These self-organized collective actions show how network resistance has enabled Chinese citizens, who have traditionally been excluded from the decision-making process of international affairs, to pose a challenge to the monopoly of international discursive rights by the state. In ensuing years, Diba has played a significant role in voicing out popular nationalist concerns in international affairs. It bombarded the Facebook page of a Swedish TV station for hosting a show that allegedly insulted China in 2018. In 2019, it targeted prominent supporters of the Hong Kong protests, including Canto-pop singer Denise Ho and pan-democrat lawmaker Claudia Mo. These cases modify the traditional model of "strong government, weak civil society" in international diplomatic affairs, forcing the state to actively respond to the new challenges brought by netizens. On one hand, the state has increasingly recognized the fact that all diplomatic activities must be sufficiently accountable to the sovereign people, because every attitude, behavior, or decision, may trigger resistance from the network. On the other hand, network resistance is also strengthening the autonomy of the popular challenge to the states' agenda-setting on international affairs. Not only can demonstrations of the sovereign people leverage pressure effectively on the actions of the state, but they can also strengthen the negotiating power of the state in global conflicts.

Recent signs of network resistance in international affairs show a new trend: the horizontal connectivity has gradually affected official media discourse and agenda-setting models, thus any international event could become a source of online contention. Compared to the traditional diplomacy which was highly centralized and bureaucratized, the network community can transcend the limitations of space to self-organize, engage in real-time communication, congregate rapidly, and respond. The range of discourse and mobilization is broadened, no longer focusing on single states, and also includes foreign companies (such as controversies on Dolce & Gabbana), treatment of historical relics (such as auctioning off looted relics) and cultural products (such as TV shows). Original boundaries between politics, economics, and culture are being blended in the new political space. Since network resistance is always floating and unpredictable, official control over discourse has become increasingly difficult. In this process, we observe a unique phenomenon of power transference, that netizens gradually participate in the fight over international discursive hegemony, and the traditional state's monopoly on diplomatic power is weakening.

5. Demanding Representation and Accountability

In the network age, the expression of popular sovereignty has become more direct and independent. The people are no longer mere invisible, anonymous "authorizers" hiding behind the state, but rather active political subjects who exercise sovereignty of their own volition. The proliferation of network-based mobilization makes it possible for the people to interact with state power in intricate ways beyond dichotomous formulations of opposition or complicity. Network resistance is characterized by voluntary participation, open debate, and diverse social organization forms. It seeks to question the representativeness and legitimacy of the entity exercising sovereignty, and asks for power-sharing and fairer treatment. It has opened up a new political space for recognition in the existing framework. Despite the obvious limits of these self-organizations, we suggest that their democratic potential should be fully accounted for. Network resistance, in our view, is not against state power, but is rather a new force that demands the state be more accountable and responsive to popular wills.

In recent years, we can observe how soaring nationalistic sentiments online in China has coincided with the government's turn to a more assertive and hardline style of diplomacy.[29] Future studies could consider what Schneider asks in his discussion of China's digital nationalism: how could the state accurately gauge the dynamics of network media when its patriotic education policy has primed citizens with the parameters of nationalism, and when media politics tend to emphasize these parameters even further?[30] Second, in an increasingly precarious international environment where China's new diplomacy style has generated pushback,[31] how could network resistance negotiate with the state? The state, Rousseau reminds us, needs to actively bear the responsibility for rationally guiding the people to pursue happiness.[32] As network resistance plays a more prominent role for China's domestic and international politics, its implications for the future of China and the world must be examined critically.

Notes

1. Wang, "Depoliticized Politics," *New Left Review* 41 (2006): 29–45.
2. Wang, "Depoliticized Politics," 29.
3. See, for example, Huhe et al., "Creating Democratic Citizens: Political Effects of the Internet in China"; Lin, "Mediating Embodied Protest: Performative Body in Social Protests in the Internet Age in China"; Xue and van Stekelenburg, "When the Internet Meets Collective Action: The Traditional and Creative Ways of Political Participation in China".
4. Poster, *What's the Matter with the Internet?*
5. Dhanapala, "China's Civil Society and Public Mobilized in Response to COVID-19".
6. Liu, "Demanding State Intervention", in *The New Global Politics*, 234–50.
7. Li, "The Emergence of the Human Flesh Search Engine and Political Protest in China".

8 Corsetti, "As the Red Cross Faces Criticism for Its Handling of Coronavirus Medical Supplies, Donors Turn to the Han Hong Foundation".
9 Hollingsworth and Thomas, "China's Red Cross is Under Fire for Not Getting Supplies to Coronavirus Hospitals. That's a Problem for the Government".
10 Chen, "Identity Theft Robs a Woman of College".
11 Bloomberg, "Chinese College Entrance Exam Scandal Sparks National Outrage".
12 Ibid.
13 Tan, "How a Stolen Identity Exposed Chinese Exam Fraud."
14 Shan and Luan, "China Considers Criminalising College Admission Identity Theft After Hundreds of Such Alleged Cases."
15 Guo, "Woman Who Set off #MeToo in China Still Looking for breakthrough".
16 Lin and Yang, "Individual and collective empowerment: Women's voices in the #MeToo movement in China."
17 Fincher. *Betraying Big Brother: The Feminist Awakening in China.*
18 Guo, "Woman Who Set off #MeToo in China Still Looking for Breakthrough".
19 Hardt and Negri, *Multitude: War and Democracy in the Age of.*
20 Ibid., 332.
21 See Tan, "How a Stolen Identity Exposed Chinese Exam Fraud"; Wang Hui. "The Crisis of Representativeness and Post-Party Politics".
22 Steve Hess, "Foreign Media Coverage and Protest Outcomes in China: The Case of the 2011 Wukan Rebellion," *Modern Asian Studies* vol. 49, no.1 (2014): 177–203.
23 Hess, "Foreign Media Coverage and Protest Outcomes in China", 20.
24 Vukovich, *Illiberal China.*
25 Bjola and Jiang, "Social Media and Public Diplomacy".
26 Leng, "Taiwan President-elect Tsai Ing-wen's Facebook Page Bombarded with Comments Attacking Any Move by Island Towards Independence".
27 Ibid.
28 Wang, "We Are All Diba Members Tonight: Cyber-nationalism as Emotional and Playful Actions Online".
29 Zhang et al., "Nationalism on Weibo: Towards a Multifaceted Understanding of Chinese Nationalism".
30 Cheng, "Challenging China's Wolf Warrior Diplomats".
31 Schneider, *China's Digital Nationalism*, 228.
32 Zhu, "Interpreting China's Wolf-Warrior Diplomacy".

Bibliography

Bloomberg, "Chinese College Entrance Exam Scandal Sparks National Outrage." *Bloomberg*, June 30 (2020). Available online: https://www.bloomberg.com/news/

articles/2020-06-30/chinese-college-entrance-exam-scandal-sparks-national-outrage (accessed July 31, 2020).

Bjola, Corneliu., and Jiang, Lu. "Social Media and Public Diplomacy: A Comparative Analysis of the Digital Diplomatic Strategies of the EU, U.S. and Japan in China," in *Digital Diplomacy: Theory and Practice*, edited by Corneliu Bjola and Marcus Holmes, 71–88. London: Routledge, 2015.

Calhoun, Craig. "Nationalism and Cultures of Democracy." *Public Culture* vol. 19, no. 1 (2020): 151–73.

Chen, Qin. "Identity Theft Robs a Woman of College." *Inkstone*, June 25 2020. Available online: https://www.inkstonenews.com/society/china-trends-identity-theft-robs-woman-college-and-novak-djokovic-feels-heat/article/3090411 (accessed July 31, 2020).

Cheng, Dean. "Challenging China's Wolf Warrior Diplomats." *Backgrounder*, July 5, 2020. Available online: https://www.heritage.org/sites/default/files/2020-07/BG3504.pdf (accessed August 1, 2020).

Corsetti, Gabriel. "As the Red Cross Faces Criticism for Its Handling of Coronavirus Medical Supplies, Donors Turn to the Han Hong Foundation." *China Development Brief* (February 3, 2020). Available online: https://chinadevelopmentbrief.cn/reports/news/as-the-red-cross-is-criticised-for-its-handling-of-coronavirus-donations-the-public-turns-to-the-han-hong-foundation/ (accessed Aug 1, 2020).

Dhanapala, Sivanka. "China's Civil Society and Public Mobilized in Response to COVID-19." *CGTN*, February 17, 2020. Available online: https://news.cgtn.com/news/2020-02-17/China-s-civil-society-and-public-mobilized-in-response-to-COVID-19-O8kETslvq0/index.html (accessed July 31, 2020).

Fincher, Leta. Hong. *Betraying Big Brother: The Feminist Awakening in China.* New York: Verso Books, 2018.

Gao, Li. "The emergence of the Human Flesh Search Engine and political protest in China: exploring the Internet and online collective action." *Media, Culture & Society* vol. 38, no. 3 (2015): 349–64.

Guo, Rui. "Woman Who Set off #MeToo in China Still Looking for breakthrough." *South China Morning Post* (December 28, 2019). Available online: https://www.scmp.com/news/china/politics/article/3043702/two-years-woman-who-set-metoo-china-still-looking-breakthrough (accessed July 31, 2020).

Hardt, Michael, and Antonio Negri. *Multitude: War and Democracy in the Age of Empire.* London: Penguin, 2004.

Hess, Steve. "Foreign Media Coverage and Protest Outcomes in China: The Case of the 2011 Wukan Rebellion." *Modern Asian Studies* vol. 49, no. 1 (2014): 177–203.

Hollingsworth, Julia, and Natalie Thomas. "China's Red Cross is Under Fire for Not Getting Supplies to Coronavirus Hospitals. That's a Problem for the Government." *CNN*, February 7, 2020. Available online: https://edition.cnn.com/2020/02/06/asia/red-cross-china-donations-intl-hnk/index.html (accessed August 2, 2020).

Huhe, Narisong., Min Tang, and Jie Chen. "Creating Democratic Citizens: Political Effects of the Internet in China." *Political Research Quarterly* vol. 71, no. 4 (2018): 757–71.

Leng, Sidney. "Taiwan President-elect Tsai Ing-wen's Facebook Page Bombarded with Comments Attacking Any Move by Island Towards Independence." *South China Morning Post* (January 21, 2016). Available online: https://www.scmp.com/news/china/policies-politics/article/1903627/taiwan-president-elect-tsai-ing-wens-facebook-page (accessed August 3, 2020).

Li, Gao. "The Emergence of the Human Flesh Search Engine and Political Protest in China: Exploring the Internet and Online Collective Action," *Media, Culture & Society* vol. 38, no. 3 (2015): 349–64.

Lin, Zhongxuan. "Mediating Embodied Protest: Performative Body in Social Protests in the Internet Age in China." *Media, Culture & Society* vol. 41, no. 6 (2018): 863–77.

Lin, Zhongxuan, and Liu Yang. "Individual and collective empowerment: Women's voices in the #MeToo movement in China." *Asian Journal of Women's Studies* vol. 25, no. 1 (2019): 117–31.

Liu, Shih-Diing. "Demanding state intervention: New opportunities for popular protest in China," in *The New Global Politics: Global Social Movements in the Twenty-First Century*, edited by Harry E. Vanden, Peter N. Funke, and Gary Prevost, 234–50. New York: Routledge, 2017.

Poster, Mark. *What's the Matter with the Internet?* Minneapolis: University of Minnesota Press, 2001.

Rousseau, Jean-Jacques. *The Social Contract*, trans. D. Matravers. Ware: Wordsworth Editions, 1998.

Schneider, Florian. *China's Digital Nationalism*. New York: Oxford University Press, 2018.

Shan, Yuxiao, and Ingrid Luan. "China Considers Criminalising College Admission Identity Theft After Hundreds of Such Alleged Cases." *The Straits Times*, July 3 2020. Available online: https://www.straitstimes.com/asia/east-asia/china-considers-criminalising-college-admission-identity-theft-after-hundreds-of-such (accessed August 2, 2020).

Tan, Yvette. "How a Stolen Identity Exposed Chinese Exam Fraud." *BBC News*, July 9 2020. Available online: https://www.bbc.com/news/world-asia-china-53316895 (accessed July 31, 2020).

Tsai, Lily L. *Accountability without Democracy: Solidary Groups and Public Goods Provision in Rural China*. Cambridge: Cambridge University Press, 2007.

Vukovich, Daniel F. *Illiberal China: The Ideological Challenge of the People's Republic of China*. Basingstoke: Springer, 2018.

Xu, Bin. "Moral Performance and Cultural Governance in China: The Compassionate Politics of Disasters." *The China Quarterly* vol. 226 (2016): 407–30.

Xue, Ting, and Jacquelien van Stekelenburg. "When the Internet Meets Collective Action: The Traditional and Creative Ways of Political Participation in China." *Current Sociology* vol. 66, no. 6 (2018): 911–28.

Wang, Hui. "Depoliticized Politics, from East to West." *New Left Review* (2006): 29–45.

Wang, Hui. "The Crisis of Representativeness and Post-Party Politics." *Modern China* 40, no. 2 (2013): 214–39.

Wang, Zhe. "We Are All Diba Members Tonight: Cyber-nationalism as Emotional and Playful Actions Online," in *From Cyber-Nationalism to Fandom Nationalism: The Case of Diba Expedition In China,* edited by H. Liu. London: Routledge, 2019.

Zhang, Yinxian., Jiajun Liu, and Ji-Rong Wen. "Nationalism on Weibo: Towards a Multifaceted Understanding of Chinese Nationalism." *The China Quarterly* vol. 235 (2018): 758–83.

Zhu, Zhiqun. "Interpreting China's Wolf-Warrior Diplomacy." *The Diplomat*, May 16 2020. Available online: https://thediplomat.com/2020/05/interpreting-chinas-wolf-warrior-diplomacy/ (accessed August 2, 2020).

"Probability and Reality Do Not Always Coincide": Uncanny Modernity in Kleist's *Michael Kohlhaas*

Louis Lo

1. Introduction

The complicated narrative of the Heinrich von Kleist (1777–1811) novella *Michael Kohlhaas* (1810) contains an intertwining mixture of realistic and fantastic literary devices.[1] Set in Saxony and Brandenburg in the sixteenth century, the story is based on an historical figure, Hans Kohlhasen (*c.* 1500–40), who took revenge against the state by developing a feud against Saxony when his demands for justice were not met in a court of law. Kleist's innovation is to add fantastical narrative centered on the character of a "gypsy," the double of the hero's dead wife, whose fortune-telling ability empowers his resistance. The labyrinthine narrative develops like a baroque motif. I explore the implications of Kohlhaas's paradoxical acts of transgression: Kohlhaas is simultaneously resisting the state (by attacking its representatives by organized banditry) and conforming to the law (by actively demanding a lawsuit) in order to pursue justice, but his resistance cannot be achieved without the gypsy woman. Instead of regarding the two threads (realistic, developed from the historical chronicle writing tradition; and fantastic, developed from the fairy-tale tradition) as separate, this essay interprets the mixing of literary styles in the novella as a whole, assuming that the fantastic element is part of the entire narrative.[2]

I will compare and contrast two notions of modernity: "calculating modernity" (a term I coined) and Deleuze and Guattari's notion of "uncanny modernity." The former, usually regarded as modernity proper, emphasizes reason, individual freedom, and technology promoted by Enlightenment ideology, whereas the latter is seen as anti-modern, primitive, mythical, and excessive. Calculability, promoted by rational thinking and the Enlightenment, gives rise to vengeful thinking (*lex talionis*, or an eye for an eye, or "measure for measure"), whereas uncanny modernity subverts the very notion of revenge and justice. Drawing on Kant and Nietzsche, Derrida calls "the principle of equivalence, the *jus talionis* between the crime and the punishment, and between the injury and the price to be paid," a rationally and morally pure calculation.³

The term "uncanny modernity" is taken from Deleuze and Guattari's discussion of Kleist's work:

> Why is it then, that the most uncanny modernity lies with him [Kleist]? It is because the elements of his work are secrecy, speed, and affect. And in Kleist the secret is no longer a content held within a form of interiority; rather, it becomes a form, identified with the form of exteriority that is always external to itself.⁴

In Kleist's novella, the two contrasting concepts of modernity work together, problematizing such notions as revenge, justice, and resistance. Via an analysis of Deleuze and Guattari's reading of Kleist's writings, I explore the two faces of modernity, in order to show that there is something uncanny about modernity, which is manifested as "secrecy, speed, and affect." Kohlhaas's submission to law, which could be seen as a revenge against the state for his transgression, makes revenge uncanny and can no longer be recognized as resistance. Nietzsche's Zarathustra defines revenge as "the will's ill-will toward time and its 'it was.'"⁵ For Zarathustra, the spirit of revenge is created by an "ill-will" toward time, because time is always moving forward, and therefore what has happened in the past cannot be undone. The revenger takes action partly because he cannot accept the unchangeable "it was." So, for Nietzsche, revenge is a reaction against something that happened in the past and cannot be changed, and the dominant emotion motivating revenge is *ressentiment*—bitterness, or rancor.⁶ The ending of the novella shows how a revenge-taker submits to the power of the uncanny that engineers his revenge, taking up a non-personal dimension, and thus resists a reactionary understanding of revenge as *ressentiment*.

The narrative tells the story of Kohlhaas, a hard-working and honest horse-dealer who takes revenge against the state after a series of unjust and tragic events, triggered by the illegal removal of his two black horses by the Junker Wenzel von Tronka when Kohlhaas is crossing the border from Brandenburg to a market in Saxony. The horses are maltreated during their detention at Tronka Castle, and Kohlhaas's stable-boy is beaten up. After a few failed attempts at bringing the case to court—including letting his wife approach the Elector's castellan which results in an accident that costs her life—but believing that it is his duty to stop this injustice, Kohlhaas attacks Tronka Castle. His goal is to capture the Junker, whom he thinks is responsible for having illegally demanded a border-crossing permit which is a "mere fabrication,"[7] according to the Chancellery at Dresden.

Kohlhaas's attack fails since the Junker escapes to Wittenberg, but he *does* succeeds at burning down the castle. Kohlhaas posts a few proclamations calling for "every good Christian"[8] to help him catch the Junker, and later styles himself "an emissary of the Archangel Michael, who has come to punish with fire and sword all those who shall stand on the Junker's side in this quarrel."[9] While much could be said of the implicit critique of Christianity, I cannot explore this topic here. It is sufficient to say that Kohlhaas identifies himself as a good Christian which, for him, justifies his violent actions.

The increase in manpower of Kohlhaas's group (people who joined his campaign, started with Kohlhaas and seven grooms, rapidly rises to 400, and then to thousands) constitutes a threat to the state. After attacking major sites including Wittenberg and Leipzig, Martin Luther intervenes by posting proclamations, condemning Kohlhaas's "blind passion" and his "personal vengeance," calling him "a rebel" and arguing that his sovereign "knows nothing"[10] about his case. Upset by Luther's accusation, Kohlhaas breaks into his house and forces him to listen to his defense; he wants to prove Luther wrong in thinking him unjust by maintaining that he was forced to defend himself because he had been cast out from society. Although Luther does not sympathize with Kohlhaas, he requests safe conduct for Kohlhaas to Dresden so that he can renew his lawsuit. Replying to Kohlhaas's demand that he hear his confession, Luther asks Kohlhaas to forgive his enemy. But Kohlhaas refuses: "even the Lord did not forgive all his enemies. Let me forgive the Electors, my two sovereigns, the warden and the steward, the lords Himz and Kunz and whoever else has done me wrong in this affair; but, if it is possible, let the Junker be compelled to fatten my blacks for me again."[11] It echoes Kohlhaas's thoughts upon his wife's pardoning the Junker on her deathbed: "May God never forgive me as I forgive the Junker!"[12] Luther denies him the holy sacrament and Kohlhaas leaves in sorrow.

Kohlhaas is granted an amnesty and safe-conduct to Dresden by the Elector of Saxony and his court is opened on the advice of Luther. He disbands his troops and accepts the arrangement of having three bodyguards, who will be dismissed as soon as Kohlhaas requests it, promised by the Prince. Johann Nagelschmidt, one of Kohlhaas's henchmen, plunders the countryside as his deputy even after he is disbanded. Although Kohlhaas dissociates himself from Nagelschmidt, the Tronka family uses this as an excuse to prolong the lawsuit. Noticing an increase in the number of guards in Kohlhaas's lodging, Kohlhaas abandons his claims and attempts to leave the state, but he falls into a trap set by the Elector of Saxony when he accepts Nagelschmidt's offer of helping him to escape. His "confession" letter is published to discredit him and he is put on trial for conspiracy. He makes no defense and is sentenced to be executed by quartering and burning.[13]

The narrative then takes a 25-page detour (out of a total of sixty-nine pages) with the episode of the gypsy woman, which will be discussed later. Intending to show off his political power, the Elector of Brandenburg intervenes and demands Kohlhaas be handed over to Berlin. His violent acts in Saxony will be judged by Brandenburg law, and his case against the Junker will be dealt with by a Saxon attorney. The Elector of Saxony, powerless to refuse, decides to appeal to the Holy Roman Emperor, whose representative will prosecute Kohlhaas for breaking Imperial peace. The Berlin court sentences Kohlhaas to be decapitated.[14] He accepts the verdict with satisfaction, provided that his horses are returned to him in full health and that the Junker is sentenced to a two-year imprisonment. He receives both a letter from Luther and the sacrament of Holy Communion. A mass of people attends his execution and mourns his death.

2. Calculating Modernity: Kant and Luther

The story is framed by references to counter-historical writing, as can be noted from its subtitle: "From an Old Chronicle." It opens:

> About the middle of the sixteenth century there lived beside the banks of the River Havel a horse-dealer called Michael Kohlhaas, the son of a schoolmaster, who was one of the most *honourable* as well as one of the most *terrible* men of his age. Until his thirtieth year, this extraordinary man could have been considered a paragon of civil virtues. In a village that still bears his name he owned a farm where he peacefully earned a living by his trade; his wife bore him children whom he brought up in the fear of God to be hard-working and honest; he had not one neighbour who was not indebted to his generosity or his fair-mindedness; in short, the world would have had cause to revere his memory, had he not pursued one of his *virtues* to *excess*. But his sense of justice made him a *robber* and a *murderer*.[15]

Kohlhaas's excessive nature is underlined in the first paragraph. Being honorable and terrible coexist because of his fair-mindedness, while his banditry and murderous tendencies are caused by his pursue of justice.

Kohlhaas is obsessed with a Kantian notion of justice:[16] the narrator says that his sense of justice "was as fine as a gold-balance."[17] He thinks that "it was now his duty to the world at large to exert all his powers in securing redress for the wrongs already perpetrated and protection for his fellow citizens against such wrongs in the future."[18] Despite Kohlhaas's initial, "selfish" demand that his horses should be restored to health, this is a moral duty that he is willing to fulfill, and which can be seen as a Kantian moral demand. Immanuel Kant argues that there is an objective principle which takes the form of a moral command, a "categorical imperative" that would "present an action as of itself objectively necessary, without regard to any other end."[19] Kant discusses duty and its relation to legality:

> The concept of duty thus requires of action that it objectively agree with the law, while of the maxim of the action it demands subjective respect for the law as the sole mode of determining the will through itself. And thereon rests the distinction between consciousness of having acted according to duty and from duty, i.e., from respect for the law. The former, legality, is possible even if inclinations alone are the determining grounds of the will, but the latter, morality or moral worth, can be conceded only where the action occurs from duty, i.e. merely for the sake of the law.[20]

The "categorical imperative" implies a new mode of subjectivity based on the calculability of injury or harm done to a person and its equivalent "compensation"—indeed "measure for measure" assumes calculability, impersonality, and abstraction. The subject engenders what Andreas Gailus terms an "impersonal passion."[21] Gailus argues that Kant's works after *Critique of Practical Reason* are an attempt to close the gaps between personal and moral subjectivity, and between desire and duty, because for Kant morality is built on the opposition between "the satisfaction of desires on the one hand, and the fulfillment of ethical demands on the other."[22]

Moral actions require the refusal of the "ordinary self," in Kant's words, "life and its enjoyment,"[23] in favor of a self which is free from the demands of life. It is exactly the pain that goes with this conscious choice in which man "discovers the sign of his freedom and a regard for himself as a moral being."[24] Gailus contrasts Kant's subjectivity with Kohlhaas's based on their differences concerning this question of renunciation. The Kantian subject renounces subjectivity but preserves the necessity of reason, whereas Kohlhaas "sacrifices both subjectivity and reason."[25] Gailus points out a contradiction in Kohlhaas's "moral heroism":

> While justice depends on the balancing of equivalents, and thus on an independent measure of value. . ., Kohlhaas's insistence on the restoration of his

horses implies a principle of justice based on the balance of identicals whose exclusive value lies in their simple identity.... At the heart of his madness lies the utter denial of difference: between equivalents (*these* horses), between past and present (*prior* to the conflict), and ultimately between instance and law, singularity and principle.[26]

Kleist's novella can be read as a critique of the Enlightenment values of rationality and subjectivity, because although Kohlhaas acts according to a moral duty, the "insanity of [his] blind passion"[27] is so murderous that it eventually overwhelms the very principle that has driven it. But "subjectivity" and "reason" imply a rational subject, and these are the very values that the Enlightenment embraces.[28] Kohlhaas's insistence may be seen as a symptom of the subjectivity produced by Enlightenment culture: a subject who seeks revenge not as personal vengeance, but as a duty demanded by the categorical imperative.[29] The categorical imperative makes everything impersonal and abstract because the demand of the categorical imperative is only possible when things are calculable. This is also the premise of *lex talionis*, and the reason Nietzsche remarks that "the categorical imperative smells of cruelty."[30] It is cruel because of its rationality, impersonality, and calculability.

Luther as a religious revolutionary figure is important to the text and to my analysis. In a sense, Kohlhaas's repeated proclamations in writing are imitating Luther's nailing of the Ninety-Five Theses to the door of Wittenberg's Castle Church on October 31, 1517 as a revolutionary act. Luther's regressive reactionary judgement of Kohlhaas and Kohlhaas's seemingly revolutionary act seem to be a chiastic exchange, i.e. an exchange of identity with each other. Commenting on representations of Luther's rebellion and on Dürer's sketches of monuments to the rebellious peasants, Stephen Greenblatt points out Luther's problematic position as a revolutionary religious figure during the German Peasants' War of 1524–6. While being rebellious himself, Luther condemned the peasants who demanded the abolition of serfdom as rebels and "the agents of the devil."[31] The Luther of *Michael Kohlhaas* sides with the historical Luther whose reactionary ideas are presented in texts like "Against the Robbing and Murdering Hordes of Peasants."[32] Kohlhaas is marginalized by Luther's disapproval, and his betrayal, and thus becomes an outcast, or even a "foreign invading power."[33] It is Kohlhaas's revolutionary spirit, which resembles Luther's former revolutionary act, that Luther cannot take. In a way, Luther recognizes the heterogeneity in Kohlhaas before the latter knows it himself. Kohlhaas's subversive resistance means he must become an outcast.

The subjectivity of Kohlhaas as a revenge-taker is two-fold, and is illustrated in his debate with Luther. After Luther questions Kohlhaas about the definition of an outcast, Kohlhaas replies:

> I call that man an outcast...who is denied the protection of the law! For I need that protection if my peaceful trade is to prosper; indeed it is for the sake of that protection that I take refuge... in that community. Whoever withholds it from me drives me out into the wilderness among savages.[34]

Luther does not approve of Kohlhaas as a rebel. In the letter he writes to the Elector of Saxony asking for safe conduct, Luther suggests that

> the situation would best be remedied if Kohlhaas were treated not so much as a rebel in revolt against the crown but rather as a *foreign* invading power, for which status, indeed, the fact that he was not a Saxon subject to some extent qualified him.[35]

This contradicts Luther's own assertion that no one has become an outcast from society "so long as states existed." Kohlhaas is outside the law, an "outcast" who is "denied the protection of the law"[36] and hence a criminal. This, he thinks, gives him license to use violence against those whom he thinks are not on his side. Alternatively, he can be seen as taking revenge on himself because he has internalized the law. In the former case, what he wants is "punishment of the Junker according to the law; the restoration of the horses to their former state; and damages for what I and my groom ... suffered from the violence that was done to us."[37] He submits himself to the law and is willing to accept punishment.

It seems that there are two laws working in *Michael Kohlhaas*.[38] Kohlhaas's open letter to Nagelschmidt warns that he will give "him over to the full vengeance of the law"[39] for the acts of murder and arson committed after the publication of the amnesty. Kohlhaas's concept of law is in the figure of an avenger. This recalls his identification as "an emissary of the Archangel Michael, who has come to punish with fire and sword."[40] Law is a figure of revenge, like the Archangel Michael. But there is another uncanny law of chance which is at work. And ironically the "vengeance of law" takes the form of a law which also kills Kohlhaas as a figure of revenge.

3. Uncanny Modernity and Kleist's War Machine

Kohlhaas's uncanny act of taking revenge against the State, and his eventual execution, are analyzed by Deleuze and Guattari, who pick up the "war machine" feature in Kohlhaas (and its creator Kleist), who is never understood by the State. They define the war machine as possessing absolute possibility and the potential for change. Invented by the nomads, the war machine is exterior to the State.

> Throughout his work, Kleist celebrates the war machine, setting it against the State apparatus in a struggle that is lost from the start.... [Kohlhaas]'s war machine can no longer be anything more than banditry. Is it the destiny of the war machine, when the State triumphs, to be caught in this alternative: either to be nothing more than the disciplined, military organ of the State apparatus, *or to turn against itself*, to become a double suicide machine for a solitary man and a solitary woman? Goethe and Hegel, State thinkers both, see Kleist as a monster, and Kleist has lost from the start.[41]

The two possible outcomes for Kohlhaas as a war machine, maintained Deleuze and Guattari, are that he is disciplined and eventually absorbed into the state apparatus, or that he turns against himself until nothing is left in his subjectivity, his "interiority." Kohlhaas is an absolute "outcast" (as he calls himself), not only in the sense that he is not protected by the community, but that he operates on secrecy, speed, and affect. The war machine sides with exteriority, producing an effect so that "the Self (*Moi*) is now nothing more than a character whose actions and emotions are desubjectified, perhaps even to the point of death."[42] In contrast to Kleist, Goethe and Hegel are committed to State thinking, and they cannot accept passion because it is something which cannot be reconciled with State apparatus. Deleuze and Guattari identify the "East" in Kleist, "the Japanese fighter, interminably still, who then makes a move too quick to see." They continue,

> Could it be that it is at the moment the war machine ceases to exist, conquered by the State, that it displays to the utmost its irreducibility, that it scatters into thinking, loving, dying, or creating machines that have at their disposal vital or revolutionary powers capable of challenging the conquering State?[43]

The war machine is scattered and returned, and is appropriated by the State apparatus, just as Kohlhaas is executed by the State. But his revenge against the Elector of Saxony is achieved thanks to a secret (a note passed to him by the gypsy woman about the future of the Elector's reign), the nature and significance of which he is unaware. It is revealed to him shortly before he is executed. The revelation of the secret and the destruction (Kohlhaas swallows the note shortly before his execution) that ensues constitute Kohlhaas's revenge act with a touch of uncanniness.[44]

A mysterious episode, "The Story of a Gypsy Woman," is inserted after Kohlhaas's two death sentences when the story arcs in a new direction:

> *Now it happened at this time that* the Kingdom of Poland, for reasons not known to us, was involved in a dispute with the House of Saxony, and was repeatedly

and urgently pressing the Elector of Brandenburg to make common cause with the Poles against the Saxons.[45]

This showcases how the pursuit of justice depends on the power of the uncanny exemplified in the character of the gypsy woman. The episode acts as a *leitmotif* inasmuch as it takes up the phrase "it happened that." While Kohlhaas is being transferred to Berlin for state trial, "it happens that"[46] the Elector of Saxony is invited by the Lord Sheriff to a great stag hunt on the Saxon border, the same spot where Kohlhaas will later spend a night. The Elector was the first love of the Lord Sheriff's daughter, Lady Heloise, now the wife of Kunz the Chamberlain. At her request, the Elector agrees to disguise himself as a huntsman and visit Kohlhaas with her. The Elector notices a small lead locket hanging from Kohlhaas's neck, and asks him about it. Kohlhaas replies, "there is a strange story connected with this locket,"[47] and tells a first-person narrative. He describes how he got the locket from a gypsy woman on the day of his wife's funeral, from where he set off on his quest to capture Junker von Tronka, and how he witnessed an encounter between the gypsy woman, the Elector of Saxony, and the Elector of Brandenburg in a town hall. He saw the gypsy woman telling fortunes in the marketplace, and was astonished when she suddenly came to him, handed him a piece of paper, and called him by his name, saying, this is "an amulet, Kohlhaas the horse-dealer; keep it safely, one day it will save your life,"[48] and then vanished. At this point, the Elector of Saxony collapses. After he has regained some strength, he sends a man to ask Kohlhaas for the piece of paper in exchange for his freedom, but he replies, "you can send me to the scaffold, but I can make you suffer, and I mean to do so!"[49]

The Elector's health condition deteriorates and his efforts to prolong Kohlhaas's life are in vain. Upon the request of the Chamberlain, Saxony tells a story that complements Kohlhaas's, about the day that he and the Elector of Brandenburg encountered the gypsy woman in Jüterbock. He reveals that his companion Brandenburg meant to destroy the woman's soothsaying reputation, but their efforts were in vain as she managed to prove herself to be a powerful prophetess. After reading Saxony's palm, she said, "I shall write down three things for you: the name of the last ruler of your dynasty, the year in which he will lose his throne, and the name of the man who will seize it by force of arms."[50] That paper was sealed and handed to Kohlhaas, a bystander.

The Chamberlain, meanwhile, conspires to find a rag-seller on the streets of Berlin who is old enough to imitate the gypsy woman, so that he can send her to visit Kohlhaas and trick him into giving back the piece of paper. But it turns out that that old woman *is* the same gypsy. The narrator says, and indeed (for probability and reality do not always coincide) it chanced that something had happened here which we must report, though anyone who so pleases is at liberty to doubt it: the Chamberlain had committed the most appalling of blunders, for in the old rag-seller whom he had taken from the streets of Berlin to play the part of the gypsy-woman, he had picked upon the mysterious gypsy herself whose part he wanted to have played.[51]

Kohlhaas notices "a strange resemblance between her and his deceased wife Lisbeth,"[52] including her gestures, features, bony hands, and even the mole on her neck. He fails to extract any useful answers from her, except her promise that he will find out who exactly she is when they meet again; this turns out to be the day of his execution, the day following the Palm Sunday. Instead of giving a logical explanation, which is assumed in narrative and a feature of the Enlightenment, the narrator just leaves it up to the power of the uncanny.[53] Rationalism, which begins the narrative, ends up unable to explain the event. Apart from the ironic tone the Kleistian narrator adapts, and the explanation given in the parenthesis—"(for probability and reality do not always coincide)"—this inability is also shown in an inconsistency regarding the details of how many days Kohlhaas has waited before setting off for von Tronka's castle.[54] The impossibility of telling a consistent story could be a critique of Enlightenment thought, as discussed above.

Uncanniness does not only reside in the gypsy woman's resemblance of Kohlhaas's wife, but also in the coincidence of the Chamberlain's taking the very same gypsy from a Berlin street to play the role of the mysterious gypsy-soothsayer who met the Elector of Saxony. Dickens notes the high probability of chance encounters in London: as a character in *Nicholas Nickleby* says, not without a sense of self-reflexivity, "I don't believe now . . . that there's such a place in all the world for coincidences as London is."[55] Calculability is undone by coincidence; calculating modernity by uncanny modernity.

This inserted episode crosses the textual border of the story when the narrative comes to an end. On the Monday after Palm Sunday, when Kohlhaas is in the procession moving to the place of his execution, he shakes hands with a mournful crowd of his friends. The castellan of the Electoral palace hands him a note, which he says is from a strange old woman. The paper warns him of the Elector of Saxony's secret plan to retrieve the paper after his burial, and the note is signed "Your Elizabeth."[56] Kohlhaas cannot grasp what the castellan is saying about the woman's identity. Before he turns his head to the scaffold, Kohlhaas unseals the paper and reads it. Then, "fixing his gaze steadily on the man with the blue and white plumes [the Elector of Saxony] who is already beginning to harbour sweet hopes, he [sticks] it in his mouth and swallow[s] it."[57]

The paradox in *Michael Kohlhaas* is that while his revenge is far from being transgressive (as he insists on submitting to the law), his *story* transgresses the boundary between literature and history (which has no place for figures like the gypsy woman). John R. Cary argues that there are two invisible powers that engineer Kohlhaas's revenge: one is the power of the dead that returns alive, and the other is pure chance.[58] We could understand these powers by using Freud's term "the uncanny."[59] The gypsy woman is the representative power of the cultural margin, the feminine, the absolute other; she is the double of Kohlhaas's wife, and therefore is ghostly and mythical. Calculating modernity gives way to uncanny modernity regarding Kohlhaas's resistance.

Freud notices that in German, the word "*unheimlich*" (uncanny), the negation of the word "*heimlich*" (homely, familiar), collides with the meaning of "homely": the uncanny as the familiar and unfamiliar at the same time.[60] He argues that there is something uncanny around the traces of something desirable repressed in the past, which keeps on returning in the form of chance encounters.[61] It is the uncanny that informs the sense that Kohlhaas's revenge is not engineered by detailed planning, but by a force represented by the gypsy woman, who resembles Kohlhaas's dead wife. This power of the uncanny, of chance, of the irrational, also makes possible and complicates Kohlhaas's revenge. Turned upside down, the plot includes comic elements and chance incidents that are crucial to Kohlhaas's revenge. This carnivalesque mode uses a tiny incident to turn the main plot into an uncanny story. The effect is so great that the main plot can no longer support the subplot's supernatural tendency. As the protagonist in this detour, the gypsy woman's power even tears apart the narrative itself. The very notion of justice is problematized when the revenger is eventually executed, as if saying he is devoured by the very notion of justice.

The power of the dead returning to life is instanced in the Dresden market scene in which Kohlhaas is asked to identify his horses from the hands of the knacker. The animals are so worn out that they seem "on the point of dropping down dead at any minute,"[62] a pair of horses "on whose account the state [has] been rocked to its very foundations."[63] The incident turns out to be a riot because the Elector of Saxony's Chamberlain is not sensitive to the people's fear and contempt of the horses, as they are technically dead if they have been handed over to the knacker. Although the horses' appearance is not described directly in the market place when Kohlhaas is asked to identify them, it is described as going "against all custom and decency"[64] for the Chamberlain's groom to touch them. So, for the people in Dresden, the horses are technically dead unless their honor is restored by a ritual, alluded to at the end of the story, when they at last appear before Kohlhaas' eyes. They are outside the community, just as Kohlhaas is an outcast.

There is something uncanny about the horses in the sense (on the narrative level) that they disappear and return more and more frequently, and at the end are restored physically and spiritually, "now shining with health and pawing the ground with their hooves"[65] where they were once "a pair of scrawny, warn-out nags, their bones protruding like pegs you could have hung things on, their manes and coats matted together from lack of care and grooming."[66] And after the Dresden market scene, the horses are described as dead by Count Kallheim in response to the Elector of Saxony's enquiry of the feasibility of providing monetary compensation, as "in any legal sense they are dead because they have no value, and they will be physically dead too before they can be taken from the knacker's yard to their lordships' stables."[67] So, given the various extreme changes in condition, the horses are "magical and mysterious."[68] In an earlier incident, at Jüterbock, a dead stag appears unexpectedly (dragged by the butcher's dog) as a sign to prove the gypsy woman's predictive power when she is challenged by the Elector of Brandenburg. If we take into account that Kohlhaas is sentenced to death in the farmhouse at Dahme, Kohlhaas is also by that time on the side of the uncanny; so is the gypsy woman, in the form of the resurrected Lisbeth. All of these otherworldly powers make Kohlhaas's quest for justice possible, the incalculable nature of which therefore begins to show.[69]

It is the power of the uncanny that restores justice, while the power of chance subverts the notion of justice. If Cary is right, that the ending of *Michael Kohlhaas* indeed "leaves the source and nature of justice as mysterious as ever,"[70] we may argue that even if justice is restored, it can be achieved only through revenge (whether by law or by personal action), and that the concept of justice is also strange, beyond the bound of rationality, uncanny. The power of pure chance is not necessarily just; in fact, it is unjust if we consider the representation of the two Electors. The Elector of Saxony at the end is "physically and mentally a broken man,"[71] whereas the Elector of Brandenburg, whose bodyguard kills Kohlhaas's wife—the act that actually sets off his revenge—is on the side of justice by this stage. Brandenburg is the true cause of Kohlhaas' suffering, but it is Saxony that ultimately suffers most. If we consider in defence of the Elector of Brandenburg, that he actually does not know what his guard had done to Lisbeth and is therefore not responsible for her death, we can argue equally that the

Elector of Saxony is not responsible, since—according to Luther—he does not know it is "the state officials [who] suppress lawsuits behind his back or make a mockery of his otherwise sacred name without his knowledge."[72] The two Electors are neither particularly corrupt nor particularly good. It is pure chance, as the narrator says—"it happened at this time"[73]—that Poland and the House of Saxony are in dispute, and that Brandenburg can take advantage of this to make common cause with the Poles.

It is not just coincidences and the ghostly which are uncanny, but also the text itself. The most important act of writing in the novella is the prophecy written by the gypsy woman, and that belongs to the other realm in which the story operates. The story is initiated by Kohlhaas's lack of a permit, which is a "mere fabrication,"[74] and ends with the swallowing of the gypsy woman's paper.[75] The novella shows how an illegibility in the center of the text is exposed when the text is read repeatedly. Hillis Miller argues that the text of *Michael Kohlhaas* posits a new law in literary study as long as it is not rationalized in the institution of literary studies.[76] The heterogeneity of the text performs in the reading of it as long as no "justified" reading is given. The eating of the paper enables Kohlhaas to make words act, but the act requires him to be beheaded. The reading of the gypsy woman's paper acts as an emblem of law: it is that which cannot be read, but possesses power because of both its readability and its unreadability. By eating the paper, the subject submits to the law, and yet revolutionizes his own body to make the paper and the text performative. The text includes law, history, the "old chronicle," and the novella itself.

4. Conclusion

The power of the uncanny operates a vengeance not in the name of justice. It is Kohlhaas who demands justice to be restored even to himself, and that brings about his own death. He willingly accepts his beheading, and at the same time he takes revenge on a person who does not necessarily deserve the revenge. As a war machine, he is lost before he starts, as Deleuze and Guattari maintain. His resistance ends up assisting the head of state. Julian Reid compares Deleuze's war machine with the Nietzschean "struggle of free men" against the forces of *ressentiment*' and argues that Deleuze is inspired by Nietzsche to "differentiate[s] between the warrior-thought of Nietzsche and the legislator-thought of the Enlightenment."[77] Kohlhaas as a war machine could be understood as a way of going beyond *ressentiment*.

Notes

1. Heinrich von Kleist, "*Michael Kohlhaas*," in *The Marquise of O-' and Other Stories*, trans. David Luke and Nigel Reeves (Harmondsworth: Penguin, 1978), 114–213 (114).
2. Critics usually regard the novella's narrative as two parallel parts: the realistic style associated with Kohlhaas's quest and the fantastic style with the gypsy woman. For example, the translators of the novella call the gypsy woman episode a "bizarre and fantastic sub-plot." David Luke and Nigel Reeves (trans.), "Introduction," in *"The Marquise of O-" and Other Stories* (Harmondsworth: Penguin, 1978), 7–49 (27). Also, Henry Pickford distinguishes the two styles as the "primary" (documentary, historical chronicle) and "secondary" (fairy tale) narratives. Henry Pickford, "Thinking with Kleist: *Michael Kohlhaas* and Moral Luck," *The German Quarterly* vol. 86, no. 4 (Fall 2013): 381–403 (398).
3. Jacques Derrida, *The Death Penalty*, 2 vols., ed. Geoffrey Bennington, Marc Crépon, and Thomas Dutoit, trans. Peggy Kamuf (Chicago and London: The University of Chicago Press, 2014), vol. 1, 107.
4. Gilles Deleuze and Félix Guattari, *A Thousand Plateaus: Capitalism and Schizophrenia*, trans. Brian Massumi (London: The Athlone Press, 1980), 355.
5. Friedrich Nietzsche, *Thus Spoke Zarathustra*, trans. Graham Parkes (Oxford: Oxford University Press, 2005), Part 2, Section 20, 121.
6. Nietzsche, "*On the Genealogy of Morals*," in *On the Genealogy of Morals and Ecce Homo*, trans. and ed. Walter Kaufmann and R. J. Hollingdale (New York: Vintage, 1989), Essay 1, Part 3, 44.
7. Kleist, "*Michael Kohlhaas*," 118.
8. Kleist, "*Michael Kohlhaas*," 143.
9. Kleist, "*Michael Kohlhaas*," 148.
10. Kleist, "*Michael Kohlhaas*," 149; 150.
11. Kleist, "*Michael Kohlhaas*," 155.
12. Kleist, "*Michael Kohlhaas*," 137.
13. Kleist, "*Michael Kohlhaas*," 185.
14. Kleist, "*Michael Kohlhaas*," 204.
15. Kleist, "*Michael Kohlhaas*," 114, my emphasis.
16. It remains a matter of debate whether or not Kleist read Immanuel Kant (1724–1804), whose three Critiques were published from 1781 to 1790. For the extent to which Kleist was influenced by Kantian thoughts, see D. F. S. Scott, "Heinrich von Kleist's Kant Crisis," *The Modern Language Review* vol. 42, no. 4 (October 1947): 474–84.
17. Kleist, "*Michael Kohlhaas*," 120.
18. Kleist, "*Michael Kohlhaas*," 121.

19 Immanuel Kant, "Foundations of the Metaphysics of Morals (1785)," in *Critique of Practical Reason and Other Writings in Moral Philosophy*, trans. and ed. Lewis White Beck (London: The University of Chicago Press, 1949), iv, 413, 73.
20 Kant, *Critique of Practical Reason and Other Writings in Moral Philosophy*, trans. and ed. Lewis White Beck (London: The University of Chicago Press, 1949), v.81, 188.
21 Andreas Gailus, *Passions of the Sign: Revolution and Language in Kant, Goethe, and Kleist* (Baltimore: The John Hopkins University Press, 2006), 27.
22 Gailus, *Passions of the Sign,* 117.
23 Kant, *Critique of Practical Reason*, v.89, 195.
24 Gailus, *Passions of the Sign*, 117.
25 Gailus, *Passions of the Sign*, 118.
26 Gailus, *Passions of the Sign*, 118–19, original emphasis.
27 Martin Luther addressing Kohlhaas in an open letter; see Kleist, "*Michael Kohlhaas*," 149.
28 For an account of how Enlightenment thought arrives at such definition of man, especially the role played by law, see Zeev Sternhell, *The Anti-Enlightenment Tradition*, trans. David Maisel (New Haven & London: Yale University Press, 2010), 52.
29 Lacan maintains that Kant's *Critique of Practical Reason* should be read together with Sade's *Philosophy in the Bedroom*. See Jacques Lacan, "Kant with Sade," in *Écrits*, trans. Bruce Fink (New York and London: W. W. Norton & Co., 2006), 645–68.
30 Nietzsche, "*On the Genealogy of Morals*," 2. 6. 501.
31 Stephen Greenblatt, "Murdering Peasants: Status, Genre, and the Representation of Rebellion." *Representation* 1 (February 1983): 1–29 (7).
32 Martin Luther, "Against the Robbing and Murdering Hordes of Peasants," in *Luther's Works*, 55 vols., ed. Helmut T. Lehmann (Philadelphia: Fortress Press, 1967), vol. 46, 50.
33 Kleist, "*Michael Kohlhaas*," 156.
34 Kleist, "*Michael Kohlhaas*," 152.
35 Kleist, "*Michael Kohlhaas*," 156, my emphasis.
36 Kleist, "*Michael Kohlhaas*," 152.
37 Kleist, "*Michael Kohlhaas*," 153.
38 Margarete Landwehr maintains that "Kleist exposes the limitations of the law (and of language) by portraying the legal/illegal dichotomy demarcating justice from revenge as arbitrary and reductive explanations of behaviour." See Landwehr, "The Mysterious Gypsy in Kleist's *Michael Kohlhaas*: The Disintegration of Legal and Linguistic Boundaries." *Monatshefte* vol. 84, no. 4 (Winter 1992): 431–46 (436).
39 Kleist, "*Michael Kohlhaas*," 176.
40 Kleist, "*Michael Kohlhaas*," 148.
41 Deleuze and Guattari, *A Thousand Plateaus,* 355, original emphasis.

42 Deleuze and Guattari, *A Thousand Plateaus*, 356.
43 Deleuze and Guattari, *A Thousand Plateaus*, 356.
44 Apart from being uncanny, there is another dimension in the gypsy woman episode. J. Hillis Miller argues that the episode is "performative," in the sense that the telling makes something happen. *Michael Kohlhaas* "establishes the law of the absence, unavailability, or failure of the law" (103–04). See J. Hillis Miller, *Topographies* (Stanford: Stanford University Press, 1995), 80–104.
45 Kleist, "*Michael Kohlhaas*," 186, my emphasis.
46 Kleist, "*Michael Kohlhaas*," 188.
47 Kleist, "*Michael Kohlhaas*," 190.
48 Kleist, "*Michael Kohlhaas*," 192.
49 Kleist, "*Michael Kohlhaas*," 195.
50 Kleist, "*Michael Kohlhaas*," 201.
51 Kleist, "*Michael Kohlhaas*," 205–06.
52 Kleist, "*Michael Kohlhaas*," 206.
53 Sternhell, *The Anti-Enlightenment Tradition*, 104.
54 Antony Stephens, *Heinrich von Kleist*, 251.
55 Charles Dickens, *Nicholas Nickleby* (London: Penguin, 2005), 530. See also Neil Forsyth, "Wonderful Chains: Dickens and Coincidence." *Modern Philology* vol. 83, no. 2 (November 1985): 151–65.
56 Kleist, "*Michael Kohlhaas*," 210. The text remains ambiguous whether or not the signed "Your Elizabeth" signifies Kohlhaas' wife "Lisbeth."
57 Kleist, "*Michael Kohlhaas*," 213.
58 John R. Cary, "A Reading of Kleist's *Michael Kohlhaas*." *PMLA* vol. 85, no. 2 (Mar 1970): 212–18.
59 Sigmund Freud, "The 'Uncanny,'" in *The Standard Edition of the Complete Psychological Works of Sigmund Freud vol. 17 (1917-1919)*, trans. James Strachey et al. (London: The Hogarth Press, 2001), 217–56. For a full account of the uncanny and alienation in *Michael Kohlhaas*, see Richard Kuhns, "The Strangeness of Justice: Reading *Michael Kohlhaas*." *New Literary History* vol. 15, no. 1 (Autumn 1983): 81–4. There is a contradiction in the sense of justice to be achieved, as noted by Kuhns, who argues that "Justice is done out of strangeness . . . . Neither belief in legal rationality nor faith in divine righteousness would allow us to find an appropriate set of feelings toward Kohlhaas's death" (88). See also Jo Collins and John Jervis (eds), *Uncanny Modernity: Cultural Theories, Modern Anxieties* (New York: Palgrave Macmillan, 2008).
60 Freud, "The 'Uncanny,'" 226.
61 Freud, "The 'Uncanny,'" 245.
62 Kleist, "*Michael Kohlhaas*," 166.
63 Kleist, "*Michael Kohlhaas*," 166.
64 Kleist, "*Michael Kohlhaas*," 170.

65 Kleist, "*Michael Kohlhaas*," 211.
66 Kleist, "*Michael Kohlhaas*," 119.
67 Kleist, "*Michael Kohlhaas*," 173.
68 Kuhns, "The Strangeness of Justice," 81.
69 For an account on how the Gypsies and Bohemia become images of "counterculturalism" in the youth movement of 1830 and the European revolution of 1848, see Evelyn Gould, *The Fate of Carmen* (Baltimore and London: The Johns Hopkins University Press, 1996), ch.1.
70 Cary, "A Reading of Kleist's *Michael Kohlhaas*," 218.
71 Kleist, "*Michael Kohlhaas*," 213.
72 Kleist, "*Michael Kohlhaas*," 153.
73 Kleist, "*Michael Kohlhaas*," 186.
74 Kleist, "*Michael Kohlhaas*," 118.
75 Clayton Koelb observes that Kleist's novella "is a tale of reading and writing," arguing that it is this "mere fabrication" which motivates the narrative, and that invites various forms of writings, including contracts, writs, letters, petitions, declarations, notices, proclamations, certificates, passports, reports, sentences, prophecy, and finally the chronicle itself. Kohlhaas's final eating of the paper is an act of incorporation, which incorporates himself into the body of history. See Koelb, "Incorporating the Text: Kleist's *Michael Kohlhaas*," *PMLA* vol. 105, no. 5 (Oct 1990): 1098–1107 (1105).
76 J. Hillis Miller, *Topographies*, 103–04.
77 Julian Reid, "Deleuze's War Machine: Nomadism Against the State," *Millennium: Journal of International Studies* vol. 32, no. 1 (2003): 57–85 (60, 77). See also Gilles Deleuze, *Nietzsche and Philosophy*, trans. Hugh Tomlinson (London: Continuum, 2007).

Bibliography

Cary, John R. "A Reading of Kleist's 'Michael Kohlhaas.'" *PMLA* 85.2 (Mar 1970): 212–18.
Collins, Jo, and John Jervis, eds. *Uncanny Modernity: Cultural Theories, Modern Anxieties*. New York: Palgrave Macmillan, 2008.
David, Luke, and Nigel Reeves. "Introduction," in *The Marquise of O-' and Other Stories*, trans. David Luke and Nigel Reeves. Harmondsworth: Penguin, 1978, 7–49.
Derrida, Jacques. *The Death Penalty*, 2 vols., ed. Geoffrey Bennington, Marc Crépon, and Thomas Dutoit, trans. Peggy Kamuf. Chicago and London: The University of Chicago Press, 2014, vol. 1, 107.
Deleuze, Gilles, and Félix Guattari. *A Thousand Plateaus: Capitalism and Schizophrenia*, trans. Brian Massumi. London: The Athlone Press, 1980.
Deleuze, Gilles. *Nietzsche and Philosophy*, trans. Hugh Tomlinson. London: Continuum, 2007.

Dickens, Charles. *Nicholas Nickleby*. London: Penguin, 2005.
Forsyth, Neil. "Wonderful Chains: Dickens and Coincidence." *Modern Philology*, vol. 83, no. 2 (November 1985): 151–65.
Freud, Sigmund "The 'Uncanny,'" in *The Standard Edition of the Complete Psychological Works of Sigmund Freud vol. 17 (1917–1919)*, trans. James Strachey et al. London: The Hogarth Press, 2001.
Gailus, Andreas. *Passions of the Sign: Revolution and Language in Kant, Goethe, and Kleist*. Baltimore: The John Hopkins University Press, 2006.
Gould, Evelyn. *The Fate of Carmen*, Baltimore and London: The Johns Hopkins University Press, 1996.
Greenblatt, Stephen. "Murdering Peasants: Status, Genre, and The Representation of Rebellion." *Representation* 1 (Feb 1983): 1–29.
Kant, Immanuel. "Foundations of the Metaphysics of Morals" (1785), in *Critique of Practical Reason and Other Writings in Moral Philosophy*, trans. and ed. Lewis White Beck. London: The University of Chicago Press, 1949.
Kant, Immanuel. *Critique of Practical Reason and Other Writings in Moral Philosophy*, trans. and ed. Lewis White Beck. London: The University of Chicago Press, 1949.
Kleist, Heinrich von. "*Michael Kohlhaas*," in "*The Marquise of O-' and Other Story*, trans. David Luke and Nigel Reeves. Harmondsworth: Penguin, 1978.
Koelb, Clayton. "Incorporating the Text: Kleist's Michael Kohlhaas." *PMLA* vol. 105, no. 5 (Oct 1990): 1098–1107.
Kuhns, Richard. *New Literary History* vol. 15, no. 1 (*Autumn* 1983): 73–91 (81–4).
Lacan, Jacques. "Kant with Sade," in *Écrits*, trans. Bruce Fink. New York and London: W. W. Norton & Co., 2006.
Landwehr, Margarete. "The Mysterious Gypsy in Kleist's *Michael Kohlhaas*: The Disintegration of Legal and Linguistic Boundaries." *Monatshefte* vol. 84, no. 4 (Winter 1992): 431–46.
Luther, Martin. "Against the Robbing and Murdering Hordes of Peasants," in *Luther's Works*, 55 vols., ed. Helmut T. Lehmann. Philadelphia: Fortress Press, 1967.
Miller, J. Hillis. *Topographies*. Stanford: Stanford University Press, 1995.
Nietzsche, Friedrich. "*Thus Spoke Zarathustra*," in *The Portable Nietzsche*, trans. and ed. Walter Kaufmann. Harmondsworth: Penguin, 1976.
Nietzsche, Friedrich. "*On the Genealogy of Morals*," in *On the Genealogy of Morals and Ecce Homo*, trans. and ed. Walter Kaufmann and R. J. Hollingdale. New York: Vintage, 1989.
Pickford, Henry. "Thinking with Kleist: Michael Kohlhaas and Moral Luck." *The German Quarterly* vol. 86, no. 4 (Fall 2013): 381–403 (398).
Reid, Julian. "Deleuze's War Machine: Nomadism Against the State." *Millennium: Journal of International Studies* vol. 32, no. 1 (2003): 57–85 (60 and 77).
Sternhell, Zeev. *The Anti-Enlightenment Tradition*, trans. David Maisel. New Haven & London: Yale University Press, 2010.

10

Resistance in the Mysticism of Kabir and Jaspers

Amita Valmiki

The concept of resistance is understood in different ways in relation to its use in different circumstances. Generally speaking, the concept has a dual aspect: first, it refers to the rebel taking action against an atrocious regime; and second, it refers to the regime's resistance against the rebels. Obviously, action against the atrocious regime is affirmative, in the sense of pursuing justice and establishing a just society, while the regime's resistance may lack this affirmative dimension. This text concentrates on social resistance by comparing the writings of Kabir (c. 1440–1518), the mystic-saint from North India, and Karl Jaspers (1883–1969), a German philosopher in the existentialist tradition.

Throughout the centuries, history has proven that resistance has been part of human beings´ ingrained "virtue" (if I am allowed to use the term). Thus, it is a truism to say that resistance is the action taken by individuals and groups when they perceive an existing phenomenon to pose a threat, a sort of intimidation to the existing scenario; and the perception of such threat elicits resistance. M. K. Gandhi, B. R. Ambedkar, and Karl Marx all resisted the existing morphology of their times by either using the weapon of non-violent resistance (*satyagraha*/ holding on to truth/soul force or truth force) or by adopting a different religion— in their cases, Neo-Buddhism or revolution respectively.

Andrew Reeve believed that political philosophy focuses on two sides of the same coin: one is what we ought to do; and the other what we *actually* do. It is a shibboleth that philosophy is positioned and swayed by political activity. Though philosophy stands on a progressive pedestal, it is often contaminated by the power-politics of a particular perspective. Marx was not against theoretical philosophy, but asked for a suitable philosophical doctrine.[3] This is quite similar to Ambedkar's reasoning. In connection to the political aspect of resistance, its social aspect needs to be discussed since these two domains overlap and share many traits. Hobbes' philosophy is crucial at this juncture. His political philosophy stands in contrast to many other political thinkers, including some who lived after his time. Thus, Hobbes' philosophy could be considered as rebellious not only against Plato and Aristotle, but also against Locke, Rousseau, Kant, and even Rawls. Instead of resisting "the absolute sovereign," Hobbes' "social contract theory" asks for submission to the sovereign authority. For Hobbes, resistance should be understood in a social context, and thus to resist man's "real nature" is selfish. Therefore, to avoid a war-like situation, surrendering oneself to authority seems to be the best possible solution as it curbs the natural instincts and avoids unnecessary bloodshed. Though criticized severely, Hobbes' understanding of resistance is very different to that of his predecessors or successors. As noted in the book *Hobbes and the Law of Nature*,

> J. W. N. Watkins argued that Hobbes's laws of nature are not moral but prudential, and resemble a doctor's orders to a patient rather than moral rules.[4]

In the social domain, over the years resistance has been manifested in many of the realms of social life; for example, between rigid orthodox patriarchs and social reformers, between conventionalists and liberals, or between religious orthodoxies and revolutionary saints and mystics (those who rebelled against prevailing fundamentalism and fanaticism to create space for religious freedom and community, thereby leading to harmony). Groups of philosophers are no exception to this form of social resistance. For instance, the empiricist John Locke spoke firmly about the rights of citizens against their oppressive dictators. He argued that rulers who violates the human rights of their citizens in fact violate the bond of trust authorized to them. Thus, one has the right to revoke a tyrant's commands. Jean-Jacques Rousseau maintained that humanity had in fact become enslaved by political, cultural, legal, and economic customs and institutions. Therefore, resistance to this kind of tyrannical and oppressive regime is necessary for any civilization. According to him, therefore, both individualist and republican conceptions in politics and in the social sphere should join forces to secure for the democratic rights of every citizen.

Revisiting Gandhi, his socio-political resistance towards the imperial rule of the British was *satyagraha* (as noted earlier), a "non-violent resistance" or "civil resistance." He brought about the amalgamation of socio-political action and spirituality, once thought to be an impossible activity, but manifested successfully by Gandhi. His resistance movement would be customized and deployed all over the world; later it was adopted by Martin Luther King, Jr. and Nelson Mandela. It commanded respect from philosophers and reformers globally. He questioned and broke the traditional mold of religious formalism to ascend towards spiritualism. Leo Strauss, a German Jew, can be compared to Gandhi as he too was critical of existing dogma and adopted Socratic political philosophy. His views created bitter opposition in academia and intellectual circles during his lifetime. The abiding theme of Strauss' mature philosophic thinking was what he called the "theologico-political problem"; one that is quite similar to a problem formulated by Spinoza. This position is also very similar to Kabir's and Jaspers', as we shall see later.

The revolutionary activity of mystics who resisted superstitions in Indian society led to a "reformation" that heralded positive change.[5] For example, the Northern Indian bhakti movement (the path of devotion) was championed by Kabir, Guru Nanak (founder of Sikhism), and others: these mystics/saints spoke the language of the masses, breaking the shackles of high-caste Brahmins' authority over worshipping God in highly Sanskritized language.[6]

Kabir, a great mystic from Benares (Uttar Pradesh, Northern India), talked about the ecstatic experience of the "Real," the "Truth," or the "God."[7] For him, the rituals and practices of different religions had no use "if the purpose of mental one-pointed concentration on God was forgotten." Although little is known about Kabir's personal history, it is thought that he was born to a family of Muslim weavers (or brought up in one). If this is the case, his family was most probably recent converts from the prevalent faith of the common people of the time, in which Gorakhanath was held in great reverence. Therefore, they worshipped both Allah (the God of Muslims) and Ram (the God of Hindus).[8] Kabir disliked the bigotry and superstitions of all formal religions, as he influenced by both the *bhakti* (devotion) of Vaisnavism and Islamic *Sufism*. His writing was completely devotional, and he named his Lord as *"Allah-Ram."* As a result, however, he was persecuted by both Hindus and Muslims. S. N. Dasgupta remarks:

> With him (Kabir) and his followers, such as Ruidas and Dadu, we find a religion which shook off all the traditional limitations of formal religions, with their belief in revealed books and their acceptance of mythological stories, and dogmas and creeds that often obscure the purity of the religious light......When Kabir's parents found that they could not subdue his Hindu tendencies they wanted to circumcise him, and at this he said:
>
>> Whence have come the Hindus and Mussulmans? Who hath put them in their different ways?
>>
>> Having thought and reflected in thy heart, answer this—who shall obtain Heaven and who Hell.
>>
>> *Bijak*[9]

The subjective inwardness in relation to God that was upheld by Kabir's predecessors was popularized by Kabir himself. We find in him an open challenge to the existing socio-philosophical ideologies that existed at that time. The resistance to orthodoxies and dogmatic conventions is very obvious in Kabir's writings and had been initiated by Kabir's so-called teachers. As P. D. Barthwal notes:

> These precursors of Kabir represent an intermediate position between *Saguna* (qualified) and the *Nirgunas* (unqualified) schools......The tendency to break the bond of caste in the sphere of religion, Monism, the all-absorbing Love of God and a quietistic and resigned life, is all there. These teachers can, thus be said to have prepared a path......for Kabir, who carried these tendencies to the extreme.[10]

Kabir says:

> I searched for God for years and years and I could not find him. Then I dropped the whole idea and I became still and loving.........Now I know the way......... it is not in formalities, but in an informal friendliness with the existence.[11]

So, Kabir in fact recommended *bhakti marga* (the path of devotion) as he felt that only the path of devotion exalts man, and elevates him from a mundane level to spiritual heights while (existentially speaking) still remaining very much grounded to this world. (This view coincides with the "theistic existentialism" of Søren Kierkegaard and Karl Jaspers.) Kabir's resistance has been truly reformatory, however. His writings seem to show the same rebellious zeal of the *Lokayat* (the *Charvaka* philosophy of materialism in Indian philosophy), although of course we must not forget the core difference between these two philosophical approaches.[12] His resistance to rigid conventions, and his demonstration of the path for salvation, are revealed in various collections of Kabir's songs:

1. *Bijak* (of *Kabir panth* [sect]);
2. Songs in *Adi Guru Granth*; and
3. The *Kabir Granthavali* (questionable authenticity)—compiled by Dadu Panthis, followers of the sixteenth-century saint, Dadu.

His reformatory writings show us his theistic existential character. Kabir denounced vigorously religious practices followed by Hindus at that time,[14] resisting the organized religion that did not allow an individual to take flight and transcend the boundaries created by the authoritarians. Therefore, his poems are more about a socio-political struggle that later settles in a realm of spirituality that is accessible to all, especially the marginalized and the subalterns. Kabir believed in "dialogical communication," and therefore he recited his poems (to his disciples, who wrote them down later) in the vernacular language with which most people were familiar. Jaspers adopted a similar approach when he acquainted his readers with the concept of symbols and ciphers. These would transcend the objectification of religious language to reinstate the universal code of communication, which is an ongoing process. The ciphers would accentuate a much-needed dialogue between various thought systems in order to create a level playing field on which all could live in harmony leading to a balanced and fair society. In Kabir's time, many dialects and languages were spoken in Northern India. This enhanced the poetic language and simultaneously brought people together; another aspect shared with Jaspers and his take on religious philosophy.

Like Kabir, Jaspers resisted the formalistic religion that promised to make spiritual experience accessible to all, but failed to do so. For Jaspers, formalized religion is based on objectified truths that do not accept the diverse ways in which truth is verbalized. Like Jaspers, Kabir believed in complete "unity" as a concept that one cannot arrive at by arguments. Like Kierkegaard and Jaspers, Kabir also believed in the "inwardness" of subjective consciousness where God-realization can occur. The mystics believed that they sang these songs because "Truth requires to be sung." St. Dyaneshwar (from Maharashtra, Western India) said: "There is no bondage or liberation, there is nothing to accomplish. There is only the joy of expounding." Therefore, there are no rational arguments. Both the mystics' and the existentialists' approach belittled the importance of reason, and both also emphasize that everyone has the choice to "become." Saints of the medieval period in India believed that becoming is realizing the Truth that is One, while existentialists concentrated on the universal concept of becoming. Though the joy of becoming is immense for the mystics, the existentialists may say that joy may or may not follow in the process of becoming. Again, both emphasize the concept of "hope" that exists for all to become. But the "essence" of becoming for Kabir (or for any mystic) is "God," while the existentialists "denied the essence." While the two perspectives may differ, both are characterized by an open approach that emphasizes freedom. Whether freedom causes joy or dread is inconsequential. Kabir says in *Bijak*:

> You and I are of one blood; one life exists in us both. From one mother the world is born, what then is this sense of separateness? We have all come from the same country; we all drink from the same fountain; yet the ignorant divide us into innumerable sects.[15]

Karl Jaspers began his career as a psychologist, but by the early 1920s he turned to philosophy. He exerted influence on three major branches of philosophy, namely, epistemology, the philosophy of religion, and political theory. It was not philosophy, but his writings on governmental conditions in Germany and his ideas on reorienting moral-democratic education that would later influence the Federal Republic of Germany. Jaspers' contribution to German politics is noteworthy. His approach, dealing with pragmatic field of politics, was more like that of a mystic's since he did not back any single faith. This is suggestive of his predilection for both North German Protestantism and the religious philosophy of Kant and Kierkegaard. His philosophical contributions had already been indicated in his books on psychology, especially his book *Psychology of World Views* (1919). Though not well documented, the existential viewpoint is reflected in this book, which he developed in his typical "Jaspers-style". He resisted punctilious philosophy, instead examining and deliberating on anthropological and experiential questions in philosophy. For this he was reprimanded by Rickert and Husserl as they thought he vitiated the philosophical realm by treating the subject as he had other disciplines. Jaspers restored Kantian philosophy though he disagreed with Neo-Kantians. His emphasis was not on Kant's deontological approach in a categorically imperative and formalist doctrine of self-legislation; instead, Jaspers brought Kant's metaphysical experience, Kant's spontaneously decisive freedom, and Kant's views on an authentic inner life (in analogy to the mystic Kabir's disagreement with similar positions) to the forefront of his thought. It is therefore very conspicuous that Jaspers shared the mystics' approach. Since Jaspers was married to a Jewish woman, he felt quite threatened by Heidegger's support for the National Socialists in 1933. Jaspers' works in the 1930s thus carefully avoided political theories, and he concentrated more on the inner religious aspects of his philosophy. Again, it is quite apparent that he was dazzled more by Nietzsche's psychological approach than his philosophical perspective, believing that philosophical claims need no formal verification but should instead be understood as expressions of "underlying mental dispositions." So, like Nietzsche, he believed in resisting both rationalistic Puritanism and the idea of realizing the absolute truth or absolute knowledge. Like Heidegger and Nietzsche, he could not accept that human existential issues should be tackled externally and indifferently; but they need to be viewed literally, i.e., "existentially." There was one element of Nietzsche's philosophy that Jaspers could not align himself with, namely Nietzsche's "naturalistic vitalism." Thus, he emphasized "subjectivity" as a locus of truthful transcendence like Kierkegaard, a theme which is not found in Nietzsche's work. Schelling also exerted some influence on

Jaspers. Like Schelling, Jaspers believed in re-invoking the truth of revelation, that which goes against the rational evidence of epistemology. This again reveals a similarity to Kabir's mystical philosophy of resisting formal epistemological approach towards existential issues.[16]

Though influenced by these philosophers, he was very much averse to the idea of "progress" and "transcending the past" in order to move toward true philosophy. He was really interested in the quest for eternal truth and the great traditions offered by China, India, and the West. The fact that these philosophical traditions offered relative truths about the ultimate of which they had revelations was specific to their state of mind and condition. These are different paths leading to the Eternal Truth. According to Jaspers, the claim made by philosophers in the past to offer "true doctrinal philosophy" was inadmissible; for him, they offered only relative truths. This made Jaspers distinct as a mystic who refutes doctrinal and theoretical graduation——that is, where one tends to become fanatic and where "real communication" is impossible. This reminds us of mystics singing and narrating stories in the vernacular. In his book *The Perennial Scope of Philosophy*, Jaspers says: "Philosophy proper must reject the idea of progress, which is sound for sciences."[17]

The concentration on "being" where existential problems can be addressed created a link between Jaspers and the mystics (especially Kabir, Guru Nanak, and others) who spoke of "*Ek Nirankara*" (the only unqualified One). He believed that the sciences in recent times have inclined to become communal (as they have drawn boundaries among themselves). Stumpf, in his book *Socrates to Sartre*, points out that Jaspers (like the mystics) wanted to have a unified, secular, and single science of Being. He writes:

> It would seem that a universal science could be formulated by bringing together in some form of unity of all the particular sciences. Could not the unified sciences constitute a single science of being, of total reality?[18]

According to Jaspers, though science has expanded its reach by ways of discoveries and inventions, sciences are succored by a constrained boundary-line formula that withhold them to accept the Being as Being; [this is to say that its objectivity seems to be a hurdle where it does not allow "to think beyond".] Sciences objectify the Being (name it be called God, or Ultimate, or Absolute) and structure "the Being" which applies more generally to all beings. This makes the Being too local. It is thus obvious that Jaspers resisted natural sciences. Therefore, at this juncture, it has to be noted that Jaspers believed that philosophy has to revisit its own field and reconstruct itself. Unlike the mystical approach,

"Science, he argues, is sub-philosophic because it does not deal with the unique inner experiences of concrete individual human beings."[19] As an existential philosopher, Jaspers believed that "Existence is something that can never become a mere object; it is the 'Source' whence springs my thinking and acting." At one point he could connect with Hegel, who raised philosophy to the level of science. This is because Jaspers could objectify truth as he insisted (again like the mystics) that "truth is subjectivity";

> ...that philosophizing means communicating not about objects or objective knowledge but about the content of personal awareness produced by the individual's inner constitution. Existential thinking, says Jaspers, is "the philosophic practice of life.[20]

Thus, Jaspers arrives at the conception of "genuine communication." Existence does not mean hoarding knowledge, ego-centrism, and their consequence in solipsism; but it involves a dialogue between individuals to further the genuine communication of "becoming real."

Jaspers' theistic existentialism accentuates "interpersonal communication studies" through the inner self that does not claim any finalizability where there are restraints on the thought process. Instead, he encourages the embrace of the manifold and variegated expressions on the same subject, viz. God. Therefore, one has to enlarge and widen the horizons of our "disciplinary thinking." As a result, there is a constant need to encourage communication and thereby build up the solidarity that leads to humanity. Like Kabir, who believed in humane values—which evolve through ongoing communication—a complimentary echo can be found in Jaspers' "dialogical possibilities of Existenz-with-Existenz communication."[21] Jaspers was of the opinion that the philosopher should be concerned with devising and construing an environment where universal dialogical communication between human beings is possible. He notes that the channel of the possibility of universal communication is bifurcated in dual spheres; one is "philosophical logic," which is inevitably ingrained in every discourse; the second is that as human beings we are subject to a common historical background that built a common platform for all to live together. This commonplace pre-historical to historical journey in the sphere of philosophy lays the groundwork for universal communication. Therefore, the basic concern of philosophy is to evolve plausibility and credibility to increase the expanse of communication to the widest possible extent.[22] At this very juncture, a person reaches a state of illumination; a radiance where s/he is introduced to oneself and to others in a fundamental way. In the process, one recognizes oneself in relation to others.

Jaspers distinguished orthodox and dogmatic religious ideas among the multiple symbols and myths found in different religions and religious sub-sects that allow one to search in his/her own way to the Ultimate that is God. He believed that the authentic revelation of true faith would neither encroach on nor remove human freedom. Thus, one has to keep a positive view of religion and God. Views on both can be expressed in a variety of ways, on many levels, and in many languages. Because of these views, though Jaspers personally never appreciated being described as "existentialist," his entry into existentialism cannot be underestimated. He took the human situation into consideration. The human angle is always reflected in his philosophy (this may be because he was psychiatrist and lectured on psychology.) A human being can be considered an empirical entity, living in this world of experience. Through observation, Jaspers discovered the unique character of human consciousness, which he called *Bewusstein*, "and most importantly and distinctively how finite incompleteness of human being points to a transcendent 'beyond'; name 'it' God." The personal intuitive aspect is very important for realization of the truth. His book *The Perennial Scope of Philosophy* (pg. 19f) mentions following points:

1. His dissatisfaction with his empirical achievements.
2. His submission to the absolute (the unconditional moral imperative).
3. His urge for unity—pressing beyond all empirical diversity to its basic source.
4. His indefinable memory of pre-creation, pre-world existence (comparable to Platonic reminiscence).
5. His consciousness of immortality (i.e., his writing even now above time while living in time.).[23]

To conclude, it seems that both Kabir and Jaspers have one very important thing in common, and that is they are both "existential mystics." Their main interest was not theoretical but practical. "Karl Jaspers was a Christian much as he was a German. This is because he never chose to be either. He applied both the terms to himself descriptively rather than eulogistically.' So, one can even call them both spiritual or existential pragmatists.

Both Jaspers and Kabir emphasize the will rather than either intellect or intuition. I think the same parallel can be drawn among all theistic mystics, as well as theistic existentialists like Jaspers and Kierkegaard. Like Kabir, Jaspers writing is mystical, and there is unavoidable paradox and a "Necessary Paradox," which is beyond logic-proper and is over-simplistic. Both have a mystic's approach;[25] that do not try to prove the "object" of the "subjective experience" but feel strongly that the intuitive "real truth" demands boundless communication. For Jaspers, it is a rational demand that one has to transgress the boundaries for communication. The resistance that is revealed in Jaspers and Kabir is quite explicit in their need and demand for ongoing communication that is been thwarted by authoritarian religions of the world. In Jaspers' case, the orthodox Christian faith, and in Kabir's case, the caste system in Hinduism and Hindu-Muslim dichotomy, restricts communication as one cannot transcend the paradigm set by religious scriptures; where "the others" are not included. By means of communication, this boundary is transcended. In the course of this transcendence (term it "becoming" in an existential sense), the benefits are twofold for an individual: first, the self-realization of the infinite power of dialogue that lies within the individual; and second, through dialogical communication the realization of "existential universal camaraderie," that feeling of common cause that leads to solidarity.[26] The echo of this can be heard in Kabir, who (as noted) communicated to his disciples via innumerable poems in regional languages so that through dialogical communication he could establish "unity in diversity" (as emphasized by Jaspers.).

The resistance to a formal pattern of thinking, or conventional means of practice in religion, or in the social sphere where religion plays a pivotal role, is characteristic of both Jaspers and Kabir. By communicating, this mentality can be overcome.

The existential love affair that they both built up in their writings is a clear resistance to the traditional way of seeking "the truth." Jaspers is averse to the concept of (so-called) "progress" and one finds the same in Kabir.

Both Jaspers and Kabir resisted ghettoization—along with the "clash of civilizations"—and the resultant consequence of their resistance is an acceptance of pluralistic cultures as highly beneficial and enticing. They rebelled against the conservative attitude of preserving individual identity and belittling "the others," be they religious, ethnic, racial, caste-based, or gender-related. Organized belief systems typically deprecates the subalterns, those who are always left behind and persecuted. Tagore described this kind of organized religious sect as "an artificial average."[29] This runs parallel to Jaspers' ideology. Like Kabir, Jaspers believed in fellowship and cooperation, which binds the populace in a loving and patient bond.[30] For harmony and peace in society, it is vital to live with differences and to celebrate diversity is very important. In fact, the first lecture delivered by Jaspers was entitled "Illumination of Existence," and he preferred that title to "Existential Philosophy" because he resisted the idea of a "formal school of thought" that might impose barriers on people, confining their thought to the four "walls" of the school. Kabir was similar inasmuch as he was also against "the six schools of Indian philosophy."[31] Both believed that "existence" is always an actuality with open-ended possibilities. This kind of actual existence transcends the way of projecting oneself beyond the objective self and empirical world; but this can be achieved in actual empirical existence. Jaspers believed that one can accept different traditions, as all strive to achieve transcendental truth. Therefore, philosophical faith and religious faith *can* come together without betraying each other. Kabir also chose an interiorized view of religion, where the *sahaja* ("easy," "spontaneous," or "with oneself") state was ultimate aim of devotion. One experiences this state through freedom, which Jaspers advocated.

To sum up the ideas of Jaspers in Kabir's words:

> . . . The *Puran* (Hindu Holy Scriptures) and *Koran* are mere words; lifting up the curtain I have seen. . .[32]

Kabir articulated what he experienced; and he knew that all other things are not true (the scriptural arguments put forward by the upper-caste Brahmins), a fact which Jaspers would probably not deny. Like Socrates and Kierkegaard, Jaspers and Kabir brought high philosophy down to the earth and sowed the seeds of mutual love, understanding, concord, and peace among in their respective countries.

The two quotes at the beginning of the article are very relevant in the context of Jaspers and Kabir. For Jaspers, mere existence has no meaning in itself; it is meaningful in affinity with "freedom," however. Similarly, power has the potential to curb freedom, rendering existence meaningless. Power needs supportive means of communication, the dialogue that restores unity. Therefore, one has to decipher the ciphers and symbols used in many religions to make the hidden meaning more vocal and bring forth unification.[33] Kabir shares those sentiments. As noted above, Kabir recited his poems in a variety of Northern Indian spoken dialects, which helped him encourage the social metamorphosis needed during his lifetime (and which is equally relevant today). For him, these dialects deliver the nuances of virtues that have absolute existential value. Therefore, the second quote (at the chapter's beginning) by Gandhi reveals the close links between Jaspers and Kabir: adaptability cannot be taken for granted as mere imitation, but matures to generate the potential to resist something that shuns the freedom of dialogue-based communication and champions the cause of unification and solidarity. Kabir and Jaspers agree on the concept of "encompassing", which permeates everything and from which existential issues are comprehended and transcended; ultimately, both nod to *Existenz* (as the *Dasein* or *Geist* that has transcended the objectivized world while being grounded in the empirical world).[34] In both Kabir[35] and Jaspers, as an existential individual "I" am introduced to myself; but knowing exists only in relation to "others". Therefore, *Dasein* is known in its bona fide form as *Existenz*, as being among other beings in the world. At any case, and at any cost, resistance to canonical version transcends to evolve a better human culture.

Notes

1. Wayne Gabardi, *Negotiating Postmodernism* (Minnesota: University of Minnesota Press, 2001), 76.
2. N. B. Sen, *Wit and Wisdom of Mahatma Gandhi* (New Delhi: New Book Society of India, 1960), 26.
3. Iain McLean and Alistair McMillan, *The Concise Oxford Dictionary of Politics* [Third Edition] (Oxford: Oxford University Press, 2009).
4. Perez Zagorin, *Hobbes and the Law of Nature* (Princeton: Princeton University Press, 2009), 108.
5. This feature of resistance is very typical to mystic/saints as mentioned by R. D. Ranade in his book *Mysticism in Maharashtra* (1933); Ranade mentions very empathetically that there are two types of mystics, one, quietist and the other, activist. But without moral concern a mystic is not a mystic.
6. *Sanskrit*—a language spoken only by upper-caste Brahmins, scholars, teachers and kings, overall, the elite group.
7. The words Real, Truth, and God are usually capitalized, as these words in the *Vedanta* philosophy of Hinduism believe that the world is unreal, fleeting, and that the only "real" part of it is God, called Brahman.
8. Though there is difference of opinion among scholars regarding the historical data.
9. Surendranath N. Dasgupta, *Hindu Mysticism* (New Delhi: Allied Publishers, 1926), 157–8.
10. Pitambar D. Barthwal, *Traditions of Indian Mysticism* (New Delhi: Heritage Publishers, 1978), 250.
11. *Sacred Space: Breaking Conventions*. Agencies. Times of India (April 11, 2000).
12. As the *Charvakas* belong to atheistic non-Vedic materialist school of Indian philosophy, while Kabir embraces the concept of God though absolutely in an unconventional manner.
13. Max Arthur Macauliffe, *The Sikh Religion: It's Gurus, Sacred Writings and Authors*, vol. 6. (New York: Cambridge University Press, 2013), 145.
14. Swami Abhayananda, *History of Mysticism: The Unchanging Testament* (Olympia, WA: Atma Books, 2012.), 33.
15. Jaspers' resistance to formal religion is palpable in the quote, "…he (Jaspers) argues that religion is essentially justified by its ability to speak about human qualities, which

cannot be reduced to formal motives or attributes. It forfeits this justification, however, not where it spiritualizes material human interests, but where it objectivizes the possibilities of human transcendence by incarcerating these in doctrines, dogma or laws." See Chris Thornhill, *Karl Jaspers: Politics and Metaphysics* (New York: Routledge, 2002), 209. The same rebellious demeanor is found in Kabir while confronting formal religion. Kabir too overtly resisted the ceremonial religion with fixated dogmas. As noted by Evelyn Underhill, "…the whole approach of piety, Hindu and Moslem alike—the temple and mosque, idol and holy water, scriptures and priests—were denounced by this inconveniently clear-sighted poet (Kabir) as mere substitute for reality, dead things intervening between the soul and its love— …" See Rabindranath Tagore, *Songs of Kabir* (Auckland: The Floating Press, 2010), 14.

16 Karl Jaspers, *The Perennial Scope of Philosophy*, trans. by R. Manheim (London: Routledge and Kegan Paul, 1950), 166–7.

17 Samuel Enoch, Stumpf, *Socrates to Sartre* (New York: McGraw-Hill Book Company, 1966), 461–2.

18 Ibid, 462.

19 Ibid, 463.

20 Ronald D, Gordon, "Karl Jaspers: Existential Philosopher of Dialogical Communication." *South Communication Journal* vol. 65, no. 2–3 (2000), 105–18.

21 Jaspers, Ashton (trans.) *Philosophy and the World; Selected Essays by Karl Jaspers* (Washington, DC: A Gateway Edition, 1989), 296–7.

22 Jaspers, *The Perennial Scope of Philosophy*.

23 Vinay Dharwadkar, Kabir, *The Weaver's Song*, trans. Vinay Dharwadkar (New Delhi: Penguin Books, 2003), 202.

24 "The Greek word *mysterion* is rooted in the other Greek words such as *mystos* which means 'keeping silence' and *myein* which means 'closed lips.'" Michael Hickey, *Get Real: Reality and Mystery* (Maryland: University Press of America, Inc., 2011), 37.

25 Jaspers notes, "The demand for boundless communication testifies to the solidarity of all men in potential understanding." See Jaspers, *The Origin and Goal of History* (Westport, CT: Greenwood Press, 1976), 247.

26 Abhayananda, *History of Mysticism: The Unchanging Testament* (Bijak, Sabda 43), 333.

27 Tagore notes that Kabir did not accept the absolute claim of theism nor of monism; in fact, he cannot be quoted as a founder of any sect. Therefore, Kabir could affirm of a pluralistic society with difference of opinion. He was a poet who spoke like a Sufi that appealed to inter-caste and inter-religious congregation. See Manjulika Ghosh and Raghunath Ghosh, *Language and Interpretation: Hermeneutics from East–West Perspective* (New Delhi: North Book Centre, 2007), 220.

28 Huber comments, "Hannah Arendt as well as Karl Jaspers unfolded the insight that moral responsibility transcends the realm of individually accountable actions." See Wolfgang Huber, *Christian Responsibility and Communicative Freedom: A Challenge*

for the Pluralistic Societies, Collected Essays, ed. Willem Fourie (LIT Verlag, 2012), 11. Arendt and Jaspers resonates to Kabir's literature where they were against Germany's anti-Semitic approach; whereas Kabir was against the dominance of upper-caste Brahmins and the ill feeling between Hindus and Muslims.

29 The six schools of Indian philosophy are: *Nyaya, Vaisheshika, Samkhya, Yoga, Purva Mimamsa,* and *Uttar Mimamsa* (also known as *Vedanta* or *Upanishads*); these are orthodox, *Vedic,* and theistic schools based on formalistic philosophy.

30 Vinay Dharwadkar Kabir, trans. Tagore, *Songs of Kabir* (New Delhi: Penguin Books, 2003), 14–15.

31 It is "illustrated via Jaspers that ciphers or symbols illuminate each representative universe of discourse." See Robert Allen Evans, *Responsible Talk about God* (Leiden: E. J. Brill, 1973), 155.

32 William Desmond notes, "We humans are not the encompassing of Encompassing. Still there is a sense in which for Jaspers we humans are the Encompassing; we are not determinate things but as *Existenz* participants in the truth in this more ultimate sense." See Claire Elise Katz and Lara Trout, *Emmanuel Levinas: Critical Assessments of Leading Philosophers* (London : Routledge, 2005), 96.

33 Evelyn Underhill records, "That Supreme Spirit whom he (Kabir) knew and adored, and to whose joyous friendship he sought to induct the souls of other men, transcended all metaphysical categories and all creedal definitions. See O'Neill, *Unstruck Music: Spiritual Poetry of Kabir* (J. P. O'Neill, 2008), 12.

34 NOTE TEXT MISSING

35 NOTE TEXT MISSING

Bibliography

Abhayananda, Swami. *History of Mysticism: The Unchanging Testament.* Olympia, WA: Atma Books, 2012.

Jaspers, Karl. *Philosophy and the World: Selected Essays by Karl Jaspers*, trans. E. B. Ashton. Washington, DC: A Gateway Edition, 1989.

Barthwal, Pitambar D. *Traditions of Indian Mysticism.* New Delhi: Heritage Publishers, 1978.

Dasgupta, Surendranath N. *Hindu Mysticism.* New Delhi: Allied Publishers, 1926.

Evans, Robert Allen. *Responsible Talk about God.* Leiden: E. J. Brill, 1973.

Gabardi, Wayne. *Negotiating Postmodernism.* Minnesota: University of Minnesota Press, 2001.

Ghosh, Manjulika, and Raghunath Ghosh. *Language and Interpretation: Hermeneutics from East–West Perspective* (N. B. U. Studies in Philosophy, vol. 11). New Delhi: North Book Centre, 2007.

Gordon, Ronald D. "Karl Jaspers: Existential Philosopher of Dialogical Communication." *South Communication Journal* vol. 65, no. 2–3 (2000): 105–18.

Hickey, Michael. *Get Real: Reality and Mystery.* Maryland: University Press of America, Inc., 2011.

Huber, Wolfgang. *Christian Responsibility and Communicative Freedom: A Challenge for the Pluralistic Societies,* Collected Essays, ed. Willem Fourie (LIT Verlag, 2012).

Jaspers, Karl. *The Perennial Scope of Philosophy,* trans. R. Manheim. London: Routledge and Kegan Paul, 1950.

Jaspers, Karl. *The Origin and Goal of History.* Westport, CT: Greenwood Press, 1976.

Kabir, Vinay Dharwadkar, trans. *The Weaver's Song.* New Delhi: Penguin Books, 2003.

Katz, Claire Elise, ed. *Emmanuel Levinas: Critical Assessments of Leading Philosophers.* New York: Routledge, 2005.

Macauliffe, Max Arthur. *The Sikh Religion: Its Gurus, Sacred Writings and Authors,* Vol. 6. New York: Cambridge University Press, 2013.

McLean, Iain, and Alistair McMillan. *The Concise Oxford Dictionary of Politics,* 3rd edn. Oxford: Oxford University Press, 2009.

Miron, Ronny. *Karl Jaspers: From Selfhood to Being.* New York: Rodopi, 2012.

O'Neill, J. P., ed. *Unstruck Music: Spiritual Poetry of Kabir.* J. P. O'Neill, Morrisville: Lulu, 2008.

Ranade, Ramchandra D. *Indian Mysticism in Maharashtra,* 1st edn. Pune: Aryabhusan Press, 1933.

Sen, N. B. *Wit and Wisdom of Mahatma Gandhi.* New Delhi: New Book Society of India, 1960.

Stumpf, Samuel Enoch. *Socrates to Sartre.* New York: McGraw-Hill Book Company, 1966.

Tagore, Rabindranath. *Songs of Kabir.* Auckland The Floating Press, 2010.

Thornhill, Chris. *Karl Jaspers: Politics and Metaphysics.* New York: Routledge, 2002.

Zagorin, Perez. *Hobbes and the Law of Nature.* Princeton: Princeton University Press, 2009.

11

On Dissent Against Public Health Interventions: A Phenomenological Perspective During the COVID-19 Pandemic

Tarun Kattumana and Thomas Byrne

0. Introduction

Amidst the emergence of the COVID-19 pandemic in 2020, governments around the world set in place large-scale non-pharmaceutical interventions. These interventions refer to activities or mobilizations undertaken to reduce the basic reproduction rate, or average number of infections generated by each infected case over the course of their infection, and limit the spread of the virus.[1] Examples include social distancing, large-scale lockdowns and school closures among others. While these measures were implemented based on the best scientific understanding available at the time, protests sprang up in response across different parts of the world. These protests occurred in two waves: the first during April and May of 2020 as the initial COVID-19 control measures were implemented; the second in early August responding to the extension of said restrictions.[2] At the time of writing in mid-March of 2021, a third wave of protests can be seen in certain parts of the world.

There has been a tendency for the media narrative in the Global North to characterize dissent against public health interventions as an expression of those emphasizing individual liberties over public benefits. However, it is crucial to recognize said dissent as a global phenomenon with diverse context specific motivations. In this chapter, we follow Edmund Husserl's phenomenology to argue that under specific conditions public health directives can be alienating and exacerbate the context specific drivers enabling dissent against large-scale non-pharmaceutical interventions.

Before proceeding, it is important to briefly clarify Husserl's reputation as a philosopher concerned with transcendental consciousness. To many it maybe unclear what resources such a perspective can have for distinctly political issues, especially given that Husserl himself acknowledged that his philosophy is "entirely unpolitical."[3] Indeed, as Karl Schuhmann notes, the term *Politik* appears fewer than ten times in the first twenty Husserliana volumes.[4] Furthermore, any reference to transcendental philosophy immediately evokes a Kantian heritage that is commonly understood to emphasize individual subjectivity at the cost of inter-subjectivity. We begin by clarifying the inter-subjective character of Husserl's transcendental phenomenology before briefly discussing the political potential of his thought.

Husserl is well aware that invoking the term "transcendental" evokes Immanuel Kant. Yet, Husserl is no Kantian, despite having a complicated relationship with Kant's philosophy.[5] One important point of difference is that Husserl uses the term transcendental in the "broadest sense."[6] Much can be said (and indeed has been) of Husserl's "broad" use of the term and it will not be possible to give a detailed account here. It suffices for our current purposes to note that as a part of this broadening Husserl sees his philosophy as focusing on the inter-subjective character of the transcendental. As Husserl notes in his lecture *Kant and the Idea of the Transcendental*,

> Finally, one must pay careful attention to the fact that a possible transcendental subjectivity in general is not merely to be understood as a possible singular but rather also as a possible communicative subjectivity, and primarily as one such that purely according to consciousness, that is to say, through possible intersubjective acts of consciousness, it encloses together into a possible *allness* a multiplicity of individual transcendental subjects.[7]

In line with this insight, Dan Zahavi argues that this "occasions an intersubjective transformation of transcendental philosophy" that results in a "*decisive broadening* of the transcendental field of objects."[8] Consequently, Husserl enables investigations into domains that "a classical (Kantian) transcendental philosophy would relegate to an empirical-mundane province without any transcendental relevance."[9] Therefore, Husserl's transcendental phenomenology is applied to "domains previously reserved for other disciplines such as psychopathology, sociology, anthropology, and ethnology."[10] This broadening of transcendental inquiry has many implications. Zahavi argues that "*one of the most radical consequences* of an inter-subjective transformation of transcendental philosophy consists precisely *in opening up the possibility of dissent.*"[11] In other words, the transcendental character of Husserl's phenomenology does not disqualify, but rather enriches the application of Husserlian concepts to the issue of dissent.

At the same time, however, we stress that it is not necessary to employ methodological components of transcendental phenomenology (epoché and the reduction) when applying Husserlian phenomenology. Zahavi notes that applied phenomenology must take a heterodox approach that is selective in its use of phenomenological material or run the risk of misconstruing concepts/operations originally formulated for specific philosophical purposes.[12] Accordingly, our application of Husserlian phenomenology to dissent against large-scale COVID-19 control measures restricts its focus to the implications that follow from Husserl's critical treatment of science in his last major work *The Crisis of the European sciences and Transcendental Phenomenology* (henceforth: *Crisis*).

With respect to the political potential of Husserl's phenomenology, we follow Don Idhe's claim that Husserl holds a "distinctly contemporary" view of science, i.e., that "science presupposes and remains cultural, historical, anthropological all the way down."[13] However, emphasizing the inter-subjective features of science does not imply compromising or downplaying value of scientific inquiry. Indeed, the defense of the latter is central to Husserl's philosophy. At a time when the political and social character of science is no longer restricted to academic discourse, but is an explicit feature of public contestations, we argue that Husserl's philosophy of science has the potential to be sensitive towards both the loss of confidence in scientific expertise and the motivations underlying public contestations of science. This chapter extends the political potential of Husserl's treatment of science in the *Crisis*, where Philip Buckley argues

> ... that part of the crisis consists in being lost in the social and political world, that is, in accepting what has been given as self-evident ... thereby formulating solutions to the crisis in the same worn out and sedimented concepts and language that are in fact part of the problem.[14]

To clarify, and following Sean Petranovich, Husserl distinguishes between two kinds of crises.[15] The first, or explicit crises, are immediately evident to us when we live through them. Writing in the 1930s, the explicit crises worrying Husserl's contemporaries included economic, political, cultural, and religious crises. The explicit crisis examined in this paper is the COVID-19 pandemic and dissent against much needed public health recommendations. The second, or implicit crises, are not immediately evident to those living through them. An example of this, following Husserl's discussion, is the crisis of the sciences. Husserl argues that, because the sciences have been undeniably successful, we have come to overlook the fact that the sciences are undergoing a crisis.[16] This overlooking results in our forgetting that we might be extending worn out concepts resulting from a misguided scientific world-view, that inadvertently contributes to and is part of the explicit crises that confront us. Our working example in this chapter is the implicit crisis concerning the discrepancy between the population level benefits vis-à-vis individual/group level benefits of public health interventions. The discrepancy between these two levels underlies the explicit crisis of the COVID-19 pandemic and dissent against public health recommendations.

This chapter is divided into four sections. The first section explicates Husserl's analysis of the crisis of the European sciences. Section two sets up a parallel between Galilean science and public health to extend the implications of Husserl's critical treatment of the former to the latter. This section examines the discrepancy between the population and individual level benefits of COVID-19 control measures following the prevention paradox as influencially articulated by epidemiologist Geoffrey Rose. The third section situates our analysis within the context of dissent against large-scale public health interventions around the world. The paper concludes with a brief consideration of the scope and implications of our argument.

To avoid possible misunderstandings, we make three preliminary clarifications. First, it is important to stress that there is a significant gap between identifying the conditions that enable dissent against public health recommendations and endorsing the specific forms that such dissent can take. In this chapter we undertake the former task (identifying conditions) and not the latter (endorsing the specific forms such dissent can take, e.g., protests that deny the need or value of COVID-19 restrictions). Second, when extending Husserl's phenomenology to global political concerns we are confronted by Husserl's Eurocentrism. While identifying potential resources in Husserl's thought, it is important to not overlook these limitations. What we hope to undertake is, following Kenneth Knies, a highly *qualified* account that fully acknowledges Husserl's blind-spots.[17] Lastly, the present analysis concerns dissent against COVID-19 control measures in 2020. Further research is required when extending our claims toward more recent examples of dissent against public health directives.

1. Husserl's Historical Treatment of the Crisis of the Sciences

Husserl's investigation of the crisis of the sciences, is primarily undertaken in his long and famous analysis of Galileo Galilei. Husserl's analysis of Galileo may initially seem to take the discussion away from the COVID-19 pandemic. Yet, crises do not take place in a vacuum and the current crisis is the result of a long historical process. As such, any critical examination of this contemporary crisis, which focuses only on how it manifests itself in the present, would likely be limited. Accordingly, by discussing Husserl's historical analysis of the sciences, we will begin to outline the conditions that set the stage for the emergence of dissent during the COVID-19 pandemic, which we will explicitly discuss in section three.

Before proceeding, a quick methodological clarification on Husserl's analysis of Galileo. Husserl does not put forward a strict historical treatment if this is understood to mean a factual study of the life and times of Galileo Galilei. As Husserl notes,

> All [merely] factual history remains incomprehensible because, always merely drawing its conclusions naively and straightforwardly from facts, it never makes thematic the general ground of meaning upon which all such conclusions rest.[18]

A factual analysis of history would focus on certain events and figures. However, it is never clear why these moments as opposed to others are worthy of our attention. In contrast, Husserl's treatment undertakes the task of "*clarifying history by inquiring back into the primal establishment of the goals, which bind together the chain of future generations.*"[19] In other words, Husserl's analysis of history concerns how certain events are meaningful and continue to influence the attitudes of successive generations. In this regard, Husserl does not undertake a factual study of the historical Galileo, but is better understood analyzing Galileo's legacy that continues to influence and be meaningful to those inside and outside of the scientific community. To avoid possible confusion, we will use the term "Galilean science" as opposed to Galileo when referring to the object of Husserl's inquiry.[20]

1.1 Husserl's Critical Analysis of Galilean Science

Although an inherently complicated episode in the history of science, the tension between Galileo and the Catholic Church continues to be meaningfully associated with the rise of scientific authority in the West and its claims to objective truth.[21] Additionally, Galilean science inaugurated an influential "style" of scientific thinking that, as Aron Gurwitsch notes, posits a "cleavage between the world as it presents itself in the perceptual experience of everyday life, and the world as it is in scientific truth."[22] This cleavage was the (indirect) result of scientific investigations that employed specific methods and techniques. In this section, we follow Husserl's attempts to clarify these methods and techniques. Crucial to this clarification is shedding light on the differences between the ideal objects of geometry and the perceptual objects in everyday experience, or the "life-world."

Ideal geometrical shapes are "'pure' shapes which can be drawn in ideal space—'pure' bodies, 'pure' straight lines."[23] They do not vary or change over time. Moreover, pure geometrical objects are never found in our lived experience. We never perceive an ideal straight line, an ideal triangle, or an ideal sphere. In contrast, perceived objects of the life-world are immediately given to and around us, e.g., trees, coastlines, rocks, cars, and so on. Their properties can vary and change over time. In its search for objective knowledge, Galilean science aims to transition from the varying character of our perceptual experiences to invariant truths. This is achieved by executing the technique of idealization, which repeatedly perfects indeterminate and varying aspects of perceptual objects to attain ideal geometrical figures. For instance, the roughly straight line in perceptual experience is constantly perfected to attain an "invariant and never attainable pole" of the most ideal form of straight-ness.[24]

For Husserl, the technique of idealization reduces the inexact features of a perceptual object, or secondary qualities, to its primary qualities. The former refers to qualities like color, that ostensibly pertain only to the subject's relation to the object. However, the subject's perception of color can fluctuate depending on various contextual factors, for example, visibility conditions. Conversely, primary qualities are purportedly mathematizable and understood to inhere in the object independent of a subject's relation to it. In the case of color, the corresponding primary quality would be wavelength. Given that primary qualities can be calculated in an "exact" manner unlike secondary qualities, color is reduced to wavelength for the purposes of precise measurement. Therefore, via the process of idealization, one can execute an "indirect mathematization" of secondary qualities in terms of primary qualities.[25]

Yet, by subsuming all perceptual features of the sensible world under mathematizable primary qualities, secondary qualities eventually attain a reduced status. As the historical Galileo notes, "tastes, odors, colors, etc., are nothing but *empty names* ... they inhere only in the sensitive body, such that *if one removes the animal, then all these qualities are taken away and annihilated.*"[26] In other words, secondary qualities become "empty names" and are not taken to be objectively present in the world. Underlying this outlook is the assumption that only that which inheres in the object, irrespective of the subject, is objectively real. This represents the underlying motivation of Galilean science to achieve the renaissance ideal of a "universal knowledge, [that is] absolutely free from prejudice, of world and man."[27]

However, this accomplishment has its limitations. As previously mentioned, only mathematizable primary qualities fulfil the criteria set by Galilean science. This would imply that the mathematizability of a quality is the measure of its reality. What Galilean science sets out to achieve is to extend this insight from the qualities of individual objects to the concrete world as such.[28] This eventually leads to a complete mathematization of reality where the objective aspects of nature are taken to be those that are mathematical. As Husserl notes,

> Mathematics and mathematical science, as a *garb of ideas* ... encompasses everything which, for scientists and the educated generally, *represents* the life-world, *dresses it up* as "objectively actual and true" nature. It is through the garb of ideas that we take for *true being* what is actually a *method*.[29]

Consequently, Husserl writes that "through Galileo's *mathematization of nature*, *nature itself* is idealized [and] under the guidance of the new mathematics nature itself becomes—to express it in a modern way—a mathematical manifold [*Mannigfaltigkeit*]."[30] In other words, nature becomes a mathematical domain, thereby excluding un-mathematizable features of subjective experience.

1.2 Alienation and the Mathematization of Nature

The above critical treatment of the Galilean mathematization of nature might give the impression that Husserl is against applying mathematics to empirical phenomena. But this is certainly not the case. Husserl has always seen the use of mathematics to understand empirical phenomena as a helpful and indeed, indispensable tool for the success of the sciences. Even in his earliest manuscripts from 1891, Husserl concluded, concerning mathematical symbols in particular,

> Upon the conscious application of symbols, the human intellect raised itself to a new and truly human level. And the progress of intellectual development runs parallel with progress in symbolic technique. The magnificent development of the natural sciences, and that of the technology based upon it, constitute above all else the pride and glory of recent centuries.[31]

Throughout all stages of his oeuvre, Husserl would continue to highlight the value of mathematics and mathematization. Toward the end of his philosophical career, Husserl claims that mathematics was an accomplishment that represented a "triumph of the human spirit" and its development has allowed for "inductions with an efficiency, a degree of probability, a precision, and a computability that were simply unimaginable in earlier times."[32]

What directs Husserl's criticism is the privileging of mathematizable qualities over secondary qualities. In other words, Husserl is critical of granting mathematizable qualities the status of objective reality while reducing the secondary qualities, and by extension common-sense experience in the lifeworld, to the status of an "empty name."[33] To be precise, Husserl has a problem with,

> ... the *surreptitious substitution* of the mathematically substructed world of idealities for the only real world, the one that is actually given through perception, that is ever experienced and experienceable- our everyday life-world.[34]

The life-world represents the larger whole. As seen above, the mathematical world of idealities is made possible by idealizing objects in the life-world. These idealities are thus dependent upon the life-world. The surreptitious substitution consists in the mathematical world of idealities being detached from the life-world and then being conceived of as an all-encapsulating whole that can act as a substitute for the life-world—and all this, despite only being a dependent part of the life-world.

The problem with the "surreptitious substitution" is that Galilean science instantiates a *fundamental reversal*: what is a dependent part is taken to be the whole, one that relegates the subjective experience of the world to mere opinion, prejudice, or subjective appearance. As Gary Gutting notes: "[a]ny scientific description of the world is essentially incomplete in that it inevitably omits major dimensions of our life-world experiences."[35] A famous instantiation of this is physicist Arthur Eddington's distinction between two tables.[36] The first table, or commonplace table, refers to the substantial perceptual object that is a part of our daily activities in the life-world. The second (scientific) table differs in that it is not given to the senses and consists mostly of emptiness scattered with electric charges. Eddington sees the scientific table as "objectively real" while the common place table gets relegated to the status of mere subjective appearance. This represents the surreptitious substitution where the scientific table claims the status of being objective reality, thus leaving no legitimate place for the common place table of the life-world.

When a subject's concrete ways of engaging with objects, such as tables, are eschewed from scientific reality, it becomes unclear what the subject is dealing with when interacting with the common-place table. This has a double effect. First, the domain of scientific reality can become *enigmatic* when it diverges from everyday experience. Second, as Richard Tiezen notes following Husserl, this could lead to a form of "alienation from reality" for the subject when her everyday experience is not taken as a part of objective reality.[37]

Admittedly, the implications of feeling alienated from the enigmatic character of Eddington's scientific table can seem trivial and may not lead to widespread dissent. But the alienation experienced is far from trivial when science deals with matters of social impact, like control measures during the COVID-19 pandemic. In the next section, we will identify further features of scientific practice that enables dissent against expert recommendations when combined with the alienating and enigmatic character of scientific objectivity.

2. Parallel between Husserl's critique of Galilean science and public health

In this section, we extend the implications of Husserl's treatment of Galilean science towards public health practice. In making this extension, we are not claiming that the specifics of Galilean science applies to public health. To avoid such conflation, we first identify the basis for a parallel between Galilean science and public health. Beginning with a brief description of public health, Dean Rickles notes that:

> Public health concerns the health of *populations* of people, rather than *individual* people... [i]t deals with *aggregates* of measurements of properties of individuals and is therefore a statistical science, facing the many (technical, epistemological, and metaphysical) problems that this inevitably involves.[38]

Public health deals with populations rather than individuals and is a mathematical science that is heavily reliant on statistics. In other words, like Galilean science, public health practice is heavily reliant on sophisticated mathematics which is applied to populations in the empirical world. As Rickles notes, this makes public health liable to certain criticisms. Before elaborating on how said criticisms resonate with Husserl's treatment of Galilean science, it is crucial to discuss why public health requires statistics.

Public health is heavily reliant on statistics owing to its focus on populations. This is because the population of a country or region is not immediately given. For instance, strolling along Belgian streets we see individuals or large groups but never the entire population of the Belgium. To constitute the entire population, we start with individuals immediately perceived and extend our horizon to constitute a collective. However, such extensions are not antithetical to perception but are constitutive of its character. As Husserl famously notes: "[e]xternal perception is a constant pretension to accomplish something that, by its very nature, it is not in a position to accomplish".[39] Similarly, public health practitioners are also constrained by the fact that they are dealing with entities that are not directly perceivable. This limitation is overcome by starting with individual level data, aggregating it, and attaining statistical measures that represent the population level. As Daniel Reidpath notes:

> One does not measure the health of a population; one measures the health of individuals and aggregates the data. It is in the process of "rolling up" the individual level data into a single summary statistic that one delivers a measure of population health.[40]

In other words, public health is reliant on statistics as it is the medium through which populations can be intended and studied.

The public health focus on populations rather than individuals is also important in the contexts of pandemics. During a disease outbreak, individuals fall into either the high-risk or low-to-moderate risk categories. Common-sense would see medical interventions being directed at the former, or those at higher risk, rather than the latter. This represents the traditional high-risk strategy. However, epidemiologist Geoffrey Rose influentially proposes a population strategy that operates on the counter-intuitive insight that "*a large number of people at a small risk may give rise to more cases of disease than the small number who are at a high risk*".[41] Consider Rose's example of the occurrence of Down's syndrome births and its relation to maternal age.[42] Mothers under thirty tend to be at minimal risk of such an occurrence at the individual level. But this group sees significantly more births as compared to mothers over forty, who are at higher risk but see lesser number of births. Consequently, mothers under 30 generate half the cases of Down's syndrome births as a group although each individual is at low risk. Similarly, during the COVID-19 pandemic, asymptomatic individuals and those who identified themselves as unlikely to contract SARS-CoV-2 constituted the majority of the population and a majority of the cases.[43] For this reason, Rose emphasises the need for a population strategy, that focuses on reducing the risk of individuals in the low-to-moderate risk group, as a necessary supplement to the more intensive interventions for those at higher risk. Another reason in favour of a population strategy includes the fact that medical personnel and institutions have limited capacities when it comes to identifying those at high risk.[44] Moreover, any screening process would identify borderline cases where it is unclear how to proceed.[45] Lastly, a population strategy is radical in the sense that it "attempts to remove the underlying causes that make the disease common".[46] This is unlike strategies narrowly focusing on high-risk individuals that do not fundamentally engage with the factors that made said individuals highly vulnerable in the first place.[47] For these reasons and more, a population strategy was preferred in the case of the COVID-19 pandemic as it would entail a variety of non-pharmaceutical interventions like social distancing and large-scale lockdowns to deny SARS-CoV-2 new sites of infection and potential mutation.[48]

Despite these benefits, extending Husserl's critical treatment of Galilean science to public health theorizing is useful when population level reasoning aided by statistical factors like relative risk distribution or the rates of incidence within a population are applied uncritically. As previously noted, population health data is attained by "rolling up" individual health data. Accordingly, although population health is indicative of certain health features at the individual level, the two are not synonymous. Overlooking these differences can have important implications in case of serious discrepancies between the population and individual levels. On this point, and despite his support for population strategies, Rose highlights the *prevention paradox* where "a preventative measure that brings large benefits to the community offers little to each participating individual".[49] In other words, benefit at the population level following a preventive measure does not necessarily correlate with benefit for all individuals/groups within that population.

To fully grasp the implications of the paradox, we follow Stephen John in distinguishing between two senses of benefit implicit in Rose's formulation. In the first sense, the benefit of a population strategy is the avoidance of death for those targeted.[50] However, most individuals in a population fall into the low-to-moderate risk group, as was the case during the COVID-19 pandemic. Consequently, death was not perceived to be a real possibility by members of this group and therefore avoiding it did not constitute a significant benefit. The second sense of benefit, follows what John calls an "ex-ante" understanding, where most individuals in the population attain a negligible reduction of risk.[51] In this case, Rose claims that it is plausible for such negligible benefit to be outweighed by the negative consequences of the preventive intervention.[52] As will be seen in the next section, this was especially the case during the COVID-19 pandemic where large-scale non-pharmaceutical interventions were correlated with drastic economic, social, psychological, and political ramifications for individuals/groups in the population.

Here we see a repetition of the implications of, and a parallel with, Husserl's critique of Galilean science. The devastating impact of SARS-CoV-2 and the urgent need for a population strategy that limits its viral spread becomes *enigmatic* amidst a variety of economic, socio-political, and personal crises. In these contexts, Husserl articulates the public perception of science as follows:

> In our vital need—so we are told—this science has nothing to say to us. It excludes in principle precisely the questions which man, given over in our unhappy times to the most portentous upheavals, finds the most burning...[53]

During the "unhappy times" of the COVID-19 pandemic and its "most portentous upheavals," well-intentioned and necessary public health recommendations can seem to overlook the stark realities that accompany their application. Put differently, statistically based population level reasoning is surreptitiously substituted for other context specific ways of relating to the pandemic. If this is followed by experts framing public disagreement or opposition as selfish or lacking in concern for the overall benefit of the population, then complying with public interventions can become *alienating* and set the stage for dissent.

There is potential in Husserl's phenomenology to articulate a positive account of how public health could motivate collective action. A potentially fruitful, and sadly, under-examined aspect of the Husserlian corpus is his nuanced treatment of the concept of motivation.[54] Moreover, in the *Vienna Lecture*, Husserl makes clear his intention of using phenomenology to bring about a total *reorientation* of the task of knowledge towards "a *new sort of praxis*" that is capable of transforming humanity from the *"bottom up."*[55] However, elaborating on this potential for public health interventions is outside the limited ambit of the present chapter, which focuses on the specific conditions under which dissent against public health recommendations emerges.

In the next section, we engage with three types of dissent against public health interventions by considering examples from across the world. The first occurs where the public cannot comply with COVID-19 control measures owing to structural and context specific reasons. When these issues are overlooked and the control measures are imposed, experts and policy makers are perceived to be insensitive to the lived reality of the pandemic. The second concerns how those in power use the threat posed by SARS-CoV-2 to extend and impose their authority in draconian ways, leading to public dissent against the co-opting of public health interventions. The third transpires when political forces use the economic and social distresses brought about by the pandemic to arouse public opposition against scientific institutions and experts.

Before proceeding, it is important to stress the analysis in the next section does not play devil's advocate for those opposing public health recommendations.[56] As just noted, we follow Rose's defense of the numerous benefits of a population strategy. This cannot be legitimately contested in any of the cases that will be discussed in the next section. But following Rose also implies paying need to the prevention paradox where population level benefits of a preventive intervention does not necessarily lead to benefits for individuals/groups in the population. Our approach is limited to identifying those instances where the implementation of social distancing or large-scale lockdowns, when combined with an overlooking of the stark realities that follow, sets the stage for dissent.[57]

3. Protests and the Crisis of the COVID-19 Pandemic

Thomas Carothers and Benjamin Press argue that despite their "shared anti-lockdown theme," there is significant diversity among protests against large-scale COVID-19 control measures.[58] This includes differences in the local circumstances motivating protests and the varying composition of those protesting, from urban elites to the rural poor.[59] Within this wide range, we follow Carothers and Press in identifying *three* sub-types of protests.

(1) The first concerns protests following the devastating socio-economic impact of COVID-19 restrictions. Consider the Indian context, where lockdowns have further marginalized workers in the informal sector, who subsist on daily wage labor, which cannot be undertaken with social distancing.[60] Additionally, those in the informal sector are not always present in official records and thus often overlooked by government initiatives during the pandemic.[61] To emphasize the extent to which this group was overlooked, it is worthwhile to consider the manner in which lockdowns were imposed. India declared a 21-day lockdown at midnight of March 24, 2020. This extended to shutting down public transport, thereby transforming millions of migrant workers into refugees overnight. Unable to survive in the cities, these workers were then forced to walk back to their villages, which were often hundreds of miles away; with many dying on the way.[62] It is impossible to overemphasize a news report noting that "a lockdown to stave off a pandemic is turning into a humanitarian crisis."[63] When the lockdown was extended in May, migrant workers in Mumbai protested by demanding travel back to their homes. This was met with police violence.[64]

In Chile, Magdalena Gil and Eduardo Undurranga note that by "overlooking critical socio-spatial factors such as segregation, sanitation, and overcrowding, decision-makers were blind to the potential consequences of their strategy of localized lockdowns."[65] Around 400,000 households in Chile have more than 2.5 persons per room.[66] In the capital city Santiago, 56 percent of households live in less than 70 square meters and have only one toilet.[67] In these conditions, it is not possible to follow social distancing measures. These structural features were not immediately evident to policy-makers, however, as evidenced by the Chilean health minister's public acceptance of this fact on May 28, 2020.[68] Public demonstrations in light of these events have been met with police violence, with one protester saying: "You go out to ask for bread or say you are hungry, and in response they shoot teargas."[69]

In South Africa, public health efforts were initially lauded for their swift response. However, control measures were not sensitive to the social context and this resulted in aggravating already existing social and economic disparities. The urban poor were confronted with a food crisis that required swift action through emergency relief measures.[70] In some cases, this led to protests when the promise of food parcels never materialized.[71] For these reasons, Alexander Broadbent[72] and colleagues argue that,

> It is unhelpful to characterise lockdown scepticism as a neoliberal political stance. Lockdown is demonstrably not egalitarian in either its costs or its benefits. We must assess lockdowns and other measures holistically, remembering that the costs will mostly fall, as ever, on the global poor.[73]

While this view attempts to understand the drivers of an anti-lockdown sentiment, it has also been criticized for overlooking the specific ways in which COVID-19 disproportionately impacts racial minorities.[74] This resonates with the African American experience in the United States, where the infection rate in black counties is three times higher than white counties, with the mortality rate being six times higher.[75] As Clyde Yancy notes, "if race per se enters this discussion, it is because in so many communities, race determines home."[76] Yancy continues that, being "able to maintain social distancing while working from home, telecommuting, and accepting a furlough from work but indulging in the plethora of virtual social events are issues of privilege. In certain communities these privileges are simply not accessible."[77] Similarly, public health authorities in the UK have reported that persons from Black, Asian, or Minority Ethnic (BAME) backgrounds were at a higher risk of dying from COVID-19 than white British citizens.[78]

The socio-economic devastation of COVID-19 is not restricted to the global south or to minorities in high income countries. In a study designed to be representative of the adult population in the UK, Atchison and colleagues note that while a majority of the respondents were worried about COVID-19, only less than half of the respondents reported adopting social distancing measures.[79]

Further analysis showed that respondents who were separated, divorced, widowed, or never married were less likely to adopt social distancing measures.[80] Those who constituted the lowest household income bracket were six times less likely to work from home. Respondents without a degree level qualification were less likely to be able to work from home as compared to those with a degree.[81]

The COVID-19 Pandemic and public health control measures have been experienced in different ways by different people. For some, the pandemic and its restrictions have been a harsh reminder of the precariousness of their socio-economic status. For others, their structural inability to follow COVID-19 control measures has made explicit that the ability to comply is itself a privilege. When this is coupled with a mischaracterization of the public's inability to comply as a lack of willingness to follow expert recommendations, COVID-19 restrictions become a sign of insensitivity to the stark realities brought about by the pandemic. Consequently, the continued imposition of control measures further exacerbates feelings of exclusion, thereby setting the conditions for emergence of dissent.

(2) The second sub-type of protests react against the co-option of COVID-19 control measures by those in power. In Kenya, protesters accused the Kenyan police of excessively enforcing COVID-19 restrictions that led to avoidable deaths.[82] In the Philippines, Cambodia, and Thailand, the pandemic has been used as an excuse for governments to extend emergency powers.[83] This power was not just used to impose lockdowns, but also to censor and curb dissent against those in power. In Serbia, thousands of protesters opposed President Aleksandar Vučić for imposing restrictions to curb dissent after a contested election.[84]

In the above-mentioned examples, the mapping of COVID-19 restrictions onto previously existing socio-political fault lines have explicitly politicized the pandemic. This further testifies to the feeling that control measures are motivated by political interests and disproportionate to the threat of SARS-CoV-2. Consequently, the threat posed by the pandemic becomes enigmatic and following COVID-19 restrictions becomes alienating, as it implies willfully complying with draconian political interests.

(3) The third and last sub-type of protests generally takes place in high income countries and opposes the manner in which lockdown measures infringe on individual freedoms. These protests can be characterized as "big tent" demonstrations bringing together varying interests from business advocates to vaccine skeptics.[85] In the United States, these protests have also vocalized grievances like the opposition to abortion, immigration, support for Donald Trump, and issues pertaining to the second amendment in the American constitution.[86] Former President Donald Trump contributed to these protests by downplaying the impact of the pandemic,

politicizing COVID-19 control measures, refusing to wear a mask, and disparaging his own public health officials.[87] Additionally, Trump drew strong associations between the state of the economy and public health interventions claiming "'we cannot let the cure be worse than the problem itself'".[88] This intermingling between politicians in power and dissent against public health interventions is not restricted to the United States. In Brazil, President Jair Bolsonaro distanced himself from COVID-19 control measures and encouraged his supporters to ignore these restrictions.[89] In Germany, far-right groups have been accused of instrumentalizing the pandemic to further their message.[90]

Depending on one's ideological lens, these movements are portrayed very differently. For some, these protests represented spontaneous "grassroot" movements. For others, they represented an "AstroTurf" operation funded by interest groups.[91] In both cases, public health recommendations are forced operate within the framework of already existing socio-political polarization. When this is coupled with prominent figures mischaracterizing the intended benefits of COVID-19 restrictions, the stage is set for dissent against public health recommendations.

An objection could be raised that the examples mentioned above concern dissent against government policy rather than science or public health. In response, we argue that a strong distinction between science and government policy is a curious one to draw during a pandemic where scientists have been rightly asked to play an important role in policy-making. For this reason, although it is important to distinguish between science and government policy, we argue that a strong separation between the two is untenable during the COVID-19 pandemic. Furthermore, we note that it has been increasingly hard for the public to differentiate between science and government policy. Especially given that governments have been consistently emphasizing that they are "following the science" or drawing a direct association between scientific policy and the many inequalities exacerbated by the pandemic when it suits their political interests. Given that this chapter focuses on the public perception of COVID-19 control measures, we question the validity of a strong distinction between science and government policy in this regard as well.

4. Conclusion

This chapter represents a preliminary step in extending the potential of Husserl's phenomenology to engage with public contestation of science in general, and public health in particular. Phenomenologically speaking, COVID-19 control measures mean very different things in different contexts. For some, large-scale public health interventions are about limiting the spread of a deadly virus with an extremely high rate of transmission. For others, these control measures highlight their economic and social precarity, becoming an instance where already existing inequalities are exacerbated. In certain cases, public health interventions have been co-opted for draconian political purposes in a manner that was perhaps disproportionate to the threat posed by COVID-19. But not all protests necessarily reflect local concerns manifesting spontaneously, with some examples pointing to instigation and support from interest groups for political purposes. Despite these differences, dissent against public health interventions highlight the implications of Husserl's critical treatment of Galilean science. The surreptitious substitution of population level reasoning for the various context specific ways of relating to the stark realities that follow large-scale public health interventions, set the stage for dissent. Making this claim does not deny our immense gratitude to public health experts, health-care professionals, policy makers, and volunteers who have worked tirelessly to keep us safe from this threatening virus. Instead, we hope to have identified those conditions and instances that limit compliance with COVID-19 control measures and undermine the valiant efforts public health practitioners.

Notes

1 Seth Flaxman et al., "Estimating the Effects of Non-Pharmaceutical Interventions on COVID-19 in Europe." *Nature* vol. 584, no. 7820 (2020): 257
2 Thomas Carothers and Benjamin Press, "The Global Rise of Anti-Lockdown Protests—and What to Do About It." *World Politics News*, October 15, 2020. Available online: https://www.worldpoliticsreview.com/articles/29137/amid-the-covid-19-pandemic-protest-movements-challenge-lockdowns-worldwide (accessed December 14, 2020).
3 Husserl, *Husserliana: Dokumente 3*. Bd. 9. Familienbriefe, ed. Karl Schumann. (Dordrecht; Kluwer, 1999), 9, 244.
4 Karl Schuhmann, *Husserls Staatsphilosophie* (Freiburg: Verlag Karl Alber, 1988), 18; The Husserliana volumes are the main series in which Husserl's works are edited. Volumes contain both previously published books and articles in a critical edition as well as selections from unpublished manuscripts conserved at The Husserl Archives in Leuven.
5 Husserl's engagement with Kantian thought evolved significantly during his lifetime. His early engagements with Kant under the influence of Brentano could be

interpreted as being dismissive. However, there is a greater appreciation, while at the same time, an acknowledgment of crucial differences in works such as *The Idea of Phenomenology*, *Thing and Space*, *First Philosophy* lectures of 1923/24, the *Crisis* and the lecture *Kant and the Idea of the Transcendental*.

6 Edmund Husserl, *Husserliana VI*, 100/1970, *Husserliana VI. Die Krisis der europäischen Wissenschaften und die transzendentale Phänomenologie*, ed. Walter Biemel (The Hague: Martinus Nijhoff, 1976), 97.

7 Husserl, "Kant and the Idea of Transcendental Philosophy," trans. Ted Kein and William Pohl. *The Southwestern Journal of Philosophy* vol. 5, no. 3 (1974): 31.

8 Dan Zahavi, *Husserl and Transcendental Intersubjectivity: A Response to the Linguistic-Pragmatic Critique*. Athens (OH: Ohio University Press, 2001), 86; emphasis added.

9 Zahavi, *Transcendental Intersubjectivity*, 86.

10 Ibid, 86.

11 Ibid, 37; emphasis added. See also Thomas Byrne, "The Meaning of Being: Husserl on Existential Propositions as Predicative Propositions." *Axiomathes* vol. 32 (2020): 123–39.

12 Zahavi, *Transcendental Intersubjectivity*, 37; emphasis added. See also Thomas Byrne, "The Meaning of Being: Husserl on Existential Propositions as Predicative Propositions." *Axiomathes* vol. 32 (2020): 123–39.

12 Zahavi, "Applied Phenomenology: Why It Is Safe to Ignore the Epoché." *Continental Philosophy Review* vol. 54, no. 2 (2021), 270–2.

13 Idhe, "Husserl's Galileo Needed a Telescope!" *Philosophy & Technology* 24 (2011): 75. It is important to stress that Idhe is not a proponent of Husserl's philosophy of science. Furthermore, the essay cited is very critical of Husserl's treatment of Galilean science, which is discussed in the second section of this chapter. Despite this fact, we agree with Idhe that Husserl's treatment of science is similar to contemporary authors like Steve Shapin, Bruno Latour, or Donna Haraway. Moreover, we believe that by capitalizing on the similarity between those works, there is great potential to further extend Husserlian phenomenology to public contestations of science.

14 Phillip Buckley, "Political Aspects of Husserl's Call for Renewal," in *Transitions in Continental Thought*, ed. Arleen B. Dallery, Stephen H. Watson, and E. Marya Bower (New York: SUNY Press, 1994), 8.

15 Sean Petranovich, "Trust and Betrayal from a Husserlian Standpoint," *International Journal of Philosophical Studies* vol. 26, no. 2 (2018): 131.

16 Husserl, *Husserliana VI*, 1/1970, 3.

17 Kenneth Knies, "A Qualified Defense of Husserl's Crisis Concepts." *Metodo. International Studies in Phenomenology and Philosophy* vol. 4, no. 1 (2016): 27–47. See also Byrne, "Husserl's Early Semiotics and Number Signs: Philosophy of Arithmetic through the Lens of 'On the Logic of Signs (Semiotic)." *The Journal of the British Society for Phenomenology* vol. 48, no. 4 (2017): 287–303.

18 Husserl, *Husserliana VI*, 383/1970, 371.
19 Husserl, *Husserliana VI*, 72/1970, 71; emphasis added.
20 Husserl, *Husserliana VI*, 19–20/1970, 22–23.
21 Galileo's confrontation with the Catholic Church led to his condemnation in 1616 and 1633. While the predominant view finds the church was dogmatic in its inability to recognize the Copernican world-view, some historians and philosophers of science see the confrontation differently, arguing that church authorities were bringing to light blindspots in Galileo's understanding of the limits of his experimental method. See Juha Himanka, "Husserl's Argumentation for the Pre-Copernican View of the Earth," *The Review of Metaphysics* vol. 58 (2005): 628.
22 Aron Gurwitsch, *Phenomenology and Theory of Science*, trans. Lester Embree (Evanston: Northwestern University Press, 1974), 34. See Byrne, *Husserl's Early Genealogy*.
23 Husserl, *Husserliana VI*, 21/1970, 25.
24 Ibid, 22/26.
25 Ibid, 34/35.
26 Galilei Galileo, *Essential Galileo*, trans. Maurice Finocchiaro (New York: Hackett, 2008), 185; emphasis added.
27 Husserl, *Husserliana VI*, 6/1970, 8.
28 Ibid, 30/33.
29 Ibid, 50/51; emphasis added.
30 Ibid, 25/23.
31 Husserl, *Husserliana XXII*, 350/1994: 29.
32 Husserl, *Vienna Lecture*, 295.
33 Galileo, *Essential Galileo*, 185.
34 Husserl, *Husserliana VI*, 48–9 (1970): 48–9.
35 Gary Gutting, "Husserl and Scientific Realism." *Philosophy and Phenomenological Research* vol. 39, no. 1 (1978): 43–4.
36 Arthur Eddington, *The Nature of the Physical World*. (London: Kessinger, 2010), ix–x.
37 Richard Tiezen, "Science as a Triumph of the Human Spirit and Science in Crisis: Husserl and the Fortunes of Reason," in *Continental Philosophy of Science*, ed. Gary Guttin (Cambridge: Cambridge University Press, 2005), 109.
38 Dean Rickles, "Public Health," in *Handbook of the Philosophy of Science*, ed. Fred Gifford (Dordrecht: Springer, 2011), 523.
39 Husserl, *Analyses Concerning Passive and Active Synthesis: Lectures on Transcendental Logic*, trans. Antony J. (Steinbock. Springer Netherlands, 2001), 39.
40 Reidpath, "Population Health. More than the Sum of the Parts?" *Journal of Epidemiology & Community Health* vol. 59, no. 10 (2005), 877
41 Rose, "Sick Individuals and Sick Populations." *International Journal of Epidemiology* vol. 30 (2001), 431; emphasis original.
42 Ibid.

43 Gandhi et al., "Asymptomatic transmission, the Achilles' heel of current strategies to control Covid-19." *The New England Journal of Medicine* vol. 382 (2020): 2158–60; Bruckner et al., "SARS-CoV-2: An Empirical Investigation of Rose's Population-Based Logic," in *Epidemiology* vol. 32, no. 6 (2021): 809.
44 Rose, "Sick individuals and sick Populations" 430
45 Ibid.
46 Ibid, 431.
47 Ibid, 430.
48 Halperin, Ibrahim, and Connell, "Geoffrey Rose's Strategy of Prevention Applied to COVID-19." *Health Security* vol. 18, no. 6 (2020): 504.
49 Rose, *Rose's Strategy of Preventive Medicine: The Complete Original Text*, ed. Kay-Tee Khaw and M. G. Marmot, New ed. (Oxford: Oxford University Press, 2008), 47; Rose, "Sick Individuals and Sick Populations" 432.
50 Stephen John, "Why the Prevention Paradox Is a Paradox, and Why We Should Solve It: A Philosophical View." *Preventive Medicine* vol. 53, no. 4–5 (2011): 250.
51 Ibid, 251.
52 Rose, "Sick Individuals and Sick Populations" 432.
53 Husserl, *Husserliana VI* vol. 4 (1970): 6.
54 See Husserl, *Ideas for a Pure Phenomenology and Phenomenological Philosophy. Second Book: Studies in the Phenomenology of Constitution*, trans. Richard Rojcewicz and André Schuwer (Kluwer Academic, 1989), § 54 &56
55 Husserl, *Vienna Lecture*, 299; emphasis added.
56 We see a similar tendency in Husserl's discussion of relativism. In the *Crisis*, Husserl acknowledges the presence of relativism in the life-world. However, the acknowledgement is a limited one that never proceeds to undertake a defense or legitimation of relativism. Additionally, in the sections where the acknowledgment of relativism occurs, Husserl makes it explicitly clear that relativism remains an "embarrassment." This represents a continuity in Husserl's thought from his early refutations of relativism in the *Prolegomena* to *Logical Investigations* to his critical treatment of the same in *Philosophy as a Rigorous Science*. Another instance where Husserl acknowledges the reality of relativism is in his letter to the anthropologist Lucien Lévy-Bruhl. See, Husserl, *Edmund Husserl's letter to Lucien Lévy-Bruhl*. Similarly, Husserl is read more correctly as arguing that there are perpetuated by science that set the stage for dissent. But this dissent is not celebrated or valorized. Rather too much of Husserl's work in the *Crisis* is geared towards helping science improve its engagement with the public and phenomena in the life-world.
57 A similar perspective has been raised when it concerns opposition to COVID-19 vaccines. See Tarun Kattumana, "Understanding the Fear of Vaccines: How to talk about public health in the age of COVID". *Public Seminar*, July 21, 2020. Available online: https://publicseminar.org/essays/understanding-the-fear-of-vaccines/.

58 Thomas Carothers and Benjamin Press, "The Global Rise of Anti-Lockdown Protests—and What to Do About It".
59 Ibid.
60 Howell & Mobarak, "The Benefits and Costs of Social Distancing in High and Low Income Countries," *Transactions of the Royal Society of Tropical Medicine and Hygiene* vol. 0 (2021): 6–7.
61 Ibid, 6–7.
62 Soutik Biswas. "Coronavirus: India's pandemic lockdown turns into a human tragedy," *BBC News,* March 30, 2020.
63 Ibid.
64 Sanjeev Miglani and Rupam Jain, "India extends world's biggest lockdown, ignites protest by migrant workers."
65 Gil and Unduranga, "Covid-19 has exposed how 'The Other Half' (Still) Lives." *Bulletin of Latin American Research* vol. 39 (2020): 30.
66 Ibid, 29.
67 Ibid, 29.
68 Ibid, 29.
69 "Chile police using Covid-19 quarantine as pretext to crush protest, activists say." *The Guardian*, August 26, 2020. Available Online: https://www.theguardian.com/global-development/2020/aug/26/chile-police-covid-19-quarantine-protest.
70 Melissa Leach, et al., "COVID-19: Key Considerations for a Public Health Response." in Briefing, Brighton: Institute of Development Studies (2020), 4.
71 Fiona Anciano, et al., "Beyond trafficking and slavery: 'We are still waiting'—protesting under lockdown in South Africa." *Open Democracy*, April 24, 2020. Available online: https://www.opendemocracy.net/en/beyond-trafficking-and-slavery/we-are-still-waiting-protesting-under-lockdown-in-south-africa/.
72 In the case of Africa, with specific reference to South Africa, Alexander Broadbent has also argued that lockdowns are grossly disproportionate to the threat posed by the pandemic. He claims that COVID-19 is fatal to the elderly who constitute only 3 percent of the South African population, while the rest are forced to confront a recession that could be a matter of life and death given pre-existing social inequalities. See Alex Broadbent, "Lockdown is wrong for Africa." *Mail & Guardian*, April 8, 2020. Available Online: https://mg.co.za/article/2020-04-08-is-lockdown-wrong-for-africa/ (accessed October 3, 2020). Broadbent is not alone in making this point. "The Great Barrington Declaration" sees a group of epidemiologists and public health scientists express "grave concerns about the damaging physical and mental health impacts of the prevailing COVID-19 policies." They argue for "Focused Protection" or a "compassionate approach" that allows "those who are at minimal risk of death to live their lives normally to build up immunity to the virus through natural infection, while better protecting those who are at highest risk." See Martin

Kulldorff, et al., "The Great Barrington Declaration." October 4. Available online: https://gbdeclaration.org/ (accessed October 30, 2020). It is outside the scope of this chapter, and our limited expertise, to ascertain if forced protection is feasible. We limit our attention to many protests around the world that have been vocalizing frustration with the harsh realities that coincide with COVID-19 control measures.

73 Broadbent, Walker, Chalkidou, Sullivan & Glassman, "Lockdown Is Not Egalitarian: The Costs Fall on the Global Poor." *Lancet* vol. 396, no. 10243 (2020), 22.

74 Lucy Allais and Francois Venter, "Lockdown or no lockdown: we face hard choices for complex times."

75 Elissa M, Abrams and Szefler, "COVID-19 and the Impact of Social Determinants of Health." *The Lancet: Respiratory Medicine* vol. 8, no. 7 (2020): 660.

76 Clyde Yancy, "COVID-19 and African Americans," *JAMA* vol. 323 (2020): 1891.

77 Ibid, 1891–2.

78 Public Health England. *Disparities in the risk and outcomes of COVID-19* (London: Wellington House, 2020). The comment could be raised that once co-morbidities have been factored in that there was no difference between the COVID-19 mortality rates between ethnic groups. This could lead to the conclusion that more focus needs to be directed towards co-morbidities rather than how COVID-19 affects different ethnic groups differently. However, research shows that patients from ethnic minority groups were much more likely to have co-morbidities that were associated with a higher risk of dying from COVID-19 in the UK. As Krithi Ravi notes, research into ethnic disparities in COVID-19 mortality needs to consider social as well as biological factors. See Krithi Ravi, "Ethnic Disparities in COVID-19 Mortality: Are Comorbidities to Blame?" *The Lancet* vol. 396, no. 10243 (2020): 22.

79 Christina Atchison, et al., "Early Perceptions and Behavioral Response of the General Public during the COVID-19 Pandemic: A cross-sectional Survey of UK Adults." *BMJ Open* (2021), 7.

80 Ibid, 7.

81 Ibid, 12.

82 "Coronavirus in Kenya: Police kill three in motorcycle taxi protest." *BBC News*, June 20, 2020. Available Online: https://www.bbc.com/news/world-africa-53191358.

83 Leach, Meeker, MacGregor, Schmidt-Sane & Wilkinson, "Public Health Response," 6.

84 Carothers, Thomas, and Benjamin Press, "The Global Rise of Anti-Lockdown Protests—and What to Do About It."

85 Ibid.

86 Cas Mudde, "The 'anti-lockdown' protests are about more than just quarantines." *The Guardian*, April 21, 2020. Available online: https://www.theguardian.com/us-news/commentisfree/2020/apr/21/anti-lockdown-protests-trump-right-wing (accessed November 22, 2020).

87 Gideon Lasco, "Medical Populism and the COVID-19 Pandemic." *Global Public Health* vol. 15, no. 10 (2020): 1422–3.

88 Ibid, 1423.
89 Alexi Gugushvili et al., "Votes, Populism, and Pandemics." *International Journal of Public Health* vol. 65, no. 6 (2020): 721.
90 Alex Ward. "Anti-lockdown protests aren't just an American thing. They're a global phenomenon. From Germany to Brazil, from the UK to Chile, coronavirus-related demonstrations keep popping up." *Vox*, May 20, 2020. Available online: https://www.vox.com/2020/5/20/21263919/anti-lockdown-protests-coronavirus-germany-brazil-uk-chile (accessed May 21, 2020).
91 Cas Mudde, "The 'anti-lockdown' protests are about more than just quarantines." In the American example, reporting claims that the above-mentioned protests were funded by conservative interest groups like the DeVos family (Betsy DeVos being President Trump's Education Secretary). See Owen Dyer, "Covid-19: Trump Stokes Protests against Social Distancing Measures." *BMJ* vol. 369 (2020): 1596.

Bibliography

Abrams, Elissa M., and Stanley J. Szefler. "COVID-19 and the Impact of Social Determinants of Health." *The Lancet: Respiratory Medicine*, vol. 8, no. 7 (2020): 659–61.

Allais, Lucy, and François Venter. "Lockdown or no Lockdown: We face hard Choices for complex Times." *Mail & Guardian*, April 13, 2020. Available online: https://mg.co.za/article/2020-04-13-lockdown-or-no-lockdown-we-face-hard-choices-for-complex-times/ (accessed October 3, 2020).

Anciano, Fiona, et al. "Beyong trafficking and slavery: 'We are still waiting'—protesting under lockdown in South Africa." *Open Democracy*, April 24, 2020. Available online: https://www.opendemocracy.net/en/beyond-trafficking-and-slavery/we-are-still-waiting-protesting-under-lockdown-in-south-africa/.

Atchison, Christina, et al. "Early Perceptions and Behavioral Response of the General Public during the COVID-19 Pandemic: A cross-sectional Survey of UK Adults." *BMJ Open* (2021).

Barnett-Howell, Zachary, Oliver Watson, and Ahmed Mobarak. "The Benefits and Costs of Social Distancing in High and Low Income Countries." *Transactions of the Royal Society of Tropical Medicine and Hygiene* vol. 0 (2021): 1–13.

Biswas, Soutik. "Coronavirus: India's pandemic lockdown turns into a human tragedy." *BBC News*, March 30, 2020. Available online: https://www.bbc.com/news/world-asia-india-52086274.

Broadbent, Alexander, et al. "Lockdown Is Not Egalitarian: The Costs Fall on the Global Poor." *Lancet*, vol. 396, no. 10243 (2020): 21–22.

Broadbent, Alexander. "Lockdown is wrong for Africa," *Mail & Guardian*, April 8, 2020. Available Online: https://mg.co.za/article/2020-04-08-is-lockdown-wrong-for-africa/ (accessed October 3, 2020).

Bruckner, Tim, et al. "SARS-CoV-2: An Empirical Investigation of Rose's Population-Based Logic." *Epidemiology (Cambridge, Mass.)*, vol. 32, no. 6 (2021): 807–10.

Buckley, Phillip. "Political Aspects of Husserl's Call for Renewal," in *Transitions in Continental Thought*, edited by Arleen B. Dallery Stephen H Watson & E. Marya Bower, 3–20. New York: SUNY Press, 1994.

Byrne, Thomas. "Husserl's Early Genealogy of the Number System." *Meta: Research in Hermeneutics, Phenomenology, and Practical Philosophy* vol. 2 (2019): 402–29.

Byrne, Thomas. "Husserl's Early Semiotics and Number Signs: Philosophy of Arithmetic through the Lens of 'On the Logic of Signs (Semiotic).'" *The Journal of the British Society for Phenomenology* vol. 48 no. 4 (2017): 287–303.

Byrne, Thomas. "The Meaning of Being: Husserl on Existential Propositions as Predicative Propositions." *Axiomathes* vol. 32 (2020): 123–139.

Carothers, Thomas and Benjamin Press. "The Global Rise of Anti-Lockdown Protests," *World Politics News*, October 15, 2020. Available online: https://www.worldpoliticsreview.com/articles/29137/amid-the-covid-19-pandemic-protest-movements-challenge-lockdowns-worldwide (accessed December 14, 2020).

"Chile police using Covid-19 quarantine as pretext to crush protest, activists say." *The Guardian*, August 26, 2020. Available Online: https://www.theguardian.com/global-development/2020/aug/26/chile-police-covid-19-quarantine-protest.

"Coronavirus in Kenya: Police kill three in motorcycle taxi protest." *BBC News*, June 20, 2020. Available Online: https://www.bbc.com/news/world-africa-53191358.

Dyer, Owen. "Covid-19: Trump Stokes Protests against Social Distancing Measures." *BMJ*, vol. 369 (2020): m1596.

Eddington, Arthur. *The Nature of the Physical World*. London: Kessinger, 2010.

Flaxman, Seth, et al. "Estimating the Effects of Non-Pharmaceutical Interventions on COVID-19 in Europe." *Nature*, vol. 584, no. 7820 (2020): 257–61.

Galilei, Galileo. *Essential Galileo*, trans. Maurice Finocchiaro. New York: Hackett, 2008.

Gandhi M, Yokoe DS, Havlir DV. "Asymptomatic transmission, the Achilles' heel of current strategies to control Covid-19." *The New England Journal of Medicine*, 382 (2020): 2158–2160.

Gil, Magdalena, and Eduardo Undurraga. "Covid-19 has exposed how 'The Other Half' (Still) Lives." *Bulletin of Latin American Research* vol. 39 (2020): 28–34.

Gugushvili, Alexi, et al. "Votes, Populism, and Pandemics." *International Journal of Public Health*, vol. 65, no. 6 (2020): 721–22.

Gurwitsch, Aron. *Phenomenology and Theory of Science*, trans. Lester Embree. Evanston: Northwestern University Press, 1974.

Gutting, Gary. "Husserl and Scientific Realism." *Philosophy and Phenomenological Research* vol. 39, no. 1 (1978): 42–56.

Halperin, William, et al. "Geoffrey Rose's Strategy of Prevention Applied to COVID-19." *Health Security*, vol. 18, no. 6 (2020): 502–04.

Himanka, Juha. "Husserl's Argumentation for the Pre-Copernican View of the Earth." *The Review of Metaphysics* vol. 58 (2005): 621–44.

Husserl, Edmund. "Abhandlungen III, Die Krisis des Europäischen Menschentums und die Philosophie," in *Husserliana VI. Die Krisis der europäischen Wissenschaften und die transzendentale Phänomenologie,* edited by Walter Biemel, 314–48. The Hague: Martinus Nijhoff, 1976.

Husserl, Edmund. "Appendix I, Philosophy and the Crisis of European Humanity," in *The Crisis of the European Sciences and Transcendental Phenomenology,* translated by David Carr, 269–300. Evanston: Northwestern, 1970.

Husserl, Edmund. "Appendix VI, The Origin of Geometry," in *The Crisis of the European Sciences and Transcendental Phenomenology,* translated by David Carr, 353–78. Evanston: Northwestern, 1970.

Husserl, Edmund. "Beilage III. Die Frage nach der Ursprung der Geometrie als intentional-historische Problem," in *Husserliana VI. Die Krisis der europäischen Wissenschaften und die transzendentale Phänomenologie,* edited by Walter Biemel, 365–8. The Hague: Martinus Nijhoff, 1976.

Husserl, Edmund. *Analyses Concerning Passive and Active Synthesis: Lectures on Transcendental Logic,* translated by Antony J. Steinbock. Springer Netherlands, 2001.

Husserl, Edmund. *Ideas for a Pure Phenomenology and Phenomenological Philosophy. Second Book: Studies in the Phenomenology of Constitution,* translated by Richard Rojcewicz and André Schuwer. Kluwer Academic, 1989.

Husserl, Edmund. "Edmund Husserl's Letter to Lucien Levy-Bruhl," in Lukas Steinacher and Dermot Moran, *The New Yearbook for Phenomenology and Phenomenological Philosophy* vol. 8 (2008): 349–54.

Husserl, Edmund. *Husserliana IV. Ideen zur einer reinen Phänomenologie und phänomenologischen Philosophie. Zweites Buch: Phänomenologische Untersuchungen zur Konstitution,* ed. Marly Biemel. The Hague: Martinus Nijhoff, 1952.

Husserl, Edmund. *Husserliana VI. Die Krisis der europäischen Wissenschaften und die transzendentale Phänomenologie,* ed. Walter Biemel. The Hague: Martinus Nijhoff, 1976.

Husserl, Edmund. *Husserliana XII. Philosophie der Arithmetik. Mit ergänzenden Texten,* ed. Lothar Eley. The Hague: Martinus Nijhoff, 1970.

Husserl, Edmund. *Husserliana XI. Analysen zur passiven Synthesis. Aus Vorlesungs- und Forschungsmanuskripten, 1918-1926,* ed. Margot Fleischer. The Hague: Martinus Nijhoff, 1966

Husserl, Edmund. *Husserliana: Dokumente 3. Bd. 9. Familienbriefe,* ed. Karl Schumann. Dordrecht; Kluwer, 1999.

Husserl, Edmund. *The Crisis of the European Sciences and Transcendental Phenomenology,* trans. David Carr. Evanston: Northwestern University Press, 1970.

Husserl, Edmund. "Kant and the Idea of Transcendental Philosophy," trans. Ted Kein and William Pohl. *The Southwestern Journal of Philosophy* vol. 5, no. 3 (1974): 9–56.

Ihde, Don. "Husserl's Galileo Needed a Telescope!" *Philosophy & Technology* 24 (2011): 69–82.

John, Stephen. "Why the Prevention Paradox Is a Paradox, and Why We Should Solve It: A Philosophical View." *Preventive Medicine*, vol. 53, no. 4–5 (2011): 250–52.

Kattumana, Tarun. "Understanding the Fear of Vaccines: How to Talk about Public Health in the Age of COVID," *Public Seminar*, July 21, 2020. Available online: https://publicseminar.org/essays/understanding-the-fear-of-vaccines/ (accessed July 21, 2020).

Knies, Kenneth. "A Qualified Defense of Husserl's Crisis Concepts." *Metodo. International Studies in Phenomenology and Philosophy* vol. 4, no. 1 (2016): 27–47.

Kattumana, Tarun. "Understanding the Fear of Vaccines: How to talk about public health in the age of COVID." *Public Seminar*, July, 21, 2020. Available online: https://publicseminar.org/essays/understanding-the-fear-of-vaccines/.

Kulldorf, Martin, Sunetra Gupta, Jay Bhattacharya et al. "The Great Barrington Declaration," October 4. Available online: https://gbdeclaration.org/ (accessed October 30, 2020).

Lasco, Gideon. "Medical Populism and the COVID-19 Pandemic." *Global Public Health*, vol. 15, no. 10 (2020): 1417–29.

Leach, Melissa, et al. "COVID-19: Key Considerations for a Public Health Response." in *Briefing, Brighton: Institute of Development Studies* (2020): 1–20.

Miglani, Sanjeev and Rupam Jain. "India extends world's biggest lockdown, ignites protest by migrant workers." *Refuters*, April 14, 2020. https://www.reuters.com/article/us-health-coronavirus-southasia-idUSKCN21W0HI.

Mudde, Cas. "The 'Anti-Lockdown' Protests are about more than just Quartantines," *The Guardian*, April 21, 2020. Available online: https://www.theguardian.com/us-news/commentisfree/2020/apr/21/anti-lockdown-protests-trump-right-wing (accessed November 22, 2020).

Petranovich, Sean. "Trust and Betrayal from a Husserlian Standpoint." *International Journal of Philosophical Studies*, 26:2 (2018): 251–274.

Public Health England. *Disparities in the risk and outcomes of COVID19*. London: Wellington House, 2020.

Ravi, Krithi. "Ethnic Disparities in COVID-19 Mortality: Are Comorbidities to Blame?" *The Lancet*, vol. 396, no. 10243 (2020): 22.

Reidpath, D. D. "Population Health. More than the Sum of the Parts?" *Journal of Epidemiology & Community Health*, vol. 59, no. 10 (2005): 877–80.

Rickles, Dean. "Public Health," in *Handbook of the Philosophy of Science,* edited by Fred Gifford, 523–72. Dordrecht: Springer, 2011.

Rose, G. A. *Rose's Strategy of Preventive Medicine: The Complete Original Text*, edited by Kay-Tee Khaw and M. G. Marmot, New ed. Oxford: Oxford University Press, 2008.

Rose, Geoffrey. "Sick Individuals and Sick Populations." *International Journal of Epidemiology*, vol. 30 (2001): 427–32.

Schuhmann, Karl. *Husserls Staatsphilosophie*. Freiburg: Verlag Karl Alber, 1988.

Tieszen, Richard. "Science as a Triumph of the Human Spirit and Science in Crisis: Husserl and the Fortunes of Reason," in *Continental Philosophy of Science*, edited by Gary Guttin, 21–45. Cambridge: Cambridge University Press, 2005.

Ward, Alex. "Anti-lockdown protests aren't just an American thing. They're a global phenomenon," *Vox*, May 20, 2020. Available online: https://www.vox.com/2020/5/20/21263919/anti-lockdown-protests-coronavirus-germany-brazil-uk-chile (accessed May 21, 2020).

Yancy, Clyde. "COVID-19 and African Americans." *JAMA* 323 (2020): 1891–2.

Zahavi, Dan. *Husserl and Transcendental Intersubjectivity: A Response to the Linguistic-Pragmatic Critique*. Athens, OH: Ohio University Press, 2001.

Zahavi, Dan. "Applied Phenomenology: Why It Is Safe to Ignore the Epoché." *Continental Philosophy Review*, vol. 54, no. 2 (2021): 259–73.

Notes on Contributors

Thomas Byrne (T.byrne3@gmail.com)
Thomas Byrne (PhD, KU Leuven) is an assistant research professor at the Department of Philosophy and NCPRE at the University of Illinois Urbana-Champaign. He has published in *Husserl Studies*, *Axiomathes*, and *Meta*. He works on Husserlian phenomenology.

Stefan Deines (stefan.deines@gmx.de)
Stefan Deines currently works as a consultant for impact orientation, monitoring, and evaluation in the educational sector. He taught philosophy at Goethe University in Frankfurt, where he received his PhD in 2008, at the University of Gießen, the University of Macau, and at the Free University in Berlin. His areas of specialization are Critical Theory, Social Philosophy, the Philosophy of Education, Theories of Cultural Change, Aesthetics, and the Philosophy of Art. His most recent publication is a volume on the plurality and dynamics of the arts, *Die Kunst und die Künste. Ein Kompendium zur Kunsttheorie der Gegenwart* (co-edited with Georg Bertram and Daniel Feige, 2021).

Philip Hogh (philip.hogh@uni-kassel.de)
Philip Hogh is Professor for Practical Philosophy at University of Kassel. Between 2011 until 2021 he was Research Associate and Assistant Professor of Philosophy at Carl von Ossietzky University of Oldenburg. He is the author of *Communication and Expression: Adorno's Philosophy of Language* (2017), *Language and Critical Theory* (co-edited with Stefan Deines, 2017), and "Two Sorts of Natural History. On a Central Concept in Ethical Naturalism and Critical Theory" (*European Journal of Philosophy*, 2022).

Tarun Kattumana (tarunjose.kattumana@kuleuven.be)
Tarun Kattumana is a PhD candidate at the Husserl Archives, KU Leuven. He also works at The Transvaxx Project and Centre for Access to Medicines. His research concerns COVID-19, vaccine hesitancy, and phenomenology.

Shih-Diing Liu (sdliu@um.edu.mo)
Shih-Diing Liu is Professor of Communication at the University of Macau. His recent book is *The Politics of People: Protest Cultures in China* (2019).

He is now working on another book project, tentatively titled *The Feeling Nation*.

Louis Lo (louiswclo@nycu.edu.tw)
Louis Lo is Associate Professor and Director of the Institute of Visual Studies, National Yang Ming Chiao Tung University. He obtained his PhD in Comparative Literature from the University of Hong Kong in 2006. His research interests include the history of ideas, the representation of cities in literature and films, and Asian cinema. He is the author of *Male Jealousy: Literature and Film* (2008) and co-author and photographer of *Walking Macao, Reading the Baroque* (2009). His journal articles can be found in *Concentric: Literary and Cultural Studies*, *CLCWeb Comparative Literature and Culture*, *Textual Practice*, *Shima*, and *Monde Chinois Nouvelle Asie*. He has contributed chapters in a wide range of edited books including, most recently, *The Palgrave Encyclopedia of Urban Literary Studies* (2022). He is currently working on the revenge motif in literature and cinema.

Stephen R. Palmquist (stevepq@associate.hkbu.edu.hk)
Stephen R. Palmquist earned his doctorate from Oxford University (St. Peter's College) in 1987. He then taught philosophy at universities in Hong Kong for thirty-four years before relocating to Los Angeles in late 2021. His 210+ publications, translated into thirteen languages, include over 120 refereed journal articles and book chapters. Among his twelve books are: *Comprehensive Commentary on Kant's Religion within the Bounds of Bare Reason* (2016); *Kant's Critical Religion* (2000/2019); *Kant on Intuition: Western and Asian Perspectives on Transcendental Idealism* (2019); and *Kant and Mysticism: Critique as the Experience of Baring All in Reason's Light* (2019).

Alexei Procyshyn (Alexei.procyshyn@gmail.com)
Alexei Procyshyn (PhD, The New School for Social Research) is Lecturer in Philosophy at Queen's University Belfast.

Christian Schmidt (ch.schmidt@hu-berlin.de)
Christian Schmidt, PD Dr. phil. habil., is Academic Coordinator of the Humanities and Social Change Centre at Humboldt University, Berlin. His research focuses on the tension between the modern concept of freedom and social structures. His most recent book is *Karl Marx zur Einführung* (2018).

Lin Song (songlinhk@gmail.com)
Lin Song is an Assistant Professor in communication at Jinan University, Guangzhou, China. He is the author of *Queering Chinese Kinship: Queer Public*

Culture in Globalizing China (Hong Kong University Press 2021). His other works can be found in journals Asian Studies Review, Feminist Media Studies, Convergence, Television and New Media, and Continuum, and edited books *Contesting Chineseness* (Springer 2021), *Queering Paradigms VII* (Peter Lang 2018), and *The Cosmopolitan Dream* (Hong Kong University Press 2018).

Amita Valmiki (amitavalmiki@gmail.com)
Amita Valmiki is associate professor and head of the Department of Philosophy at Ramniranjan Jhunjhunwala College of Arts, Science and Commerce, and Visiting Faculty at the Department of Philosophy, University of Mumbai. She is the author of *Mystical Worlds: Social, Spiritual and Secular* (2019) and the editor of *100 Years of Indian Cinema: Issues and Challenges in Retrospection* (co-edited with Uma Shankar, Rina Pitale Puradkar, Shashi Mishra, Akshat Shetty, Pankti Chitalia, Arundhati Chitre and B. Dutta 2013). She has published more than fifty articles in various books as well as in national and international journals.

Mario Wenning (mwenning@uloyola.es)
Mario Wenning is professor of philosophy at Loyola University Andalusia. His work focuses on social and political philosophy as well as aesthetics from a global perspective. Recent publications include *The Human–Animal Boundary* (co-edited with Nandita Batra 2018, 2021), *Environmental Philosophy and East Asia* (co-edited with Hiroshi Abe and Matthias Fritsch 2022) and *Philosophy and Gambling* (2022).

Jinting Wu (jintingw@buffalo.edu)
Jinting Wu is an associate professor of educational culture, policy, and society at the State University of New York at Buffalo. She is an educational anthropologist with an interest in philosophy and cultural studies. She has conducted research on rural minority education, disability and special education, immigrant youth and families, and educational meritocracy on the global stage. She is the recipient of the American Educational Research Association Division B Outstanding Book Recognition Award for her book *Fabricating an Educational Miracle: Compulsory Schooling Meets Ethnic Rural Development in Southwest China* (2016). She is also the awardee of the 2020 Henry Luce Foundation/American Council of Learned Societies Early Career Fellowship in China Studies.

Index

Adorno, Theodor W. 6, 60, 62–5, 77
against vi, 1–4, 6–7, 9–10, 15–16, 21, 32, 35, 38, 44, 48, 53, 61, 63–4, 73, 77–9, 82–4, 100–2, 106, 117–23, 125, 132, 136, 141, 158, 163–5, 167, 173–4, 176–80, 183, 185, 191–2, 197, 200, 207, 209–10, 213, 215, 218–19, 221–3
alienating 10, 207, 215, 218, 221
Amery, Jean 6, 64
Antigone 2
Arendt, Hannah 6, 32, 48, 50, 77, 82–3, 88–90, 203–4
Asian 4, 128–30, 153, 168, 220, 236
authority v, 2, 5, 15–26, 36–7, 44, 46, 58, 106, 116, 163–5, 192–3, 211, 218

Benjamin, Walter 5, 7, 11, 13, 15, 43, 44–7, 93–6, 99–108
Brecht, Bertolt 7, 118, 120, 126
Butler, Judith 6, 77, 79, 81, 82, 85

China v, 8, 47, 114, 116–19, 122, 157, 160–1, 164–7, 197, 235–7
civil rights movement 7, 116, 126
contestation 1, 3–4, 8, 34, 40, 48, 77, 209, 223
COVID-19 6, 8, 10, 159, 207, 209–11, 215–23
    control measures 207, 210, 219, 221–3
Creon 2
critique v, 7, 44, 55, 63, 65, 74, 79, 83, 88, 93–4, 96, 100–1, 108, 116, 118–19, 123, 133, 136, 146, 162, 175, 177–8, 182, 215, 217, 236

Daoism 7, 113, 115, 117, 120, 122, 142
    Daoist 7, 113, 115–26
dissent iii, 1, 3–5, 8, 10, 116–17, 120, 123, 126, 162, 207–11, 215, 217–19, 221–3

Foucault, Michel 3, 6, 47, 79, 133, 135–8, 144

Gandhi, Mahatma 7, 116, 191–3, 201

Hegel, Georg Friedrich Wilhelm 1, 5, 38–42, 99, 180, 198
Heidegger, Martin 3, 5, 43, 45–7, 78–9, 85, 196
Husserl, Edmund 10, 196, 207–15, 217–18, 222–3

immorality 6, 54–5, 61–2
indifference v, 6, 53–5, 59–61, 63–5
irrationality 66, 78

Jaspers, Karl 9, 191, 194, 196, 199

Kabir, Das 9
Kant, Immanuel v, 5–6, 9, 15–26, 35, 53–9, 61–2, 64, 66, 93, 174, 176–7, 192, 196, 208, 236
    Kantian v, 5–6, 15, 20, 25, 41–2, 45, 61–2, 93, 101, 104, 106, 136, 177, 186, 208
    Neo-Kantians 196
Kierkegaard, Søren 9, 194, 196, 199, 201
King, Martin Luther 3, 7

lockdowns 10, 207, 217, 219–21
Locke, John 3, 192

Mao Zedong 113
    Maoist 47
Marx, Karl 3, 61, 191, 236
    Marxist 4, 5, 7, 118, 120–1, 137
    Neo-Marxist 4
#MeToo movement 8
Mill, John Stuart 3
Miller, Hillis 144, 185
modernity v, 9, 31, 173–4, 176, 179, 182–3
morality v, 6, 21–2, 53–5, 61–2, 76, 159, 177
mysticism v, 9, 191, 236

National Socialism 7, 47
negativity 1, 63, 142
nonviolence 131

passive resistance v, 7, 113, 115–16, 123, 126
pedagogy v, 8, 131, 143, 145–6
phenomenology 10, 207–8, 210, 218
probability v, 173, 182, 213
public health 6, 8, 10, 207, 209–10, 215–18, 220–3
   recommendations 10, 209–10, 218, 222

rationality 18, 74–5, 77–8, 97–101, 103, 178, 184
reality v, 2, 4, 6, 40, 42–3, 55, 59, 66, 126, 132, 139–43, 145–6, 149, 173, 182, 197, 203, 213–14, 218
relation v, 6, 17, 35–6, 39, 42, 44, 47, 53, 58–9, 61, 73–4, 84–5, 98, 101, 105, 107–8, 126, 138, 145, 158, 162, 177, 191, 194, 198, 202, 212, 216
   relationship 6, 10, 16, 18, 66, 74, 76, 97, 99, 110, 114, 138, 160, 162–4, 208
Republican Tradition 5–6, 35–6, 42
resistance ii, v, 1–9, 13, 15–16, 18–21, 23–6, 31–8, 40, 41–3, 46, 48, 53–8, 61, 64–5, 71, 73–7, 79–80, 84–5, 88, 93–4, 102, 107–8, 113, 115–24, 126, 131–43, 145–6, 155, 157–67, 173–4, 178, 183, 185, 191–2, 194, 200, 202
ressentiment 9, 174, 185
revolution ii, v, 6, 15–17, 20, 22–6, 31–2, 40–1, 65, 80–3, 87, 99, 157–8, 191
right i, iii, 2–3, 5, 7, 15–16, 19, 21–4, 32–5, 39, 41, 44, 58, 60, 63, 100–1, 103, 113, 115–17, 120, 126, 140, 145, 158–60, 162, 165, 184, 192
Rorty, Richard 6, 77, 80–2, 85

social change v, 1, 6, 43, 47, 71, 74, 79, 137, 142, 236
   social transformation v, 7, 93
Socrates 2, 197, 201, 205
Spinoza 5, 33–9, 42, 46–7, 193
spiritual v, 4, 8, 19, 117, 131–2, 137–40, 142, 144–6, 194–5, 199, 237
   spiritualism 193
   spirituality 10, 131–2, 137–8, 142–6, 192, 194
Suarez, Francisco 2
subjectivity 8, 59–60, 62, 77, 79, 132, 136–8, 141, 144–6, 158, 177–8, 180, 196, 198, 208
   inter-subjectivity 208
   transsubjectivity 140

temporality 7, 74, 82
transformation v, 3–4, 7–8, 42, 46, 74–6, 78–81, 84–5, 87, 93, 100, 107, 121, 125, 131–2, 137–8, 140–6, 208

violence v, vii, 7, 44–5, 66, 93–108, 113–14, 116, 126, 131, 157, 179, 219–20

Walzer, Michael 6, 75–8
Weber, Marx 7, 93–108
White Rose movement 7, 118–21, 126
Wilde, Oscar 6, 53–5, 60–1, 64–6
Wuwei 7, 122, 126

www.ingramcontent.com/pod-product-compliance
Lightning Source LLC
Chambersburg PA
CBHW062141300426
44115CB00012BA/1997